PRAISE for *The Literature Workshop*

Blau's book breaks new ground in teaching literature . . . and offers classroom practices that any teacher could begin to implement—and learn from!—immediately.

—**Carol Jago**
Teacher, author, educational columnist,
Director of the California Reading and
Literature Project, UCLA

THE LITERATURE WORKSHOP

THE LITERATURE WORKSHOP
Teaching Texts and Their Readers

Sheridan D. Blau

HEINEMANN
Portsmouth, NH

Heinemann
A division of Reed Elsevier Inc.
361 Hanover Street
Portsmouth, NH 03801–3912
www.heinemann.com

Offices and agents throughout the world

The author and publisher wish to thank those who have generously given permission to reprint borrowed materials:

"Sonrisas" from *Borders* by Pat Mora. Reprinted by permission of Arte Público Press, University of Huston, 1986.

"My Papa's Waltz" from *The Collected Poems of Theodore Roethke* by Theodore Roethke. Copyright © 1942 by Hearst Magazine, Inc. Used by permission of Doubleday, a division of Random House, Inc., and by Faber and Faber, Ltd.

"Pitcher" from *The Orb Weaver* by Robert Francis. Copyright © 1960 by Robert Francis. Reprinted by permission of Wesleyan University Press.

"Death of the Ball Turret Gunner" from *The Complete Poems of Randall Jarrell* by Randall Jarrell. Copyright © 1969 renewed 1997 by Mary Jarrell. Reprinted by permission of Farrar, Straus and Giroux, LLC, and by Faber and Faber, Ltd.

(credit lines continued on page 243)

Library of Congress Cataloging-in-Publication Data
Blau, Sheridan D.
  The literature workshop : teaching texts and their readers / Sheridan Blau.
      p. cm.
   Includes bibliographical references and index.
   ISBN 0-86709-540-7
   1. Literature—Study and teaching.   I. Title.

PN59 .B55 2003
807'.1—dc21   2002151042

Editor: Lisa Luedeke
Production: Elizabeth Valway
Cover design: Jenny Jensen Greenleaf
Front and back cover photos: Harvey Green
Composition: House of Equations, Inc.
Manufacturing: Steve Bernier

Printed in the United States of America on acid-free paper
07 06 05   RRD   3 4 5

For my mentor, James Gray, founder of the National Writing Project;
for the teachers of the South Coast Writing Project; and for my students past and present.

"Let the honor of your student be as dear to you as your own, the honor of your colleague
as the reverence for your teacher, and the reverence for your teacher
as the fear of heaven." (Sayings of the Fathers, IV.12)

Contents

Acknowledgments

Many colleagues reviewed manuscript versions of sections of this book and gave me responses that encouraged and corrected me, often pushing me to extend and revise my thinking. My thanks to Marjorie Roemer, Miles Myers, Deborah Appleman, Patti Stock, Angus Dunstan, Melanie Sperling, Carol Olson, Cherryl Armstrong Smith, Carol Dixon, Michael Smith, Denise Maltese, Cissy Ross, Cheryl Smith, Rosemary Cabe, Eddi Christensen, and Patricia Lai. Cristy Bruns read and commented helpfully on the entire manuscript in one of its late drafts and was indispensable in helping me solve some vexing organizational problems.

Stephen Marcus, who was the first reader of everything I wrote for twenty-five years, died unexpectedly before he could see a draft of this book. He would have gladly read every page of it and written me copious notes to interrogate and complicate my thinking and to simplify my prose. I miss him and hope my book does not suffer as much from his absence as I do.

Most of my intellectual debts are obvious in my text. Of those that are more extensive than my citations will suggest, I want to mention my indebtedness to Ruth Vinz, for modeling and advocating experimental narrative and dramatic forms for academic writing, and to Louise Rosenblatt, who remains the mentor of mentors for all teacher-educators who think about the teaching of literature. For other substantive contributions of various kinds I am indebted to Harvey Green, Mary Ann Smith, Steve Allaback, and Jeffrey Mansell.

The dedication and introduction of this book make clear my gratitude to James Gray and the National Writing Project. I want to add a particular note of thanks to colleagues at Writing Project sites where I have been invited to conduct workshops in summer institutes and continuity programs. Those workshops and the conversations around them constitute some of the earliest drafts of this book, which remains infused with the voices of the teachers and site directors who helped me think through the exercises and conceptual frameworks that I was both presenting and revising at the same time.

I am also grateful to the teacher-leaders of the National Council of Teachers of English (NCTE) and its state and regional affiliates for the many opportunities they have afforded me to conduct workshops and deliver presentations at conferences and conventions in nearly every state of the Union. My indebtedness to NCTE is also evident in my frequent references to articles and chapters in NCTE journals, research reports, and professional books.

I am most keenly grateful, of course, to the teachers I have worked with most closely at my own Writing Project site, the South Coast Writing Project, at the University of California, Santa Barbara, where I have been privileged to serve as director for the past twenty-five years. I especially want to acknowledge how much I owe to the wisdom and inspirational teaching of the teacher-leaders at my site, and to the codirectors and coordinators who so brilliantly manage our broad array of professional development programs. Space limitations prevent me from naming all who deserve to be mentioned. I will limit myself to thanking by name those codirectors and program coordinators who gave me the gift of peace of mind by professionally managing all the activities of our Project during the half-year I was on sabbatical in France completing the first draft of this book. They are Jack Phreaner, Lois Brandts, Carol Dixon, Rosemary Cabe, Rosemary Staley, Joni Chancer, Aline Shapiro, and our Project's administrative officer, Doris O'Leske. I also want to acknowledge the intellectual and material support that my Project and I have received from Jules Zimmer, the rare and exemplary dean of the Gevirtz Graduate School of Education.

Three others deserve special mention for their roles in the birth of this book. Lisa Luedeke, executive editor at Heinemann, served as midwife to this project through her encouragement and expert editorial guidance. Elizabeth Valway, Heinemann's production editor, comforted, coaxed, and instructed me tactfully and helpfully through each of the tightly scheduled stages of the production process. Bonnie Blau managed getting the permissions for this book, supplied editorial advice, and has been the beloved wife of this grateful author for forty-three years, a record that merits canonization as well as gratitude.

Much of this book was written during sabbatical leaves generously granted to me by the departments of English and education, with the support of the College of Letters and Science and the Gevirtz Graduate School of Education, at the University of California, Santa Barbara.

Finally, I want to express my appreciation to the students—undergraduate and graduate—I have been privileged to teach for more than three decades at the University of California, Santa Barbara. Much of this book is informed by what I have learned from and with my students in the classroom and in office conversations. I count the opportunity to earn my living by teaching such bright, thoughtful, and intellectually generous students as one of the great blessings of my life.

Introduction
Principles for Practice

I shall begin this introduction with the forbidden gesture of an apology for its length and its focus on theory. But I feel obliged to offer readers some account of the intellectual genealogy of the principles of practice that inform this book and a conceptual frame for the practices that this book exemplifies. In truth, I think that the rationale for the practices modeled here will emerge for attentive readers as they read the chapters that focus on practice, and (as the body of this book will make evident) I much prefer and trust that sort of empirical process for communicating the theory behind my practice. But some readers want to know what they are getting into conceptually and why it might be worthwhile before they set out on an intellectual journey with an author. It is for these readers and for the clarity of my own thinking about the model of instruction that has come to characterize my own teaching that I have written this introduction. Readers who do not have much patience with theory and intellectual history may be better advised to read this introduction after they have read the remainder of the book, when the workshops that constitute the heart of this volume will have, I hope, justified an interest in where they came from and how they may be characterized conceptually as a genre of instruction. After all, I wrote this introduction (as most introductions are written) last, after I had written all the other chapters of the book. So it might also make sense to read it last.

For those who insist on reading this book in the order provided by the table of contents, I'll start as interestingly as I know how, with a story—a personal story that may explain much of what I am trying to do in this book and how I came to care about doing it. Then I'll turn to a more general characterization of the critical and pedagogical milieu in which all of us who are English teachers (of a certain age at least) have operated over the past three decades or more, during which my own teaching has become increasingly built around literature workshops.

A Pedagogical Awakening

Early in my own teaching career (with a couple of years of high school teaching already under my belt), when I was in graduate school and teaching freshman English in a university as a TA, I found myself one day in the not unusual situation of teaching a difficult belletristic essay I had never myself been taught. I was not unprepared, of course, because I had read the essay the night before and gotten myself ready to teach it. Yet in the middle of teaching this particular class of freshmen, all of whom had impressed me as stunningly bright and thoughtful young people (though not so much younger than I was at the time), I suddenly began to wonder why it was that I seemed so much more competent as a reader of the text than they did. I knew that they were no less intelligent than I, and I could think of nothing in my education, in this particular essay, or in my interpretive skill that could account for why I was able to interpret for my students what they appeared to be incapable of interpreting for themselves. The difference between us, I realized (and promptly told them), lay largely if not entirely in our roles and in what we saw ourselves responsible for. Given my responsibility to interpret the text for this class of extraordinarily bright undergraduates, I had worked hard at the task the night before and come to class prepared to discuss the essay in ways that would illuminate its difficulties and advance our inquiry into textual or conceptual problems that deserved further interrogation. But convinced as I was that these students were all as intelligent as anyone I knew, I realized that any one of them could have done the same sort of work I had done the night before and learned the text in that way far better than they would learn it through my delivery of my interpretation and understanding to them.

What struck me most powerfully at that moment some forty years ago was a paradoxical irony that I have experienced over and over again since then: that the intellectual work I was doing as a teacher was teaching me more than anything I could do for my students would teach them! If my job was to ensure that my students were learning as much as possible, then I had to find ways to switch roles with them, to have them take the kind of responsibility for such tasks as making sense of texts and figuring out textual and conceptual problems that I regularly undertook in my role as the teacher. I undertook these tasks in order to help my students learn the texts I was teaching them. But as long as I was engaged in the task of teaching them what my efforts to construct meaning had yielded for me, all I could do was show them what I had learned. What they would know, therefore, was that I had learned it, and their notes would record some of what I had learned. But the experience of learning was mine, not theirs. They were to a very large extent merely witnesses to it.

Some ten years after this transforming pedagogical epiphany, by now a professor on the verge of tenure in a university English department, I was still worrying about that same problem and spoke about it publicly in an address I was invited to deliver to my campus community, under the title "On the Advancement of Learning Through the Abolition of Teaching." My argument in that talk was that as long as teachers are teaching, students are not going to learn, because the kind of experience teachers have that enables them to learn what they have to teach is the experience that students need to have, if they are to be the ones who learn. Given the way teaching and learning were conducted in most classrooms, I argued, the experience of being taught was merely an experience of witnessing and possibly recording the teacher's learning, and not an experience of learning for oneself.

I have spent most of my professional life trying to solve this fundamental paradox of teaching. Fortunately, I have been able to work for nearly four decades in academic settings and as a member of professional communities where the struggle to resolve such paradoxes and problems in teaching has never been a source of embarrassment or private agony, but a respected intellectual enterprise and a focus for professional inquiry, experimentation, and research. I am speaking particularly of the overlapping communities of specialists in the fields of English education and composition studies, where such topics have always been at the center of professional discourse, and most especially of the community of site directors and affiliated teachers and researchers of the National Writing Project. As a member of the NWP community, I have been blessed for nearly twenty-five years with colleagues who have nurtured and challenged my thinking about the paradoxes of teaching while offering me a copious supply of practical strategies and a model for a classroom culture that I have been able to draw upon to reframe and resolve those paradoxes in ways that have profoundly influenced my teaching and every chapter of this book.

The Professional Context

If we look at the broader field of English studies over the past quarter-century, we see an entire professional community pedagogically perplexed over what Judith Langer (1990) once referred to as a kind of schizophrenic split between the teaching of writing and the teaching of literature at every level of instruction. As a profession, we have for the past twenty or twenty-five years tended to teach composition in ways that are process-oriented, learning-centered (or learner-centered), and collaborative while we have continued (at least until recently) to teach literature in a way that has been product-oriented (directed toward having students produce approved or standard interpretive and critical statements), text-centered (concerned with the text and interpretive and critical positions on it and not with what students might be learning through instruction about how to read it), and both competitive and top-down (with alternative readings seen as competing for the same discursive space and students competing with each other to produce readings that will win the approval of the instructor, whose own interpretive position remains the correct one [Hynds 1991; Blau 1994b]). That split has troubled many thoughtful high school teachers who have felt that their literature instruction is less vital and engaging for students than their composition instruction, and it has yielded for the college and university communities bipolar English departments, if not separated programs, with one culture of instruction prevailing in composition classes and a contradictory culture of instruction the norm for literature classes.[1]

The most influential and successful attempts of the past thirty years or more to reform literature teaching—particularly in secondary schools—have drawn on Rosenblatt's transactional theory (1938, 1978) to develolp a rich body of student-centered practices (especially Probst 1988) that honor the individual responses of students over the authoritative readings that teachers once thought it necessary to communicate to students as valid literary knowledge. But response-based classrooms, as much as they have accomplished in humanizing teaching and fostering student involvement are sometimes limited or misleading in what they accomplish intellectually, given their self-referentiality and the illusion they foster of an entirely independent and naïve reader whose response has not already been shaped and situated by the culture of school and other less visible cultural forces (Gilbert 1987; Patterson 1992, 1993; Purves 1993). Moreover, insofar as they may invite unexamined and culturally biased readings, purely response-based approaches to texts may also be inadequate to the sensitive cultural challenges posed in courses featuring multicultural literature (Hynds and Appleman 1997; Appleman, Hynds, and Marshall 1998) and equally inadequate for largely the same reasons to the demands of more traditional instructional programs focused on ancient or canonical literary works (Purves 1993; Rabinowitz and Smith 1998).

More recent attempts at reform have sought to institute practices drawn from the critical theories that have lately become dominant in graduate study in university literature departments, inviting students to engage in psychoanalytic, Marxist, feminist, deconstructionist, and other post–New Critical approaches to literary texts. In the hands of tactful practitioners with a well-informed sense of pedagogical priorities about what students of literature most need to learn, contemporary literary theory has undoubtedly enriched and revitalized literary instruction in many English classes in college and even in secondary schools (see, for example, McCormick, Waller, and Flower 1987; Moon 1990; Pirie 1997; Soter 1999; Mellor, Patterson, and O'Neill 2000a, 2000b; Mellor and Patterson 2001; Appleman 2000; Carey-Webb 2001; Scholes, Comley, and Ulmer 2002). But many literature classes committed to teaching theory and especially those that teach a particular theoretical perspective as the preferred or approved approach for the study of literature have also been vexed by some troubling pedagogical problems for teachers as well as for students.

The first is that most contemporary critical theories are driven by ideological goals or defined by a larger intellectual project in which very few undergraduate students (not to mention high school students) are likely to be invested and to which more may be openly hostile (Durst 1999). A more obvious problem for teachers is that these theories are also built on the most advanced thinking in such fields as philosophy, social theory, and psychoanalysis, which few English classes, as presently organized, have time to explore beyond the few reductive principles that may appear in the back of literature anthologies or that can be summarized in lectures. Thus, teachers who require their students in introductory literature courses to produce literary essays employing one or another of the recent ideological or poststructuralist theories are often the recipients of student essays that constitute a parody of genuine literary discourse and an exercise in what Ken Macrorie (1970) calls "Engfish," the language of students who are adopting an academic idiom that they barely understand in order to produce pretentious and usually ill-formed utterances that have almost no connection to anything they genuinely think or feel.

While my book acknowledges its roots in the transactional theory and democratic ideology of Louise Rosenblatt, it seeks to remedy the limitations of many response-based classrooms by reclaiming some more traditional critical values at the same time that it draws freely on insights and practices made available by contemporary critical theory. Its focus, however, is not on theory but on *practice* and specifically on practices for use in secondary schools and the first two years of college that will have the effect of changing the culture of instruction in literature classes, with two goals in mind. The first is to renovate the culture of instruction in literature to render it more consistent with the process-oriented, collaborative, and learning-centered practices of exemplary writing classes, largely in the interest of solving the pedagogical problem I have described as that of making students rather than teachers the responsible agents for learning in classrooms. And its second related and possibly more important goal is to make literature classrooms into communities and cultures that are more conducive than literature classrooms traditionally have been to the development of a particular constellation of literary skills or habits of mind that I shall propose as the primary constituents of literary competence and as instrumental and consequential to the study and learning of literature throughout an educational career and literate lifetime (see Chapter 10).

Nevertheless, in the course of presenting and reflecting on models for practice and in advancing a model of literary competence, virtually every chapter of this volume also participates, of necessity, in some of the most pedagogically relevant conversations of modern literary theory. "Theory is what breaks out," Gerald Graff (2001) says, "when agreement about such terms as *text, reading, history, interpretation, tradition,* and *literature* can no longer be taken for granted, so that their meanings have to be formulated and debated" (2060).

The introductory literature courses that are the focus of this volume may not be sites where sophisticated theoretical debates ordinarily break out over fundamental critical terms, but they are surely sites where agreement about the meanings of such terms cannot be taken for granted. They are also sites where an introduction to some of the difficulties of formulating such meanings is appropriate both to initiate students into the conversation of the literary community (Graff 1992), so they can begin to function as at least peripheral participants (Lave and Wenger 1991), and to sophisticate with added subtlety and complexity their understanding of and appreciation for literary texts and literary discussions. More importantly, if one is actually committed to constructing a classroom culture that honors literary processes, creates frequent opportunities for collaboration among readers, and is centered on the learner or on what is happening in the heads of students as they read and respond to literary works, there is no way to avoid raising for students and for their teachers a number of theoretical questions whose answers have practical consequences in designing lessons, in directing the behavior of readers, and in defining instructional outcomes.

The Literature Workshop

Consistent with its pedagogical orientation, this book presents most of its teaching practices and principles in the context of dramatized re-creations of workshops for teachers, where readers become participants in and witnesses to workshops that have actually been conducted with students and teachers much like themselves and (possibly) the students they teach. These workshops, in other words, are not descriptions of practices, but enactments of the very practices that teachers are reading these pages to learn and which they are encouraged to learn as participants and engaged observers rather than merely as readers. Each workshop also includes retrospective reflections on what has transpired during the workshop proper, to offer teachers an explanation and rationale for the efficacy of the workshop activities and an understanding of the goals and outcomes of the workshop in the context of a larger theory of literary competence and instruction.

   As an introduction to the teaching approach demonstrated in most of the chapters of this book, let me at this juncture invite readers to participate for a few minutes in a brief segment of a textual and instructional event of the kind that I am calling a literature workshop. This particular workshop addresses some of the difficulties that students characteristically encounter in reading poetry—difficulties that might tempt them to declare themselves incompetent readers, inadequately skilled or insufficiently prepared for the poems they are typically expected to read and understand in literature courses.

A Literature Workshop in Progress

The room may be at a college or university or at a conference center or in a public school. The participants might be college freshmen or sophomores in an introductory literature class or high school students in a typical English class. Or perhaps they are student-teachers or experienced teachers in a postgraduate or professional development program on the teaching of English, and what they are participating in is a demonstration of what might transpire in an introductory college course or a high school college prep class in English. The workshop has been in progress for some time as you join the group as a participant-observer. The leader or teacher (T) gives you a welcoming nod and then begins to sum up what you missed.[2]

   T: OK. So we have experienced a number of ways that a poem or any text might pose difficulties for its readers. It might employ unusual and confusing syntactical structures that need to be painstakingly unpacked, as we saw with the passage from *Paradise Lost*. Or its lexicon—its vocabulary—might be archaic or simply unfamiliar to us. How can we expect a modern reader to know that a "bare bodkin" doesn't refer to anything like indecent exposure? Or we may find that a poem or some other text is intertextually dense, drenched in allusions or references to other texts or literary traditions that student readers are not likely to recognize, but that are likely to become more familiar to them over time as they continue to read and especially as they engage in an organized program of literary study. That was certainly the case with the Coleridge sonnet, "Work Without Hope," where most of you felt you could grasp the gist of the poem, but many of you still felt adrift because you didn't know what to make of all the references to the pastoral tradition of poetry and the poet.

Let's now turn to another Romantic lyric composed eighteen years earlier than the Coleridge poem but one that is much more widely anthologized and more frequently studied: Wordsworth's "My Heart Leaps Up." I once heard a teacher say that this poem is impossible for readers to understand unless they know something about English Romanticism and especially about Wordsworth's own brand of Neoplatonism. Are all of you familiar with Wordsworth's Neoplatonism? Of course not. Well, let's try to read the poem anyway and see how far we can get without a lesson in its philosophical or theological background. I'll read it aloud to you twice.

> My heart leaps up when I behold
> A rainbow in the sky:
> So was it when my life began;
> So is it now I am a man;
> So be it when I shall grow old,
> Or let me die!
> The Child is father of the Man;
> And I could wish my days to be
> Bound each to each by natural piety. (virtue)
> (1807)

Step 1. (3–5 minutes) Now, read the poem on your own, three or four times. Make some notes on the problems or difficulties you encounter in trying to make sense of it. When you finish, write out any questions you still have about the poem.

Step 2. (7–10 minutes) Now, working in groups of three, share your notes and your questions with your partners. Try to solve all the problems that troubled you and see if any new ones arise. I'll ask you to report out in a few minutes and tell about your problems and how you solved them or didn't.

Step 3. (10 minutes) Report out and discuss.

T: What did you find in your groups? What problems did you encounter and did any of them resist solution in your group? Or did new ones arise? Who is willing to report for a group?

S1: We thought it was a pretty easy poem until the end. Then we had problems, but I think we may have solved them.

T: So do you still have some questions?

S2: Some of us still aren't sure what "natural piety" can mean.

S1: I know what "piety" means, but I don't get the "natural" part.

T: What does "piety" mean?

S2: It means religious, like a priest or minister is pious—or is supposed to be.

S3: Wordsworth means that he learned to be religious when he was a child, from seeing rainbows and things like that. So his piety sort of comes from nature rather than the church or Sunday school.

S4: But why does he say "and I could wish my days to be bound each to each"?

S3: Because he learns from his experience each day, going from when his life began to his adulthood to old age. And he learns to be religious at every stage, because he always has these religious feelings, like when he sees a rainbow.

S4: So why does he want to die?

S5: He doesn't want to die! He says "or let me die." He'd rather be dead than not have his heart leap up when he sees a rainbow.

S4: Now I get it!

T: Is that how most of you get it? OK. Is that it? No other problems arose in your groups?

SEVERAL STUDENTS: Yeah, right! No! Yes! Of course!

T: Well?

S6: The big problem for us was we wanted to know how the child could be father of the man.

T: For how many of you was that a problem, at least for a while? That's most of you. Of course. Please notice that there aren't any difficult words in that line or that sentence. And you also understand it perfectly as a syntactic or grammatical structure. That is, you know perfectly well what it means to say that someone is the father of someone else. Any five-year-old child can understand such a sentence. So why do you say it's a problem for you?

S2: It's backward. A child can't be the father of an adult.

S7: It doesn't say adult; it says man. And most men are children anyway, so their children have to parent them.

T: Ah. Is that what your group came up with? Or is that your own feminist reading?

S7: It's my experience. But never mind.

S8: We said it was Jesus, who is a child and is also our heavenly father. Because God is both the Father and the Son.

T: And how does that connect to the rest of the poem?

S2: That was our question.

S8: He gets his piety from God, who is both the Father and the Son.

T: Go on.

S8: God creates nature and gives us the religion we get through nature. But it all starts with Jesus, who is a child, like us. I don't know. It just seems like the right way to read that line.

T: Are you all comfortable with what we are hearing about how to interpret the line "The Child is father of the Man"?

S7: I'm comfortable with the idea that God gives us what we get through nature. But what does that idea have to do with the idea that Jesus was once a child in the manger and yet is also the father? I can't see the connection.

S9: We thought that the child refers to the speaker as a child.

T: Can you elaborate on that?

S9: Well, it says that he became religious because of his childhood experience of being inspired by rainbows. They gave him a feeling like religious awe. I know exactly what he means from surfing and also from hiking in the Sierras. And the feeling stayed with him as an adult. So he can say he learned it from his childhood. So the child he was himself is like his teacher or parent.

T: What do the rest of you think of that? Does it make sense? Do you accept that reading?

S10: We came to the same idea in our group. We are the products of our experience as children. Our adult personality as well as our neuroses are the products of childhood experiences and traumas.

T: Are the rest of you now buying that reading? I see lots of affirmatively nodding heads. Why are you buying it?

S11: It fits. It makes sense.

T: It's plausible, isn't it? Is it more plausible than any alternative presented? I agree. It has explanatory power. It fits with the other facts of the poem as we understand them. It therefore persuades us. And do we need to know something about metempsychosis or Wordsworth's Neoplatonism to understand it? Or about the Romantic emphasis on the natural powers of children? I think a lecture on those ideas as an introduction to this poem might distort your experience of the poem rather than open you up to what the poem is actually saying and doing.

You may be interested in knowing, by the way, that one of the meanings of *piety*, at least through the nineteenth century (according to the *Oxford English Dictionary*), is filial devotion or reverence toward one's parents. Do you find that an applicable definition here? I think so, too. And did you have to know it to read the poem? Not at all, even though it may now be an interesting and enriching gloss on a term used in the poem, though it might be a mistake to take that definition as the primary or dominant meaning of *piety* in this context.

So are we seriously disadvantaged as readers of this poem by our own historical position, by the fact that the poem was written two hundred years ago? Is the language closed to us? Are the experiences it honors or the ideas it advances foreign to us? Not at all. In fact, aren't we at this moment in cultural history better prepared to understand its most difficult line than most well-educated readers in 1807 might have been? Notice how Dory talked about neuroses and traumas. That's the discourse of twentieth-century psychotherapy or psychoanalysis, and it reflects the general influence of Freud and Freudianism on modern thought. Isn't it a commonplace of our age that our childhood experiences shape us psychologically into the people we are as adults? Not that you need to be aware of Freudian thought to unpack what most readers usually identify as the most important and most problematic line in this poem. Wordsworth himself died before Freud was born. But my point is that as modern readers, we may be extraordinarily well-prepared rather than culturally impaired when it comes to interpreting an idea such as the one we find in this early nineteenth-century poem about how we are shaped psychologically and spiritually by our childhood experiences. So why was the line still difficult for so many of you? Why did it puzzle you, if only for a while?

S2: It's a paradox. A child can't be the father of a man, literally, or at least biologically.

T: That's true. And yet he can in so many ways. Even biologically in the sense that we have to be children before we can be adults. So we are in that sense our own progenitors, too. OK. Did most of you find the line puzzling at least for a while? Virtually everybody. And how many of you figured it out by yourselves before you met with your group? Only a few of you. And how many of you were in groups where the discussion illuminated the line for you? That's pretty good. And how many of you knew this poem before you got here, so it never gave you a problem? Only one of you? That surprises me. So, how did all the rest of you figure it out, whether you did it by yourself or in collaboration with others? What did you do to figure it out and what resources did you draw on?

S11: We drew on Charles. He knew the poem already and told us.

T: And you believed him?

S11: Well, it seemed logical.

T: What happened where you didn't have Charles in your group?

S4: We just talked about it and tried to make sense of it and considered alternatives—like the idea of God the Father and God the Son—and it just came to us that the line wasn't mysterious or symbolic or anything, but true.

T: How did it "just come to you"?

S4: We talked about it a lot and tried to make sense of it.

T: And that, ladies and gentlemen, is one of the points of this exercise: to let you see that poetry is often difficult but not inaccessible to readers who are willing to read it thoughtfully—to do the work of making sense of it. And that sense-making work is sometimes most demanded of us by lines where the language and syntax are most familiar to us. And the difficulty of such lines is often not an indication that you are missing some crucial information about the poet's culture or religion, but an indication that the poem says something that is simply difficult to grasp or says something in a way that forces you to think hard in order to grasp it. But why, you might ask, didn't Wordsworth just tell us his idea more directly, in language that wouldn't even momentarily confuse us or cause us interpretive trouble?

S12: Because he's a poet and wants to make reading difficult.

T: I think there is actually much to that idea, though not because poets simply want to be obscure. But first, couldn't someone argue with some justice that the line isn't any harder than the idea it expresses? In fact, its difficulty might be said to derive from the economy and memorable simplicity of its expression. That is, Wordsworth employs only seven words to express an idea that it would probably take us several sentences to explain. And the rambling language of our explanation might itself be hard to understand and be quickly forgotten, while Wordsworth's line and its meaning are likely to stay with us for a lifetime.

Another way to explain the difficulty of the line is a version of Randy's perhaps flippant observation that poets like to make their texts difficult for readers. In fact, it's a commonplace of criticism that the job of a poet or any artist is to make the familiar strange and the strange familiar. That means that the function of art, including literary art, is either to enrich our lives and minds by using images and ideas from the world we know to expand our experience beyond the limited sphere of the life we actually live or to compel us to experience more vitally the ordinary life we do live by having us pay closer attention to our familiar experience.

The Russian literary theorist Viktor Shklovsky ([1917] 1994) cites a passage from Tolstoy's diaries where the great Russian novelist describes cleaning a room and then not remembering if he had cleaned it or not, so automatic and unconscious had been his activity in performing such an everyday chore. To the extent that we live our lives in such a habitual and therefore unconscious way, notes Tolstoy in his diary entry, we have not lived at all and our own lives are to us as if they had never been. Building on that point, Shklovsky argues that the function of technique in art is to "defamiliarize" our experience by representing it to us in unique and difficult ways "to increase the difficulty and length of perception, because the process of perception is an aesthetic end in itself and must be prolonged" (264). In other words, poetry challenges us with its difficulty at least in part to demand our attention and thoughtfulness, that we might pay close attention to the poem itself and thereby become more alive to the experience of reading the poem as well as to the life experience the poem represents. "Art exists," says Shklovsky "that one may recover the sensation of life; it exists to make one feel things, to make the stone stony" (264). We can add, I think, that it also serves to enliven our experience of ideas and to demand our close and prolonged attention to what we think as well as feel.

This workshop will have served its purpose if it has given you an experience of coming to understand a line that you may have felt unable to understand but that revealed itself to you through your own expenditure of time and effort (perhaps in collaboration with others). I also hope the workshop has helped you to see that poetic difficulty is not usually evidence that something is missing in you as a reader, but that what you are perceiving as your own unfortunate problem may be a built-in feature of most genuine literary experience. Yes, it is also the case that a poem may sometimes include words and phrases that are not part of your lexicon or make intertextual references that you aren't familiar with. But as we have seen, these obstacles to reading are generally recognizable for what they are and don't usually pose a fatal impediment to your participation in the poetic experience. Syntactic difficulties can sometimes seem to turn a poem into doubletalk, but these are usually resolvable with enough persistence and attention on the part of the reader. And the common difficulty of not being able to make sense within the frame of your own experience of a line that seems grammatically and lexically accessible is a difficulty you can usually address productively through resources that have always been yours. I am speaking, of course, first, of the most powerful resource at your disposal: your own concentrated attention and capacity to think. Nor should we forget the resource we are to each other, nor the intellectually productive process of discussing a problem with intelligent colleagues.

What Is a Literature Workshop and Where Does It Come From?

Looking back at what transpired in the workshop segment reproduced above, one might wonder how the discourse of that classroom is different from any other typical English class where a poem or some other text is being discussed and explicated. The teacher may seem to lead students (whether they are actually students or teachers in a professional development workshop) to produce what the teacher apparently regards as an acceptable reading of a poem. The slice of classroom life reconstructed here might then be characterized (or criticized) as a class conducted in the spirit of the old New Criticism, where the text is examined carefully under the guidance of an expert interpreter to yield a meaning that would appear to be already there for sufficiently attentive and well-informed readers to apprehend (for an alternative and more positive view of the presented exchange about poetic meaning, see Chapter 9). In that sense it may appear to be a highly traditional class, even if it happens to include some unusually vocal contributors and an opportunity for all the participants to work for a while in small groups.

Yet that description of the instructional transaction we have just witnessed ignores more than it reveals about the event as an occasion and opportunity for learning. It specifically fails to notice several crucial features of the event that render it a workshop rather than a traditional literature lesson. First, note that the segment of workshop reproduced here begins with an interpretive problem (What do you make of this poem and what problems does it present for you?) presented to students for their individual solutions and for their collective reflection, calling on them to work on the poem and their problems individually and then collectively, eventually reporting on what difficulties they encountered in the poem and how they went about trying to solve them. In other words, instruction began with a double problem posed by the workshop leader, focused ostensibly on the meaning of the poem and at the same time on the phenomenology of the problem itself: how the workshop participants experienced the problem of discerning or construing a meaning, including what dimensions of the problem were in fact problematic for them, what processes or strategies they employed in seeking a solution, what impediments they encountered, what resources they drew upon, and so on.

Furthermore, the segment of workshop shown is part of a larger workshop on a constellation of different ways in which poems or poetic passages may pose difficulties for readers. In the context of that larger lesson, the challenge of the Wordsworth poem is valuable as a case study conducted by the participants—a study of a certain kind of difficulty that a poem may pose for readers and a case study for each student participant of how he or she operates and might operate, individually and as a part of a group, in reading lines that pose such a difficulty.

So if we want to identify the features of a literature workshop as a genre or form of instruction, we can say:

1. There is the posing of genuine questions or problems that face readers of literature individually and in groups as they engage in literary study or participate in the discourse of literature.
2. There is the demand that workshop participants monitor how they experience the problems set by the assignment, along with the related demand that:
3. Participants reflect on and talk about or write about the problems they encountered and how they addressed them.

The focus of the literature workshop, in other words, is at least as much on the process of reading and producing discourse about literature as it is on the substance of the discourse produced. But it is never solely about processes and it is never about the results of a reading detached from observations, reflections, and queries about how those results were achieved.

Note that a workshop requiring students to engage in what amounts to metacognitive processing—thinking about and reporting on their own thinking in their encounter with a problem—positions students and teacher in a pedagogical relationship that entails a shared or distributed expertise. It thereby takes a large step toward dismantling the top-down structure of the classroom in a way that my lecture of some thirty years ago desiderated but could not operationally imagine. The students become valued experts because only they can know and can report on their own experiences as readers engaged with the problems they encounter. The teacher's expertise is called upon, first, in this instance at least, in selecting texts and posing problems that represent promising opportunities for acquiring particular kinds of knowledge, as well as in offering commentaries, glosses, and reflections that supplement and frame the experience of the workshop in some larger conception of disciplinary knowledge in literature.

My view of the workshop as essentially a combined case study (of texts as instances of certain challenges) and self-study or phenomenological investigation sometimes tempts me to identify the instructional model demonstrated in the following chapters not as the *literature workshop* but the *literature laboratory*, thinking of a laboratory as a site where experiments are performed and findings examined in the interest of advancing knowledge both about texts and about ways of reading them (see Elbow 1995). And in my own classes (as on occasion here) I sometimes do identify activities of the kind I dramatize on these pages as experiments, and I sometimes speak of class sessions as laboratories. But, finally, I prefer to identify the genre of instruction I demonstrate here as the literature workshop, in part because I want to identify my instructional practice with the pedagogical tradition of the writing workshop, and even more because I want to identify my practice and method in this book with the learning community and professional development tradition of the National Writing Project. And this brings me to a maverick theory of practice and a model of professional discourse that inform the rhetoric, organizational logic, and presentational method I have employed in constructing all of my workshops and in writing this book for fellow teachers.

An Antitheoretical Theory of Practice: The Writing Project Model of Teacher Development

The first site of the National Writing Project was founded in 1974 as the Bay Area Writing Project at the University of California, Berkeley. Its founder, James Gray, who was decidedly and stubbornly antitheoretical in his own orientation, founded the Project on the antitheoretical and pragmatic theory (he would insist it was simply what he had observed to be true) that the crucial knowledge needed to improve the teaching of writing in the nation's schools, from elementary schools through the university, already resided in the expertise and best practices of experienced and successful classroom teachers at all levels of education and emphatically not in educational theorists and researchers. It became the function of the Writing Project, then, to identify expert teachers or "classroom practitioners" and bring them together to share and refine their practices and expertise and eventually disseminate them to colleagues (Gray 2000).

But Jim Gray (who was then a supervisor in teacher education in English at the University of California, Berkeley) and his first cohort of colleagues in the Bay Area Writing Project found almost immediately that in order for them to demonstrate and share their best practices with one another in a usable and credible form, they had to be able to articulate the principles that informed their practices. Without a set of principles or a theory to frame demonstrated practices, the practices that were demonstrated and inevitably transformed in their adaptation or translation from one classroom setting and group of students to another—like the story passed along from one teller to another—would easily lose their originating focus and pedagogical purpose, becoming mere busywork or serving contradictory and self-defeating purposes. It therefore became a distinctive function of the leaders at National Writing Project sites to assist teachers in the Project in reflecting on their practice and uncovering and articulating the theory or principles that inform the best practices they employ in their own teaching and propose to demonstrate to their colleagues. The theory of practice informing the work of the National Writing Project begins, therefore, with practice; and it looks for the tacit theory behind the practice in the experience and intellectual history of the practitioner, in the learning needs and lives of the students in the practitioner's classroom, in the practitioner's own values and goals, as well as in the research and theory available in our professional literature.

This book is influenced by the National Writing Project model of professional development most obviously in presenting pedagogical ideas to colleagues largely in the form of demonstration lessons that model actual classroom practices, and then in reflecting on those demonstrations and their origins as a way of drawing a rationale or theory for practice from the demonstrated practices themselves. Many of its chapters can be said to represent attempts to re-create for readers the experience of participating in a typical Writing Project professional development workshop (focused on the teaching of literature).

Situated Learning in Communities of Practice

The kind of workshop that is reenacted in these chapters also puts into play an additional related theory of learning and practice that is implicitly embraced by the Writing Project professional development model and informs every chapter of this book. This theory accounts for the way that every Writing Project site functions as a community of learners, where colleagues representing all levels of education collaborate as writers, teacher-researchers, reflective practitioners, and the disseminators of professional knowledge in the interest of their own professional development and that of their colleagues in schools and colleges within and beyond the regions they serve.

These practices defining what a writing project is and does were developed largely without a prior articulated theory of practice by the first cohorts of Writing Project teachers at the University of California, Berkeley. Their practice grew instead out of the mutual professional respect that governed the work of the Writing Project teachers in and beyond their summer institutes, based partly on Jim Gray's example and partly on the high standards he imposed in selecting participants (Gray 2000). But their practices also arose from the hunger they collectively felt to replace the intellectual isolation that classroom teachers characteristically experience with what they imagined to be the collegial experience of university faculty who belong to a community of scholars (a community that the university itself has historically aspired to become, but in its modern bureaucratized corporate incarnation no longer even dreams of becoming). Out of these collective aspirations and values James Gray and his colleagues of the Bay Area Writing Project created a model for all National Writing Project sites that had even more force than a theory,[3] while it also anticipated a good deal of emerging and subsequent research and theory on the sociocultural dimensions of learning (Bloome and Egan-Robertson 1993; Santa Barbara Classroom Discourse Group 1993). It anticipated most dramatically a rich strand of research and theory about "situated learning," a term that refers to a view of learning as fundamentally social and derived from participation in what researchers in the field (Lave and Wenger 1991) call "communities of practice." In fact, the unprecedented success of the National Writing Project in influencing the practice of teachers over extended periods of time and transformatively enhancing their professional expertise has made Writing Projects themselves ideal sites for research on situated learning and on the character and opportunities for learning provided in communities of practice (Neves 2001; Staley 2001; Lieberman and Wood 2003).

Among the findings confirmed by this body of research is the unsurprising fact that teachers who participate in Writing Project invitational summer institutes and follow-up programs tend to regard their experience in the Project as the most powerful and satisfying learning experience of their academic lives and that they therefore tend to aspire to comparable sorts of experiences for their students, seeking in their classrooms to create a culture that is modeled after the Writing Project itself (Blau 1993, 1999; Floriani 1994). Having experienced what it means to learn in a community of learners, teachers are inclined to count such learning as more authoritative and authentic than any other and to think of such learning as the proper aim of their own instruction. They therefore become determined to turn their own classrooms into learning communities that will function like a Writing Project, where respect for the intelligence of every learner is the starting place for all activity, where every member is seen as a source of knowledge and expertise, and where all learners are expected and required to take responsibility for their own learning as well as for assisting others to learn. In such a community, learning entails the production of knowledge as well as its reception, and knowledge is always seen as provisional and subject to challenge and refinement (Blau 1999; Lieberman and Wood 2002).

With a similar respect for the power to learn that resides in learning communities, I have attempted in most of the chapters of this book to dramatize or recreate through constructed transcripts the experience of participating in a Writing Project workshop in a community of colleagues. More significantly, the classroom lessons demonstrated through those workshops are in every instance designed to nurture and support a classroom culture for students that enables the classroom to function like a Writing Project, which is to say, as an intellectually healthy and productive learning community, where the curriculum is largely defined by opportunities for learning (Dewey 1938; Tuyay, Jennings, and Dixon 1995; Jennings 1998; Dixon, Frank, and Green 1999) that are made available to students through their active participation as members (Kutz, Groden, and Zamel 1993).

An Additional Rule for Practice

One more principle or rule for practice in the Writing Project community deserves mention here as an introduction to the chapters that follow. It is the rule that Writing Project teachers, in conducting inservice workshops for colleagues, never present or demonstrate anything that they don't do themselves as teachers in their own classrooms. The motto of the National Writing Project is "teachers teaching teachers," explicitly and publicly eschewing the tradition (no longer so widely practiced, thanks largely to the influence of the NWP) of professional development programs in K–12 education that characteristically put working classroom teachers in the professionally humiliating role of being told how to teach (according to the latest theory or body of research) by university researchers or curriculum specialists who were themselves not teaching in K–12 classrooms and sometimes not teaching at all. Such workshops have been notoriously useless for teachers, because even if the theory presented and the research findings cited might be interesting and valid, such experts have little credibility with classroom teachers and, in fact, have almost no experience to draw upon on the question of how their ideas translate to practice with real students.

In reaction to such a professionally disrespectful and counterproductive tradition of professional development, the Writing Project adopted very early on the policy that teachers affiliated with Writing Projects and conducting professional development programs representing the Writing Project would never present any ideas for teaching that they had not employed and refined in their own classrooms with their own students. Furthermore, in making presentations to teachers, Writing Project teacher-consultants are expected to call attention to the particular context for their teaching and acknowledge how their professional authority is situated in that particular context and how much what they are presenting therefore represents local knowledge.

This book honors the Writing Project tradition of teachers teaching teachers in several ways. First, every strategy or approach to teaching that I present in this book is a version of what I actually do on a regular basis and have done over a period of years with my own students in ordinary classrooms. I am not presenting recipes or advice about what any teacher should do. I am instead demonstrating in every workshop of this book what I regularly do myself and expect to continue doing (with refinements and variations resulting from new experiments) with my own students in an introduction to literature course that I teach every year for University of California undergraduates, most of whom are sophomores (eighteen to twenty years old). Some of these students are beginning their academic careers as English majors. Most of them are non-English majors, who are enrolled in the course to satisfy a general education requirement in the humanities or another requirement for a course that includes intensive work on writing.

I have also employed many of the strategies and writing assignments presented in this book with more advanced undergraduate students in an English course called Practical Criticism and in senior seminars for English majors. In addition, I regularly conduct all the workshops presented in this book in a graduate course in English education for students enrolled in a combined master's and English teaching credential program in the Graduate School of Education on my campus. And most of these students subsequently adapt many of these workshops for use in the middle school and high school classes where they teach English as student-teachers. I have also conducted many of these workshops myself with various groups of high school students in classrooms and in special programs in various parts of the country where I have been invited to serve as a guest teacher.

Finally, all of the workshops presented in this book are also re-creations of workshops I have been conducting over the past fifteen years (some only recently) for working classroom teachers at professional conferences (especially at national and regional conferences of the National Council of Teachers of English), at sites of the National Writing Project, and in other professional development programs in schools and colleges in virtually every state of the Union. When I pay return visits to these conferences and campuses and meet workshop participants at subsequent professional meetings, teachers at every grade level from middle school to college tell me appreciative stories about how they have successfully adopted in their classes the teaching strategies I demonstrated to them in my workshop. So while I acknowledge that whatever pedagogical expertise I offer here represents local knowledge earned largely in college classrooms with the (mostly) privileged students I happen to teach, I have good evidence that most English teachers who teach across the spectrum of American middle schools, high schools, community colleges, and four-year colleges will find that the demonstration lessons re-created here are usable as shown or adaptable for use in at least some of the classes they teach.

Notes

1. The split in university English departments is particularly ironic in light of the growing focus of the literature faculty over the past thirty years on literary theories that have generally sought to disestablish the authority of texts and authors in favor of readers. Yet, in spite of the dominance of such theories and in spite of the proliferation of the related new and fertile interpretive frames for readers to use in interpreting or reconstituting literary texts, the culture of literature instruction in colleges and universities seems hardly changed and remains largely product-oriented, text-centered, and top-down. This surely demonstrates the power of cultural norms and practices over members of a culture and their resistance to change. It also supports the thesis of this book that what needs to be addressed to revitalize the teaching of literature is not so much theories about reading or literary discourse, but the culture of instruction.

2. The dialogue reproduced in this workshop segment is drawn from notes, transcripts of videotaped classes, and my memory of numerous workshops over the years and therefore represents a composite or typical workshop scene rather than any particular workshop with any particular group. Any names used to identify participants are, of course, pseudonyms. For the sake of simplicity I usually tag the participants as S1, S2, and so on.

3. The assumptions and principles of the National Writing Project, while never described in the public discourse of the Project itself as a "theory" (the very term would arouse the ire of founder

James Gray), nevertheless collectively constitute a coherent and comprehensive theory of professional development and would count as a theory according to most theoretical models of what theory is and does (see Mitchell 1985, 6). Miles Myers, who was one of the founders with Jim Gray of the Bay Area Writing Project and of the California and National Writing Projects, also asserts (personal correspondence, July 25, 2002) that while James Gray insisted on an anti-theoretical and teacher-friendly rhetoric for the Writing Project and would approve of my account of its untheorized practices, those practices were nevertheless justified even in fairly early funding proposals "by three theoretical frameworks." These Myers identifies as follows: "(1) The theory of a 'Professionalization Project' and practice communities (built largely on the work of Milbury McLaughlin and the bottom-up theorists of the late 1960s); (2) The theories of Learning (Vygotsky, Dewey, Moffett, Graves) emphasizing Activity Structures and Scaffolding; and (3) The Theories of Composition—Christensen, Moffett, Don Murray, Kinneavy, O'Donnel-Strong-O'Hare (sentence combining), others."

1

Stories from the Classroom
Lessons on Learning Literature

(In this chapter and the one that follows I want to address a pedagogical problem that college teachers of literature share with most of their secondary school colleagues: the inclination of our students to behave like consumers of literary interpretations rather than the producers of them.)That is, given a poem or short story as a reading assignment, our students may do the reading themselves, but return to our classes prepared to take notes from us on what constitutes the correct interpretation of the text. Of course, whenever we cooperate in this well-established system, we may be encouraging many students not to read the text at all. We are certainly encouraging all of them to read it without any particular interpretive responsibility. So we should perhaps refer to the system not as consumership but as welfare. It is, in any event, a state of affairs that many teachers lament but feel unable to abandon, because students are so convincing about their own interpretive dependence (Nystrand 1991, 1997; Hynds 1991).

Classroom Stories as Telling Cases

Before I present a workshop designed to change the relationship of students to such work as interpretation entails, let me tell some stories to dramatize the culture of schooling and possibly explain how a culture of interpretive dependence has been and continues to be inadvertently nourished by schools. I do not tell these stories of problematic teaching practices to suggest that our profession is filled with bad teachers. On the contrary, the teachers I describe (with the exception of one who is very young) are quite masterful. My stories are about the dilemmas and challenges of teaching for every teacher. The first two stories I want to tell are about classes I observed in secondary schools; the third one is about many classes I have observed in colleges and universities.

Story #1: Julius Caesar—"This Play Sucks"

My first story reports on a visit I made some years ago to a ninth-grade English class in a suburban high school, where the students were reading *Julius Caesar*. While I was observing instruction in this fairly typical class, I noticed a student in the back of the room behaving as many students in the back rows of classrooms in ninth grade are inclined to. As the students were ostensibly reading some assigned portion of the play, this particular student, his hand cupped over his mouth to hide the source of his disruptive noises, called aloud into the room such phrases of complaint as "This play sucks," "This play is dumb," and "This is a stupid play."

The teacher, a young man himself and new to teaching, eventually located the source of the complaints and asked the student directly what was wrong. Why was he saying that this play is stupid? The student replied that the play was stupid "because if Brutus loved Caesar so much, how come he killed him?" The teacher replied that this was not a stupid play, that it most assuredly did not suck—that it was, on the contrary, one of the monuments of Western culture and one of the greatest works in the English literary tradition. It included memorable speeches and taught us important lessons in history and so on. The complaining student was properly chastened by this little speech; the other students were confirmed in their view of the disruptive student as one whose observations deserved ridicule; Shakespeare's play was restored to its rightful place as a masterpiece; and the central ethical and moral problem of the play was comfortably avoided.

The question I would raise about this incident is—who can be said to understand the play better—the student who found it confusing and called it stupid or the students who laughed at that confusion, presumably because they did not experience it, which is to say, saw no grounds for confusion? From this incident I also derive the following principle or proposition for literature classrooms: *confusion often represents an advanced state of understanding.* That is to say, the student who is confused is frequently the one who understands enough to see a problem, a problem that less perceptive students have not yet noticed or arrived at. From this perspective we might argue that one of the chief functions of a literature class is not to present literature to students (as conventional teaching guides are likely to advise) in ways that will anticipate and prevent their confusion, but to welcome and even foster among readers the experience of confusion.

Every veteran teacher of literature has had the experience of having some student in class ask a question or offer an alternative reading that throws into doubt the teacher's own long-held interpretation of a cherished poem. Teachers who are experienced enough and confident enough to endure the confusion that such interpretive doubt now engenders, and who will with their students embrace rather than avoid the problems raised by the interpretive challenge, will invariably advance their own understanding of the poem and secure for themselves and their students a more insightful and comprehensive interpretation, and one better able to sustain further interrogation. In fact, to take the alternative route and retreat from the challenge of confusion is to endure from that point forward a kind of constant fear of future exposure and a sense of fraudulence about one's own authority as a teacher.

Notice the difference between a typical student and a professionally active English professor who both have an experience of confusion in understanding a text that they had previously assumed they understood or in reading a segment of text that suddenly contradicts for them what they know the text is conventionally thought to mean. The student is likely to think of himself as a poor reader or of the text as one too difficult for him to talk about or write about. The English professor will celebrate because he has found a problem to examine in an essay or paper that he will publish for colleagues.

Even more to the point, when we consider the value of confusion, is John Dewey's observation that confusion is the generative force or motive for the intellectual work that constitutes interpretation. In *How We Think* (1910), his classic study of the mental operations that define intellectual work in all academic and artistic disciplines, Dewey notes that the process of thinking that he identifies with authentic reflection and interpretation begins with the recognition of a problem or question that for the thinker constitutes a state of intellectual disequilibrium or confusion (11–13). We might want to add to our unconventional proposition about the virtue of confusion, then, an additional and possibly more practical observation, which is that confusion represents a necessary starting point for any act of interpretation and therefore is an essential part of the experience of literary study for any student who is to achieve interpretive autonomy.[1]

Story #2: Macbeth—*Why the Footnotes You Get Are Not the Ones You Need*

Before further examining the pedagogical consequences of such instruction as I have just described, let me tell about another class I witnessed in another high school, this time a twelfth-grade college prep English class, again studying Shakespeare, but in this case *Macbeth*. When I arrived at the classroom door a few minutes early, the teacher handed me an extra text and indicated the scene or segment of the play that he would be working on for this particular class period. It was a short scene of perhaps sixty lines, which I read over quickly before the class began. As I previewed the scene, I found that there were eight or ten lines in it that I couldn't construe comfortably or couldn't make sense of at all. I looked forward, therefore, to seeing how these lines in particular would be handled in class.

The class I saw that day was in many ways an exemplary one. The teacher went over the scene carefully, asking students to act out particularly important lines, urging them to discuss various passages in small and large groups, and making sure that students understood the scene in the context of the whole play. He also attended carefully to the language of individual lines, interpreting and glossing virtually every line in the scene—every line, that is, except the eight to ten lines that I didn't understand and had been looking forward to working on.

After class, I congratulated the teacher on his stimulating lesson and remarked on the coincidence of his attending to every line in the scene except the few that I had most hoped to find elucidated. It was no coincidence, he confessed; he didn't understand those lines either. I then asked what he supposed the students in the class thought about the unglossed lines that neither of us understood. I'm sorry to say we never checked with the students themselves, but my guess was that each of the students in the class thought that he or she must be the only person in the room who didn't understand the few lines that never got discussed. If they weren't the easiest lines in the scene, each student must have thought, the teacher would surely have attended to them.

This, by the way, is exactly what students are often encouraged to think by the parallel treatment of problematic lines in poems and prose works printed in textbooks and even scholarly editions. The editors will frequently provide glosses for all the lines a strong reader can figure out for himself in a poem, but no glosses for the lines that no reader has ever figured out. I have made it a point to examine the treatment of problematic lines in college textbooks and scholarly editions, so I can attest with some authority that this is true for many textbooks and for some of the most respected scholarly editions of major poets.

But why did the teacher—himself a strong reader and generally confident teacher—avoid the lines he didn't understand in the lesson I observed? The answer is self-evident, I suppose, given conventional assumptions about what it means to teach literature. How can one teach what one doesn't know? As if the teaching of literature were essentially a matter of a teacher teaching to students the teacher's own finished reading of a text and not what it means to engage in a reading of a text, including how a competent reader proceeds with a text that is frustratingly difficult to understand.

Just how productive an alternative teaching strategy might have been was revealed to both the teacher and myself when together we worked on the lines that had puzzled us and that had been avoided in class. I regret that I don't remember what scene we worked on or what lines, but I do remember that as we constructed plausible interpretations of the lines that had puzzled us, we felt we were gaining important insights that deepened and refined our sense of the scene and of the play as a whole. In fact, we both felt that the lines that had puzzled us were the most interesting and informative lines in the whole scene—lines that had more to teach us conceptually or about the play than any of the lines that we had managed more easily to grasp. Why should this be so? The answer, I think, is that the puzzling lines puzzled us precisely because they had so much to teach us. That is to say, their difficulty derived from the fact that they told us things we didn't already know. That is why we found ourselves unable to understand them readily.

From this experience and a lifetime of similar ones, I have derived a principle for teaching and learning that in its strongly stated and most memorable form will probably not survive the strictest scrutiny, but that I nevertheless am willing to advance heuristically as a proposition worth entertaining for its potential pedagogical value: *The only texts worth reading are texts you don't understand. Because if you understand a text as soon as you read it, you must have understood it before you read it, so you didn't have to bother reading it in the first place.* Or to rephrase it in less contentious and less memorable terms, we can say that if you can't understand what you read when you first read a text, it may be evidence that this is a text especially worth reading, because it is telling you something you don't already understand conceptually and the process of figuring it out will constitute a process of advancing or deepening your vision.[2]

Consider, for example, the most tantalizing and generally most confusing line of Wordsworth's brief and frequently anthologized lyric "My Heart Leaps Up":

> My heart leaps up when I behold
> A rainbow in the sky
> So was it when my life began
> So is it now I am a man
> So be it when I shall grow old
> Or let me die.
> The Child is father of the Man.
> And I could wish my days to be
> Bound each to each by natural piety.

Most readers who aren't already well-versed in Wordsworth will be at least momentarily puzzled by the semantic confusion invited by the paradoxical idea of the child as parent of the adult (see the introduction). But after some reflection on the concept, particularly in its context, most readers will be able to construct a meaning that feels like an insight or at least an interesting perspective (which goes beyond but might be said to include a Freudian one) on our relationship to our own personal history and experience as children and on how what we know as adults depends quite literally as well as spiritually on what we learned as children, making our childhood our tutor and in that sense our progenitor or parent. And the fact that it takes more than thirty words on my part to provide what is finally only a partial and meager explanation of an idea that is evoked more comprehensively and inclusively in the poet's seven is one measure of the power of the poetic trope.

Difficulties of this kind are offered to us by many of the texts we find most difficult yet satisfying to read. Those are the very texts and the points of confusion in those texts, moreover, that most deserve and are most richly illuminated by reflection and discussion. That is, these are the texts that can be most productively taught in a context like a classroom, where readers can most conveniently engage in such activities as discussion, reflection through writing, and collaboration in the process of interpretation. In such contexts with such texts, our most enriching opportunities arise, when we encounter the very lines and sections of text that our fear of failure will most forcefully urge us to avoid. Our task, then, to is remember the virtue of confusion and the value of what Tom Newkirk (1984) has called "looking for trouble."

Story #3: *Confessing and Forgiving*

The third story I want to tell begins not in an actual but a prototypical college literature course, say, a typical survey course in English literature or a more specialized class in a particular literary period like the Renaissance. Imagine that the instructor plans to spend some time introducing students to the metaphysical poets and has decided to focus on Donne and Herbert. Such an instructor might typically assign four, five, or more poems each by Donne and Herbert, say on Friday, and expect the students to have read them—perhaps eight to ten pages of difficult reading—by Monday morning's class.

Imagine now how a typical college student might approach such a reading assignment. Sunday night about 10 P.M. he might begin reading and actually read the words of several poems once or twice before stopping to note that he can hardly understand what they are about. He might then "read" a few more pages before falling asleep or giving up. A conscientious student might plan to get up early Monday morning and finish studying then. In the hour or so available before class, such a conscientious student might then have time to complete a reading of each of the assigned poems once or twice, but not time enough to feel competent as a reader of any of them. Moreover, the student would know that it's not necessary to understand these poems before getting to class, because the professor can be counted on to explain them in class.

And of course, the student would be right. For a typical English professor will come to class prepared to lecture on the texts assigned for that class meeting or to "discuss" the texts in class in a way that is sometimes called Socratic. In practice this means that the professor asks questions that prompt responses that eventually allow the professor to say or collaborate with his students in saying the very things that he would otherwise have said in a single uninterrupted turn, if he had been inclined to lecture. In any event, what the students do mainly is take notes, which they write in notebooks and in the margins of their books to record what, according to the instructor, the poems are presumably about and what a literate reader should know about them.

This scenario has to raise questions for us about how we can characterize the student's relationship to the texts he has been assigned. Has the student performed as a reader of those texts? Or is the professor the reader, with the student functioning largely as the recorder of someone else's reading? Louise Rosenblatt says that taking someone else's interpretation as your own is like having someone else eat your dinner for you. I would add that a steady diet of that kind will lead not only to literary starvation but to a conviction that you can never eat for yourself—at least not the gourmet food served up in literature courses. And that seems to be the conviction under which many students of literature labor, not because they haven't taken courses in literature, but because they have.

Given such a literary education, it perhaps shouldn't surprise us to encounter graduating English majors about to embark on student-teaching assignments who say (as some have admitted to me over the years) that they don't feel adequately prepared to teach literature in a secondary school because they haven't had courses covering all the texts they might have to teach. They assume, in other words, that if they haven't been taught a literary work, they won't know how to teach it.

At first glance that may appear to be the expression of a perfectly rational and natural concern. We wouldn't expect a science teacher to teach botany without having had a course in it, nor an art teacher to teach pottery without some expertise in working with clay. But when a prospective high school English teacher feels it is necessary to have been taught a text before teaching it, he or she reveals a conception of the teaching of literature as the passing on of notes, or a matter of passing on to students the correct body of information that may be said to constitute knowledge of a literary text. College teachers give it to college students, and college students who become high school teachers pass it on to their students. How else can a student know what a serious literary text means if his teacher hasn't told him?

The concern of some teachers about teaching texts that they haven't been taught also reflects an assumption about what one ought to be doing in a classroom that a great many teachers, beginners and veterans—even those quite sophisticated in literary study—may still labor under and surely labored under a generation ago. It is the assumption that literary instruction mostly entails discourse by the teacher on the text being taught (Marshall 1989; Hynds 1991; Nystrand 1991, 1997). The assumption, in other words, is that if I am going to teach a literary work, I am going to do so largely by telling students about it. As if what they need to learn is what I have to say about it. Or, more responsibly, I need to know what they need to learn, so I can teach it, which is to say, tell it to them.

I remember in my last year of graduate school sitting with a colleague in a campus coffee shop, wondering how we would teach poetry to undergraduates when we entered the new teaching jobs we expected to hold the following fall. We saw one of our professors at another table and approached him for advice. "What do you say about a poem when you're teaching a class of freshmen or sophomores?" we asked. "Don't worry about it," he said, "you'll find out when you get there." His answer, like our question, I later came to realize, shows that we all thought of the teaching of literature as a problem of finding things to tell students about the literary texts we had assigned. The essential question for a teacher, as we saw it, was how to find things to say for fifty minutes a class, three times a week, that would be interesting and useful to students.

One unfortunate pedagogical consequence of such a tradition of teaching, as a number of studies of instruction have shown us (Marshall 1989; Zancanella 1991; Hynds 1991), is that teachers who know what texts are about by virtue of having had a course that taught them are often unwilling to entertain alternative readings of those texts by students who may be reading from a different cultural or ideological perspective, no matter how plausible and even insightful the alternative reading might appear to a more flexible reader. We can conjecture about why this is so. Teachers who have been recorders of their professors' readings are likely to believe that their own intellectual authority as teachers of literature rests on the body of literary knowledge about texts that they possess, as it were, secondhand. Since they haven't constructed such knowledge for themselves, they have no confidence in their capacity to reconstruct or revise it. Thus, any challenge to their secondhand literary knowledge must be experienced by them as a challenge to their authority as teachers of literature.

Before I abandon my description of university-level teaching practices that foster the development of insecure readers and a kind of pseudoliteracy, I need to repeat my claim that such practices as I have been describing are not those of pedagogically insensitive teachers or literary oafs. They may even represent the practices that are favored by faculty evaluation systems and curricular requirements. I would at least like to be able to invoke some such constraints when I admit that not long ago, in the middle of a talk I was giving to teachers on the same topic I am dealing with here, I suddenly realized and felt compelled to confess that just the week before, in my own introductory course in Renaissance literature, I had assigned my students some ten poems by George Herbert to be read by the next class meeting. Then, at the next class meeting, feeling pressed by the promise of my syllabus and the approaching end of the academic term, I gave myself a very good lecture on those poems, filled with fascinating information about the sociology of seventeenth-century literature (Herbert's mother was a friend of John Donne's and so on) and showing students what these particular poems were about and what they achieved aesthetically, theologically, and psychologically.

What else was I to do? The academic term was rushing to its close and I wanted to be sure that my students would not leave my course without some reliable knowledge of Herbert and some understanding of his accomplishment in what I regard as some of the most intellectually satisfying, emotionally powerful, and aesthetically sophisticated poems in the English literary tradition. So I gave my students my reading and they took notes. But I would have served them better (and my syllabus worse) had I shown them how to read one poem of Herbert's so that they might read others by themselves.

For what did they learn from my syllabus-serving lesson? They learned that I love and revere Herbert's poems. And, if they trusted me, as I trust they did, that might one day encourage some of them—the few who might one day find themselves in a graduate English program, perhaps—to reread Herbert, remembering my enthusiasm for him. But they also learned that they can't read Herbert just now and that to do so surely takes specialized advanced training of a kind they haven't had. They had tried to read Herbert for an hour or so as homework and found that they weren't able to. And then I showed them how well I read Herbert. But not that they could do it themselves, as they, in fact, could, with sufficient attention and some teacherly support, in spite of the difficulties the poems might present.

I tell this story about an instance of my own participation in a mode of teaching that I am challenging not merely to demonstrate that none of us is immune to temptations to teach badly, but as a way of forgiving myself (and urging all my colleagues to forgive themselves) for such teaching. More importantly, I want to acknowledge that we often engage in questionable teaching practices for good and honorable reasons and might do so again. In this instance, it was the end of the term. It was a course in Renaissance literature and I hadn't gotten to Herbert. I didn't want my students moving ahead as English majors not having been exposed to a number of poems of George Herbert's. So I did what I could do in an hour to cover what my syllabus promised and what my sense of responsibility to the curriculum demanded. And I confess that I have made similar compromises since then. But not without realizing what I was trading off.

What Have Students Learned? A Short Reading Experiment

What is it, then, that students learn about reading literature from such typical classroom teaching practices as I have described? The answer, I think, may be found in another story that can begin here with an experiment. In the interest of this experiment, I would have readers of this chapter immediately cover up the text below where they are now reading so they can't see more than a couple of lines ahead as they read on.

The experiment requires that you time yourself with a chronometer (any timepiece with a second hand will do) as you read and interpret a short passage from Thoreau, printed below. So don't look at the passage until you are ready to start your timer. Also, if possible, as you process the passage, think about what your students would do if presented with the same passage and assignment and how it might resemble or differ from what you do.

If you are now prepared to time yourself, begin reading, observing your reading process and comparing it with what your students would do, and noting with a stopwatch or clock how much time elapses between the time you start to read the passage and the time when you feel you have arrived at a satisfactory interpretation of the following sentence:

> Sometimes we are inclined to class those who are once-and-a-half-witted with the half-witted, because we appreciate only a third part of their wit.
>
> —*Henry David Thoreau*

In workshops at professional conferences I operate a stopwatch and ask teachers to raise their hands as soon as they feel they have interpreted the sentence satisfactorily, and I call out the time every fifteen seconds or so. With a typical mixed group of, say, one hundred secondary and college teachers, five or six hands will be raised to indicate completion of the task within the first ten or fifteen seconds, then another twenty-five or thirty hands will go up by the time thirty seconds have passed. Hands will then continue to rise steadily for another thirty seconds. Most readers will complete the task with varying degrees of confidence within fifty seconds, but clearly some (including some well-known scholars who have participated in my workshops) need more time, and many finish the task still feeling uncertain about their reading.

Typically I give teachers (or students) about one full minute to read the passage before I ask them to turn to a neighbor and share their reading experience and current understanding of the sentence. I also ask them to take a minute to discuss how their students might respond to the same passage.

The point of the experiment, in case it is not apparent, is to enable teachers in my workshops (or readers of this chapter) to observe the difference between the way they engage in transactions with difficult literary texts and the way typical students do in most school settings. I therefore want to begin processing the experiment here by describing what I saw (and what most teachers have confirmed they would probably see in their classes) when I introduced this passage to a class of high school students in a suburban high school.

Some years ago I taught (as an experiment and opportunity for classroom-based research) a high school class in composition at a high school not far from my university campus. The class was a mixed group of college-bound tenth- to twelfth-grade students, most of whom were either in the eleventh or twelfth grade. Most did, as I later learned, go to college, many of them to universities and state colleges and some to community colleges.

I came to use the Thoreau passage in this class because we had been talking in the first week of the course about the differences between strong and weak or good and bad writing. The students all appeared to agree with the proposition introduced by some of their classmates that writing is good when it is easy to understand. That seemed to me a reasonable and not unprecedented definition of good writing (cf. E. D. Hirsch, *The Philosophy of Composition* 1977), but a limited and surely unsustainable one. So I decided to challenge it by bringing to them some samples of writing that I thought were very good but hard to understand. And the first place I looked for such a sample was in Thoreau's *Walden*, where I found my experimental sentence in the conclusion.

When I introduced the Thoreau passage to my class of about twenty-five high school students by writing it on the chalkboard, they looked at it for no more than the few seconds it took them to scan it from beginning to end and began complaining that it was too hard to understand. "That doesn't make any sense," they said. "You shouldn't ask us to read that . . . We're just high school kids . . . We're not English majors in college . . . You're used to college students . . . You can't give us stuff like that . . . it's above our reading level." Nobody in the class, as far as I could tell, read the passage more than once or took any time to try to figure it out. When they saw that they couldn't immediately apprehend it, they declared it too difficult for them and above their reading level.

Their response surprised me since I had brought the passage in specifically to show them a piece of prose that I thought would be difficult to read—one that I knew would require attention and concentrated effort on the part of almost any reader to make it intelligible. I hadn't warned them that this was something I expected them to struggle with, however, so when they saw it, they responded as I assume they often did to most texts that posed difficulties for them in school. They retreated, insisting on their own insufficiency as readers, which is to say, on the insufficiency of their training or of their background knowledge.

In a workshop with teachers and for readers of this chapter I would now ask, What happened to you when you first looked at the passage? Most teachers, I assume, find the passage just as difficult to read as students do, and for the same reasons: a complicated (but not inaccessible) proposition is framed in witty language that uses a logically constructed neologism (once-and-a-half-witted) and mathematical ratios to state within the structure of a single sentence an interesting and nonobvious truism. Nothing about the sentence or our prior knowledge of Thoreau or American literature makes the statement any easier for us to understand than it would be for most of our English-speaking students.

But what did you do, I ask teachers, when it didn't make sense? Read it again, they invariably answer in chorus. How many of you read it more than once? I ask. All hands go up. How many more than two or three times? Most hands go up. How many read it more than five or six times? Many hands, again.

What's the difference, then, between what we do when we can't understand a difficult text and what many of our students do? The answer suggested by this experiment is that we assume that the text must be very difficult and therefore one requiring our concentrated effort and long attention. Our students, however, assume that the same difficulty, when they encounter it, is evidence of their insufficiency as readers. Which leads me to a third proposition about literary instruction: *when it comes to the reading of difficult literary texts, the difference between us and our students is that we have a much higher tolerance for failure.*

But, of course, an intolerance for difficulty and an assumption that difficulty is a sign of one's own insufficiency are precisely what a good deal of conventional instruction in reading and literature conspires to teach our students. It is surely what the stories I have told of high school and college English classes might suggest, and it is now more than ever what is being emphatically taught through some of the most widely adopted and politically touted reading programs (for secondary as well as elementary children) that tend to move literary texts to the margins and place a premium on speed and fluency over the dysfluencies that might be required by a more thoughtful attention to meaning.[3]

The result, in any event, is that students learn something very like what Mina Shaughnessy (1977) found about the state of student knowledge of writing among many open-admission students at the City University of New York a quarter-century ago. Shaughnessy noted that many students entering the university under the new open-admissions program had little previous experience in writing and were inclined to look at evidence of revision in a manuscript-in-progress as evidence of authorial incompetence. Having no experience with the role of revision in writing, these students would look at a copy of Jefferson's manuscript of the Declaration of Independence, for example, with words crossed out and replaced, with phrases inserted between lines or in margins, with numerous emendations made on the page in the interest of felicity or consensus, and conclude that Jefferson simply didn't know how to write. If he knew how to write, they would ask, why had he made all those mistakes?

For students who have never learned that composing entails drafting and that drafting often means producing early sloppy copy to be revised and corrected, the view of writing as a one-draft process for competent writers would seem entirely consistent with experience. Their own writing they know to be filled with errors and in need of much correction. But all the writing they see in books—writing from professional writers—is perfect. Why shouldn't an inexperienced writer, not having seen anything except final drafts, assume that writing takes place only in final drafts with competent writers producing perfect copy immediately and incompetent writers making mistakes? To have a problem, therefore, or to not know how to say what you want to say with perfect fluency, becomes evidence of your insufficiency as a writer.

Similarly, readers who have never seen anything but finished readings from their teachers and whose teachers either avoid or stigmatize textual difficulties are likely to conceive of reading much the way inexperienced writers think of writing: as something that competent students or adults do in a single pass, in one effortless draft, without struggle and without frustration; struggle and frustration, they believe, are the signs of incompetence, lack of knowledge, or insufficiency in skill. And what have most students seen of the reading process of expert readers that might suggest any other view of competent reading? When do students see their teachers struggling to make sense of a difficult text or producing a reading that proceeds gradually, moving from mere confusion, to a sense of a gist, to a reading that is tentatively complete but that will still give way to a more perceptive and adequate interpretation?

[margin note: Must Model reading process for students]

In fact, given what they have experienced in literature classes, most students have never had the opportunity to learn that reading, like writing, is a process of making meaning or text construction that is frequently accompanied by false starts and faulty visions, requiring frequent and messy reconstruction and revision. And with such a limited conception of reading and such a limited view of what competent readers go through to produce literary meanings, it is hardly surprising that most student readers function largely as welfare recipients in the economy of literary interpretation and instruction. What is needed, of course, is the fishing pole and fisherman's lore that the wise benefactor gives to the poor man, instead of a handout of day-old fish.

One teaching strategy that would help to correct student misperceptions about the reading process would be for a teacher to bring a difficult and unfamiliar text to class and work through an interpretation of it (either as an individual performance or collaboratively with students), thereby providing a model of how a competent reader proceeds in moving haltingly and recursively toward a satisfactory reading and interpretation of a difficult text. Many teachers of writing at all levels do engage in such modeling of the writing process in front of, in collaboration with, and alongside their students. But most literature teachers are hesitant to take the risks that such a method would entail in the teaching of literature, and students do not always regard a teacher's virtuoso performance as a viable model for themselves (see, however, Schoenbach et al. 1999).[4]

Nor is it entirely satisfactory for literature teachers to take a sink-or-swim approach to liberating their students from the cycle of interpretive dependency. It is not enough, that is, for teachers to place difficult texts in front of students and then simply tell them that reading is a process and that they have the capacity to engage in that process and solve for themselves all the interpretive problems they might encounter. The same confusion that provokes a disciplined process of inquiry and reflection on the part of an experienced interpreter of texts may leave many students feeling lost not merely because they feel confused, but because they have no idea of what steps to take in order to enter into the interpretive process and make their confusion an occasion for learning (see Dewey 1910, 12). The approach I want to present in the following chapter is a workshop for students (and for teachers) that enables them to experience how reading is a process and how much interpretive work they can do largely on their own (and with classmates), without the assistance of an expert teacher as the authoritative reader or model interpreter or coach, except insofar as the teacher sets the conditions for having students conduct what is framed as an experiment in reading poetry. The experiment is designed to move students through a disciplined process of inquiry and reflection that will serve as a kind of initiatory and prototypical experience for them to refer to when confronted with future textual problems. It is also designed as a paradigmatic lesson for teachers who want to help students become more autonomous readers through similar experiences. Finally and just as importantly, it is designed to foster in students a set of self-management skills and dispositions such as concentration, persistence, and courage in the face of intellectual difficulties, whose disabling absence in student readers is also the legacy of the culture of instruction I have described above and whose role in the literary competence of students I will discuss at length in the final chapter of this book.

Notes

1. Robert Scholes (1985, 22), in distinguishing between the act of reading and the act of interpretation, describes the cognitive occasion for interpretation much as Dewey does, claiming that interpretation "depends upon the failures of reading," and is activated by a feeling of incompleteness on the reader's part.

2. My colleagues who specialize in helping struggling and reluctant readers become fluent and more engaged readers would urge me to qualify this proposition by noting that the weakest readers often need extensive experience with easy reading in order to become fluent enough to find pleasure in reading and to acquire sufficient confidence to believe that some struggles can be worthwhile (see Beers 2000, 2002).

3. The eminent reading researcher P. David Pearson, in a communication (Oct. 30, 2002) on the listserv of the National Reading Conference, notes that reading speed and fluency are highly correlated with reading comprehension because it is very difficult for any reader to read fluently or rapidly with proper stress patterns without comprehending what is being read. Increased speed and fluency, he says, will therefore be a "natural consequence of a solid instructional program . . . that allows students to orchestrate all the code and meaning aspects of skilled reading." This fact does not suggest, however, that it is appropriate to teach for increased speed as

an outcome. "The minute we begin explicit attempts to increase speed," he insists, "we have lost the battle. Teaching to timed tests would be like treating abnormal temperature by prescribing aspirin. Prescribing aspirin might make you look healthy in the short run, but if that is all the doctor does, you are in deep trouble. Similarly, if all a program does for slow readers is to focus on increasing their speed, they are in deep trouble."

4. The idea of modeling reading practices, however, has been successfully refined and perfected in high school classrooms by a group of classroom teachers and researchers in the San Francisco area (Christine Cziko, Cynthia Greenleaf, Lori Hurwitz, and Ruth Schoenbach) into a highly sophisticated but very practical program that they refer to as a "reading apprenticeship" program. They have implemented this program with remarkable results through their Strategic Literacy Network in urban high schools, where test scores and academic performance could have been invitations to despair. The book that emerged out of their research and practice, *Reading for Understanding: A Guide to Improving Reading in Middle and High School Classrooms* (Schoenbach et al. 1999), provides detailed guidance (as well as a rich background in theory) for classroom teachers who want to adopt such a program or incorporate some of its strategies into their own teaching repertoire. While their emphasis is on academic literacy in general, rather than on the teaching of literature, many of their strategies and principles apply to the teaching of literature and have been adopted by a rapidly growing army of middle school and high school English language arts teachers all over California and, more recently, throughout the country.

2

From Telling to Teaching
The Literature Workshop in Action

A Workshop for Developing Autonomous, Disciplined Readers

My aim here is to demonstrate—as much as I can within the limits of a written discourse—the experience I take my students through in a seminal exercise I regularly conduct for undergraduates in introductory literature courses (an exercise that has been replicated or adapted successfully in a great many middle school and high school classrooms by teachers I have worked with across the country). I regard this exercise as a prototype for a number of analogous exercises that any interested teacher who participates in this workshop will then be able to generate for classroom use in varied educational settings. The goal of such exercises, it must be kept in mind, is to foster the development of a disciplined, autonomous literacy in students while building a culture of learning in the classroom that, unlike the prevailing culture of literary dependence and subservience, promotes the literary and intellectual enfranchisement of student readers.[1] Since my discourse in this chapter is obviously directed to teachers rather than to students, what I'll actually reproduce here demonstrates in its first segment what I do in my classroom, but it provides that demonstration in the context of the workshop I regularly conduct for teachers, where I take them through the exercises I employ with my students.

The text representing my voice in the workshop as well the voices of the participants is drawn from notes and handouts I use in actual workshops as well as from memory and videotapes of numerous workshops I have conducted with students and teachers. But it is a reconstruction of a typical workshop rather than a transcription of any single one, and it is designed to create a new workshop experience for readers of this text. What I ask of readers, then, is that they participate actively, insofar as possible, in the tasks I assign during the course of this workshop, so that they will be able to think with me through that portion of the workshop where I analyze the activities we have been engaged in and draw from the experience some essential principles or guidelines for teaching and learning literature.

Some Notes on Format

In presenting this workshop, I'll give instructions and offer explanations exactly as I do in actual workshops with teachers, and I'll address readers as if they were participants in the workshop. When I want to step aside from the dramatization of the workshop in order to comment on how I am conducting it, I'll mark the text as *Commentary* and print the comment in italics. For the sake of simplicity I'll not provide even fictional names for the participants (except when they are addressed directly in conversation) in the dialogue portions of the workshop, but will identify them as S1, S2, and so on, while identifying myself as the teacher or T.

The drama within the drama of this text may cause some confusion for readers who accept my invitation to include themselves in the scene of action. The core of this workshop—an experiment in reading a poem—models quite precisely what I do in my classroom with my students and therefore represents what I usually say to my own students in the course of conducting this workshop. But it also includes discourse directed to participating teachers in their role as teachers, when I comment on how I am conducting the workshop or reflect on what has transpired in it. Yet some portions of my reflective discourse also represent what I say and what needs to be said to students in order to help them reflect on what they have just experienced in the workshop so they can become more aware and in control of their processes as readers and thereby make their reading process more disciplined and productive. I make little attempt, however, to sort out what I would say to students from what I am saying here to teachers, trusting that teachers will sort it out for themselves and distill from this workshop for teachers the ideas and conclusions they want to share with their own students.

For the essential activities of the workshop I have provided time estimates for use in planning. These will vary considerably in different classrooms with different students, though I believe that almost any teacher reading this book will find that the core experiment of this workshop plus some minimal reflection on it can be completed within the scope of a conventional fifty-minute class period, with additional reflection postponed until the next class meeting. When I conduct this workshop for student-teachers or for inservice teachers, however, I need seventy-five minutes to complete the activities and provide the extensive reflection and analysis presented here.

Most of the discussion that takes place in my classroom and in actual workshops occurs as a dialogue. Some of that dialogue is represented here. Sometimes for the sake of efficiency I forgo the dialogue format temporarily and engage in a monologue that amounts to a mini-essay, the topic of which I usually identify under its own heading. For the last segments of this chapter I abandon the dialogue format entirely and provide a series of discussions on questions raised by the workshop experience and on conclusions that might be drawn from it. My readers, I hope, will provide the monologic portions of this chapter with the missing voices of various participants, including the voices of their own students.

An Experiment in Reading a Poem[2]

Step 1: Three Readings with Notes and Questions (10–12 minutes)

T: Let us begin with an exercise, which I would like to treat as an experiment, in reading a poem. What I'll do is take you through a series of activities in working on a poem, and then we'll reflect on what happened and what the results reveal to us about the reading of poetry.

1. To begin, I'd like you to read a short poem (which I'll show you momentarily) three times. With each reading, please do what Ann Berthoff calls "noticing what you notice," which is to say, notice what you find interesting or troubling or difficult to understand in the poem, what you like about what it says, what you might want to speak against in it, what questions you have about it or any line in it, or anything else you happen to observe or feel as a reader. At the end of each reading, please do two additional things:
    a. Rate your understanding of the poem on a scale from 0–10, with zero meaning that you don't understand the poem at all, and ten meaning that you understand it perfectly (whatever that might mean).
    b. Make some notes on what you were noticing.
2. At the end of your third reading, do the routine again as in your first two readings, but also do two more things:
    a. First, write a brief account of what happened to you as a reader and to your understanding of the poem over the course of your three readings.
    b. Then, write out any questions that you still have about this poem.

When you finish writing your questions, I'll have other instructions for you. But I want to ask you not to start talking to each other about the poem or your experience of it until we get to the point where I'll ask you to do exactly that. In the meantime, it's important for the sake of our experiment to proceed step-by-step and complete each step as the experiment requires before we move to the next.

The poem that we'll be working on is Pat Mora's "Sonrisas." You'll see it on your handout with no headnote, so I'll tell you what you would learn about the poet if you read the inside cover of any of her books. She is a Mexican American poet, born in 1942 in El Paso, Texas, where she spent her childhood and went to college and graduate school. She has published successful novels, an important autobiography, several volumes of highly regarded poetry, and a long list of books (fiction and nonfiction) for children and young adults. She has taught at the University of Texas and at the University of New Mexico and served for some years as a university administrator. That's what I happen to know about her and to remember from the biographical blurbs I have read. I met her only once, when she was the keynote speaker for the 2001 NCTE Convention in Baltimore, so I can add that she is a thoughtful, intellectually generous, and attractive colleague, a compelling public speaker, and a memorable reader of her own poems. You may later want to question whether it is appropriate, given the nature of this experiment, for me to give you such information about Pat Mora. I'll be happy to talk about that later.

Sonrisas

I live in a doorway
between two rooms, I hear
quiet clicks, cups of black
coffee, *click, click* like facts
    budgets, tenure, curriculum,
from careful women in crisp beige
suits, quick beige smiles
that seldom sneak into their eyes.

I peek
in the other room señoras
in faded dresses stir sweet
milk coffee, laughter whirls
with steam from fresh *tamales*
    sh, sh, mucho ruido,
they scold one another,
press their lips, trap smiles
in their dark, Mexican eyes.

             —*Pat Mora*

T: About nine minutes have passed, and almost all of you appear to be finished reading the poem and writing about your experience and questions. Am I right? I'm always surprised at how quickly teachers do this. For those of you not quite finished, please push yourself to finish now and, if necessary to save time, skip the narrative about your experience (you probably have enough notes to remember and talk about it anyway) and go directly to your questions. Do make sure you take the time to write out whatever questions you still have about this poem after three readings.

Now that you have all had a chance to write out your questions, please rerate your understanding of the poem one more time. I realize you haven't had a chance to reread it since your last rating. Nevertheless, please write down how you would rate your understanding of the poem again now on the same scale you used before.

Before we move on to the next step in this experiment, let me do a little polling of the group about your most recent rating. How many of you rated your understanding of the poem higher in the fourth rating—the one following the writing of your questions—than you did after your third reading of the poem? Please raise your hands high and, everybody, look around the room to see the results.

Notice that about a third of the readers in the room rated their understanding of the poem higher after not reading the poem again, but writing out their questions about it. What we see here is how—not all the time for every poem, but much of the time—writing about your reading, even or maybe especially if it is only writing about what you don't understand, can be a useful way to assist you in your reading. Our students need to know this, and as teachers we need to remember it as we plan activities for our students. But maybe we need some testimony about what happened. Would any of you be willing to explain why you claimed to have a better understanding after writing your questions?

S1: I found that my questions cleared up as I wrote them.

S2: Something like that happened to me, but it was more that as I wrote my question, I realized I didn't really have a question, but I wanted to argue with the poet.

S3: I just understood the poem better as I explained what I didn't understand.

Step 2: Group Work (12–15 minutes)

T: Now please join with two other people (so you have groups of three, but please not two or four and especially not five) and share a little about what happened to you or to your understanding of this poem over the course of your three readings (ideally, if there were time, we would read aloud our accounts of our three readings) and whatever questions you still have about it.

Commentary: I prefer groups of three because groups of four take too much time and a group of two provides insufficient data on the experience to be significant for the discussants. A two-person group also increases the possibility that a serious misunderstanding won't get corrected. For that reason, when the numbers don't work out exactly, I generally use leftover students to increase some groups to four rather than allow any to stand as pairs. With more difficult poems, I have the groups of three finish their work by identifying their most refractory questions and then merge with another group and work on their collective questions.

During the group work activity I find it important to circulate around the room eaves-dropping on the group work and taking notes on what I notice of interest in how the students are thinking about the text or solving or failing to solve textual problems. I some-times will help with simple factual questions about word meanings, but in this case I refuse, during group time, to translate any of the Spanish. I do ask most groups whether they have figured out the meaning of mucho ruido. *And if they tell me they haven't, I urge them to look carefully at the phrase and at its context and try to figure it out. I also acknowledge that if they don't know Spanish, they won't be able to guess at the meaning of* sonrisas. *But I still don't tell them its meaning.*

RATING THE IMPACT OF GROUP WORK

T: It seems to me that all the groups have had an adequate chance to talk about the poem and your individual experiences in reading it. Before we do anything else, please rate your understanding of the poem one more time, now.

Step 3: Completing the Experiment and Noticing What Happened (10 minutes)

T: Now that you have rated your reading again, let us take a moment here to see if any problems remain for you as readers of this poem. And we can start by making sure that every group managed to translate *mucho ruido*. How many knew the Spanish or depended on somebody in your group who knew Spanish? That's about a third of you. And the rest of you figured it out from context?

S4: We asked Yolanda, but she was in a different group.

S3: We figured from the "shushing" and the physical setting that they were say-ing something like "too noisy."

S5: We thought *ruido* might mean rude.

T: Which brought you very close to the literal meaning. Am I correct in assum-ing that most of you, even if you don't know any Spanish beyond *mucho*, caught the gist of too much noise or made a good guess at it by looking at the Spanish words and at their context? Did some of you never figure it out? In that case, did the absence of a translation get in your way much as readers?

S6: We never talked about it and I don't think any of us know Spanish. But we never realized it was a problem. We just skipped over the Spanish phrase, I guess. The poem seemed clear to us anyway.

T: That's fascinating. I've heard that before when I've walked around to listen to teachers talk in their groups (I guess I missed yours). I usually ask each group how they are reading *mucho ruido* and, like you, they sometimes say they hadn't noticed the line at all, as if it weren't there. But I've never interrogated them about it. I confess that I've sometimes been suspicious of those groups and won-dered if they weren't just careless readers. But you seem to be suggesting that you don't have to be careless to ignore what isn't obstructing your sense of the whole. We do it all the time with words we don't know, don't we?

So what about *sonrisas*. You couldn't figure that one out, no matter how hard you tried, unless you know Spanish. No, it doesn't mean sunrises. It means smiles. What does that "ahhh" mean that I have just heard from so many of you? Why ahhh?

S7: Well, it makes perfect sense and sort of clears things up.

T: Do you mean that the poem wasn't clear for you before and now it is?

S7: No, it's just that not knowing the title bothered me and now I see it fits with everything in the poem.

S8: I think it helps to emphasize the theme of the different kind of smiles, which I saw, but might not have emphasized.

T: So for you, the extra knowledge enriches your reading, but doesn't make a significant change in it?

S9: It doesn't really change it for me. I don't see any line differently. But it adds to what it all adds up to.

T: Did you all feel you understood the poem pretty well before you had an authoritative translation of the Spanish? Sure. Virtually all of you felt you understood the poem quite well, yet many of you still had questions about it (at least about the Spanish) and you knew what your questions were (except for the one group that didn't notice the Spanish that they couldn't translate). For the most part, you knew the difference between what you understood perfectly, as it were, and what you understood vaguely or insecurely (as with *mucho ruido*) and what you really didn't understand (the title, for example); so you had some idea about what your questions were and what priority they might have and yet you felt that you still understood the poem pretty well. I'm pointing out in some detail how you think about and evaluate the state of your own understanding of this poem because I suspect that your students wouldn't think about their understanding in quite the same way.

First of all, I'll bet that many of your students would say immediately that they couldn't read the poem at all, because they don't know Spanish. Right?

S10: Yes; even without foreign phrases they say that. With an ordinary English poem, I often ask them about their understanding and they say they understand "nothing." Nothing. But it's not true because they understand a lot. But they don't understand everything.

T: That's right. It's precisely the same phenomenon. And I think we see another version of it in what looks likes the opposite case. How often have you asked students what questions they have about some piece of reading they have completed and they'll tell you they don't have any questions? But then you quickly realize they don't understand very much of what they have read. Don't you get that in your classes? I sometimes get it in my classes, too.

So let's notice several things here. First, notice that although you still had questions about the poem, you saw yourself as understanding it. That is, we can understand a text and regard ourselves as competent readers of it even though we still have questions about it. I have been reading *Paradise Lost* for more than forty years and have taught the poem twenty times or more, but I still have lots of questions about it. That there is much that I don't understand in it doesn't mean that I'm not a good reader of the poem or even an expert reader of it. Students, on the other hand, often seem paralyzed by their questions or seem unaware of their questions, which may mean that they haven't arrived at a sufficiently advanced state of understanding to know that they are confused.

My own expertise in reading Milton, for example, is partly demonstrated by my awareness of many of the problematic lines and interpretive difficulties that the poem poses for readers, including me. Unlike our students, we seem to have a fairly sophisticated capacity to recognize and talk about the condition of our understanding. We know the difference between what we do and don't understand and to what degree we do or don't understand. We are, in other words, metacognitively aware. We are able to think about our thinking, and we are therefore skilled at monitoring and being able to describe the state of our own knowledge or understanding. I have heard some experts claim that such an ability is developmental, and that children before the age of seven or eight, for example, aren't able to distinguish at all between what they do and don't understand. Many of our students act as if they are not far away from that condition. The reality may be that the problem isn't one of development, but of experience. We need to give our students at every stage lots of opportunities to talk about their emerging understanding as it falters and progresses, just as we did here.

Also notice (and this may help to explain why some students seem underdeveloped in their metacognitive abilities) that my instructions in this exercise would probably be regarded by many educators (and especially many supervisors) as poor teaching because I didn't translate the foreign terms in advance and didn't set up the lesson in a way that would anticipate and avoid all possible frustrations for students. The conventional idea about reading instruction is that a responsible teacher will preview all unknown words and teach them before asking students to read a literary work, so that the students don't experience any frustration in reading, as if reading is or ought to be a process in which one never experiences frustration and never encounters new words and always understands everything immediately. No wonder, then, that students seem daunted by any problems they encounter in reading difficult texts and seem to have little capacity to reflect on the state of their understanding and seem at a loss for what to do for themselves when they encounter interpretive difficulties. Instruction has systematically taught them to depend entirely on teachers to prevent or remove any textual difficulties they might encounter.

But let's return to the poem. What about our problems here? Did any group encounter any problems that didn't get cleared up in your group discussion and that still trouble you?

S4: I didn't think the setting for the poem had to be a school or college. Most of my group read the scene as a faculty lounge or dining area or something. I think it could describe any place where there are executives and white-collar workers and also cleaning ladies and blue-collar workers—two classes of people.

S7: Why would they be talking about tenure and curriculum if it isn't a school or college?

S11: Well, I still might not have thought about a university setting, if we hadn't been set up to think that way. That's why I thought it wasn't fair that we were told all that unnecessary information about Pat Mora. It felt like the teacher was telling us how to read the poem. And I didn't like reading it that way.

S12: I didn't listen to it anyway. I still think it could be any place where rich and poor people work.

T: You're entitled to do that, but you're going to have to take into account that the people in the room where they drink black coffee and dress in beige are talking about topics like tenure and curriculum. You could create a scenario, I suppose, for how automobile industry executives might be talking about such topics, but it would be a stretch of a kind you wouldn't have to make if you assume that they are teachers or educators talking, not necessarily in a university or college, but in some kind of educational setting. But let me address the question more directly about whether it was appropriate or not for me to give you the minimal background information on Pat Mora.

Reflections on Contextual Knowledge

It seems to me that it is unfair and generally unrealistic to ask students to read texts about which they don't have the kind of minimal information that any reader who picks up a book outside of school is likely to have. It's unfair in the sense that ignorance of some contextual facts that most readers are likely to know before they read a text can sometimes produce a reading that isn't simply a variant reading but one that the reader himself would count as invalid as soon he became aware of the relevant contextual facts. Such a reader is right to feel tricked into a mistaken reading by a teacher who provides a text without the available and needed context. (See Chapter 9 for a discussion of the experiment conducted by I. A. Richards with decontextualized poems.)

On the other hand, the academic practice of providing background information for students in introductory lectures by teachers introduces two other perils for student readers. First, it invites students to feel dependent on their teachers and to believe that their capacity to understand the text they read derives from their teacher's expertise rather than their own. Second, it often becomes a subtle way of overdetermining what sort of interpretation students will produce, prejudicing them (as I have been accused of doing in the case of the Mora poem) in favor of one particular interpretation, when others might be equally plausible, or—as I have seen in a number of instances—directing them to what amounts to a misreading of a text. Critics of an earlier generation, the New Critics, warned emphatically against the "biographical heresy" and the "historical fallacy," at least partly because they had witnessed so many instances in which literary texts were misread and inappropriately judged by critics and scholars on the basis of biographical and historical research.

There is, then, danger and the real possibility for error on either side. Teachers must depend on their own literary and pedagogical judgment to determine when they are approaching the point where they are being overly directive in providing background information for student readers, and when the absence of certain contextual facts could unfairly handicap student readers. My own rule of thumb is to provide the information that any reader would likely obtain from the jacket of a book.

That rule will serve fairly well for most modern mainstream authors, but not for more ancient authors or for works by nonmainstream writers, where the important information most students are missing may have to do with cultural practices or political or religious contexts. In such cases, we are stuck having to exercise our best professional judgment about what will promote a disabling dependence on the part of our students and what will foster their autonomy and confidence as readers. My own experience in experiments I have conducted with my students over the years is that they need far less support in the form of background information and historical contextualizing than we are inclined to provide and to believe they will need. (I take up this problem at much greater length in Chapters 4 and 9).

Step 4: Collecting the Data from the Experiment (5 minutes)

T: If there are no more interpretive questions to address at this moment, let us process the experience we have just been through. Let's begin by collecting some additional data. How many of you rated your understanding of the poem higher on the last rating than on the first? All of you. How many rated your understanding higher after the second reading than after the first? All of you. And higher after your third reading? Almost all. And higher after your work in a group? Not quite all, but clearly most of you. Will some of you say why you rated your understanding lower rather than higher after additional readings?

S12: I thought I understood the poem on my own, but when I talked to other people, I saw that the poem was more complicated than I had realized. And then I wasn't so sure I understood it all or could understand the experience of the speaker.

S3: Something like that happened to me with my third reading. I thought I understood the poem after my first two readings. But in my third reading, I saw new problems.

T: Please remember those testimonies and we'll come back to them later. In the meantime, let me ask how many of you—no matter how you rated your understanding of the poem—feel that you were helped in your reading by your work with other readers? That's all of you, though perhaps some of you are just being polite.

In any event, the first conclusion we can draw from this experience, which won't be surprising to us but might be exactly what our students need to discover, has to do with the power of rereading as possibly the best method we can employ in helping ourselves read difficult texts. I would also point to at least a tentative conclusion that I think many of our colleagues need to discover: it is about the importance of group work and the contribution that conversation with your colleagues makes to your understanding of the text, even if such conversation doesn't so much confirm your own reading as show you possibilities for alternative readings. But I'll return to that topic later and to the topic of how it happened that a few of you, especially after your conversation with colleagues, rated your understanding of the poem lower than you had on your previous reading. First, let me indulge in an extended reflection on what we have seen about the phenomenon and practice of rereading.

Rereading as a Strategy and Style of Thinking

The first observation I want to make based on our experiment will come as no news to teachers, but I believe it would come as news—at least at the experiential level—to many of our students. It's the fact that one of the most powerful strategies available to us for reading difficult texts is the obvious strategy of rereading, which, it happens, is neither obvious nor frequently employed by many readers, and is especially underemployed by those who think of themselves as (and generally appear to be) not very strong, or minimally competent, or unmotivated or reluctant readers. That many students—including college students with good grades from high school—don't recognize the value of rereading has been demonstrated to me more than once when I have monitored the conversations of my students about their processes in dealing with difficult texts.

A few years ago as I walked around my classroom, listening to my students talk in small groups about poems they had individually selected as potential additions to our class syllabus, I overheard a sophomore telling his partners that he had found a poem that he loved, even though when he first read it, he could hardly make any sense of it at all. He was initially intrigued by the poem, he said, because, though it mainly puzzled him, he could manage to discern that it was about drinking beer. Given his interest in the subject, he decided to keep working on the poem in an effort to make sense of it. So he reread it many more times and now, he said, he thought he understood it quite well and wanted to recommend it to his classmates as a poem they might all want to read. Then he added, as if still surprised by the fact, "You know, I never realized before that if you can't understand a poem, you can read it over and over until you get to understand it."

I won't claim that this one student is typical of most university sophomores, but he is surely representative of many. One would be mistaken, however, to rush from this case to the premature conclusion that many high school teachers (or even the teachers of this one student) do not regularly tell their students about the importance of rereading. If my beer-loving student hadn't heard about rereading, he might not have known what to do when he decided he really cared to understand a puzzling poem. So he hadn't entirely forgotten the advice of his teachers. It's just that it appears to have taken his compelling interest in a particular poem to finally entice him to act on that advice and discover its value to him as a reader. What students seem to need, then, on top of our exhortations about rereading, is the sort of direct and dramatic experience of rereading that my student provided for himself by struggling with a poem whose subject happened to entice him or that an exercise like the one I have just demonstrated is designed to provide.

If we need more evidence that students frequently behave as if they have never learned the value of rereading, we can look to the practice of the most popular and expensive tutoring programs that prepare students for college entrance exams and graduate and professional school aptitude exams, where (I have been told) instructors emphasize over and over (presumably because students don't appear to already know) the critical importance of judicious rereading. And if we are inclined to look for an instance of how much the role of rereading can be undervalued or misunderstood as a reading strategy for high school and college students, let me cite the case of a new handbook on strategies for helping high school students become more powerful readers, issued by the state department of education of one of our most populous and prosperous states. In this volume, which many high schools are buying for all subject matter teachers, the strategy of rereading is included, of course, but relegated to the last page or nearly the last page of the book and then described as a strategy to be taught only to the weakest readers, and specifically to those whose reading difficulties are at the level of decoding. Try telling that to the students taking the Law School Aptitude Test, to lawyers reading the law, or to anyone who actually cares about making sense of complex concepts inscribed in textually dense discourse.

Can Rereading Lead to an Impoverished Reading?

Let me now turn to the more paradoxical question of how it happened that for some readers some subsequent readings of Pat Mora's poem yielded an understanding of the poem that they rated lower than the understanding they had achieved previously with an earlier reading. Is it possible that rereading can be counterproductive?

In every instance where I have received reports of downgraded rereadings, the readers have indicated, as we have seen here, that they lowered their rating from one reading to the next because the later reading revealed to them confusions they had previously not been aware of or because (and it amounts to the same thing) they thought that they understood the poem, but discovered in their next reading that they didn't understand it nearly as well as they had imagined. My question for such readers in my classroom and here is the same: if you are at a point where you realize that your previous reading was inadequate and confused and you didn't recognize your confusion earlier, should you declare yourself one who now understands less than you did before or one who understands more?

Surely your present recognition of your previous delusion, while it means that you now have questions where you formerly had answers, is an advance beyond your previous knowledge, which, though unconfused, was mistaken knowledge, masking a confusion of which it wasn't aware. In other words, your new confusion compared with your previous unconfused false knowing represents an advance, not a decline, in your knowledge. To move ahead in the wrong direction is not progress. But to move backward in order to correct your course is.

But for purposes of the experiment I have just conducted and the requirement to rate one's understanding after a series of readings, how is a participant to treat a reading that yielded confusion where before there had been clarity, even if a mistaken clarity? To rate one's present confused reading higher than a previously overrated and more mistaken reading would seem dishonest. To rate it lower, when it actually represents an advance in understanding, also feels like a misrepresentation of the facts. The only logical solution to the problem, of course, is to change (downward) one's previous rating.

The problem of how to rate a changing understanding is, of course, a trivial one, useful only in the context of the exercise or game I conduct with my students. But it is a highly instructive and useful game to play with students precisely for what it can reveal about how the advancement of learning is often not marked by an accretion of answers and growth in certitude, but by the lessening of certitude and the addition of questions where there had formerly been answers. It is their fear of relinquishing the security of their false knowledge that often prevents students (and sometimes their teachers or any of us) from proceeding beyond an easy and readily available reading of a text to one that acknowledges problematic lines and interpretive inconsistencies, which is to say, to readings that disrupt coherence and subvert certainty. But it is precisely their willingness to surrender the security of their knowledge and to launch themselves into the abyss of uncertainty—a disposition that pragmatist philosophers embrace as "fallibilism" (Berthoff 1981, 43; Gunn 2001, 86)—that allows learners to advance in their learning, just as it is an unwillingness to risk their certainty that characterizes those most incapable of learning and most likely to value a scorable answer over a more intellectually thoughtful but less easily measured question.

Continuing the Data Collection: Questions of Reading, Interpretation, and Criticism

T: I want to continue our processing of the experiment we have just completed by asking a few questions to which the answers may seem so obvious as to make the questions hardly worth asking. First, how many of you in reading the poem found that you gave considerable effort at some stage in your reading (probably in your first reading) to the task of simply figuring out what the poem was saying at the most literal level? Virtually everybody, of course. Next, how many found that at some point you were able to see what the poem appeared to be saying, but had a problem with what it meant, or found yourself having to assume some meaning beyond what the poem literally said? In this case, the problem was probably located in the phrase about living in a doorway. What did you make of that phrase the first time you read it? Anybody?

S13: I imagined it was about a homeless person, the kind who would sleep in a doorway in the city.

T: Sure, why not? Why did you give up on that idea?

S13: It didn't work as the poem went on. It had nothing to do with the rest of what was happening in the poem.

T: Did anybody have another idea about the first lines?

S14: I thought it might be about a mouse. You know, it starts out like a Disney film, where some cute animal narrates the story. And you said Pat Mora wrote children's stories. But before I got to the end of the poem, I realized this isn't a kids' story.

S15: I thought about Disney stories, too, and I figured that it was a kind of insect living in a doorway. Like Jiminy Cricket.

T: That's terrific. I've often heard the insect reading, but I've never had him named before. Others of you, I assume, were simply puzzled for a while, not sure of what to make of this person who says she (or he?) lives in a doorway, and you remained puzzled until you decided to think of the doorway metaphorically. That is, whatever we envision in our initial reading of the line, we are likely to find as we read on that we can't interpret the statement about living in a doorway literally. The context for the line, the entire rest of the poem, forces us, if we are to make some coherent sense of the whole, to take the idea of living in a doorway metaphorically, and to recognize the idea of the speaker "living" in it as a statement not about shelter or housing, but about psychological or cultural space.

Finally, let me ask some questions about what you thought of this poem after reading and interpreting it. Before you answer, either look at your notes or try to remember how you were thinking. Is it the case that all of you made some sort of judgment about the poem either as you were reading it or at the end? Did anybody not engage in something like an evaluation of it?

S5: I don't think I evaluated it. I read it and figured it out and enjoyed it, but I didn't compare it with any other poem and say it's better or worse. I didn't make a judgment of it. And I'm still not ready to do that.

T: So you didn't think about how you found it moving or enlightening or aesthetically pleasing? Or how you found it philosophically or psychologically penetrating or superficial? You didn't find that it spoke for you or that you wanted to speak against it or some line in it?

S5: No. I was more ambivalent about it. I wasn't sure what to think about how the woman sat in one room and only peeked into the other, like she couldn't go into the other room. And I wondered if she was also a little ashamed of her background or maybe ashamed of herself for leaving her own people. And I'm still not sure what I think about this poem.

T: It sounds like you have done a good deal of reflective and evaluative thinking about this poem and are still doing it.

S5: Maybe, yes, I suppose so.

S16: Well, I liked it a lot. As a Mexican American woman, I felt it spoke for me and told my story very well.

S17: I loved it! You don't have to be Hispanic to connect with the experience.

T: Didn't anyone object to anything in this poem? Ah, I see one reluctant hand barely raised.

S15: Well, am I the only one who is offended by the stereotyping of the Anglo women? Do we all really wear beige and flash false smiles?

S18: But she's stereotyping the Mexican women even more.

S7: Yes, but she's Mexican herself.

S3: Is stereotyping OK if applies to a group where you're a member, but not to some other group?

S4: It's not stereotyping; it's talking about groups of people and characterizing them realistically.

S18: That's stereotyping. It implies that all Mexican women are cleaning ladies or cafeteria workers.

S7: No it doesn't. It implies that they are more real and know better how to live a genuine life.

S15: And that all Anglo women wear colorless clothing and drink black coffee (because they're watching their weight), and they don't know how to enjoy themselves.

S3: Who says they're Anglo women?

S4: It says that the other women flash their dark Mexican eyes.

T: Well, if the women in the first room are teachers, aren't they likely to be Anglo?

S18: Come on! How can you say that?

T: I once said it in a workshop in Hawaii, when we were dealing with the same issue in this poem. I asked, Aren't all teachers Anglo? And they laughed, of course, because in a room with about one hundred teachers, maybe twenty-five of them were Anglo. Most of them were Japanese and some were Hawaiian or Filipino or Korean or Pacific Islanders and so on. But what evidence do we have that at least one of the women among the people talking about tenure is herself Mexican?

S3: The speaker is Mexican; she says she lives between the two rooms. She identifies with both groups.

S1: Does that mean she has to be Mexican? Can't she just come from a working-class background?

S3: That's possible, but we know that the writer is Mexican American, so that's what we assume about the speaker.

T: Well, without resolving the exact ethnicity of the speaker, let me get something clear here about the descriptions of the women. How many of you would object to my speaking of how the poem stereotypes Anglo women? A lot of you would! But would anybody object to someone saying that the poem stereotypes the "professional" women or the "academic" women?

S4: I might, because I'm not sure that it's stereotyping.

T: OK. So how many of you are objecting to the charge that the poem is stereotyping anybody? That is, you are prepared to defend it against the charge of stereotyping. That's a third of you. And how many of you are objecting to my speaking of the women in beige as Anglo rather than professional or academic women? That's almost all of you. There's a big difference, isn't there? Don't we have two different kinds of objections here representing two different levels of thinking in our discussion of the poem?

That is, you might want to argue with each other about whether the descriptions in the poem constitute stereotyping, but no matter what side you take, you can also recognize the other side of the argument as a legitimate one, even if you think it is wrong. And that's because both positions are based on pretty much the same understanding of what the poem means. Any discussion of whether to call the characterization stereotyping will proceed, in other words, from what first amounts to substantial agreement about how to interpret the descriptive accounts of the women involved. So the question of whether the poem indulges in stereotyping depends on your attitude toward the characterizations of the two groups of women and not upon your understanding of how they are characterized or who they are. Right?

But when you object to my reference to the professional women as Anglo, it's a different kind of objection at a different level of meaning. Our disagreement now is not based on our attitudes toward some idea or meaning that we both construe the poem to represent or signify. The contested issue is rather one that has to be adjudicated by referring to the text of the poem itself and the meaning we may plausibly claim for it. Verification for either position constitutes a determination of what the poem says and what that means, not how we subsequently think about or want to characterize that meaning. Do you see the difference? For most of us, the question of whether the women in the first room can be referred to as distinctively Anglo is answerable in the negative, by virtue of the fact that the speaker who peers out from that room is one who identifies herself with the Mexican women in faded dresses and one who by implication is therefore Mexican herself. Thus it becomes inaccurate—not merely evidence of a different response or attitude—to refer to the women in the first room as Anglo, while it is consistent with the other facts of the poem to refer to them as professional or academic women.

Reflecting on the Data: Literary Reading and Critical Thinking

Let us now reflect on the kinds of thinking that we have identified as marking our engagement with Pat Mora's poem at various stages in our reading and thinking about it. We have all acknowledged trying at some points simply to make plain sense of the poem. And we all claim to have given some attention to finding a more abstract or metaphoric meaning for parts of the poem where the plain sense seemed more evocative than literal. Virtually all of us also claim to have reflected evaluatively on the poem, generally appreciating it as true to our own experience or as valuable for its accurate representation of a more widely experienced human dilemma. A few readers also found it intellectually or ethically compromised for its reductive characterization or stereotyping of groups of people. Other readers want to argue with that judgment and some aren't sure one way or the other.

There is surely nothing surprising about such reports from readers, nor in the fact that, despite some disagreements about meaning or value, virtually all of us appear to have engaged in similar mental operations. Yet the fact that such mental operations appear almost natural or inevitable for readers (at least for well-educated readers like ourselves) and define a repertoire of reading behaviors shared by so many readers suggests that the particular set of mental operations we have documented may represent a set of literate practices that are widely taught in schools (or somewhere else in our culture), either explicitly or perhaps tacitly in the way that many social behaviors are taught and learned through participation in a culture. That this particular set of mental operations is not natural or somehow physiologically or psychologically constitutive of literate behavior becomes evident when we look at what defines literate practice in other cultures and has defined it in various communities and periods of American cultural history. In various places and at various times, students or adults who are literate would, upon being presented with a literary text, proceed to commit it to memory or prepare to recite it aloud, or expect to be asked to recall facts about what the text describes or the events it narrates, never thinking that they might presume to uncover its broader meanings, question its truth, or reflect independently on its intellectual or ethical value (see Myers 1996 and Blau 2001).

Robert Scholes (1985), in attempting to build a model of instruction and literary competence on principles drawn from modern critical theory, identifies the same set of mental operations we have practiced and reported here as the fundamental skills that underlie all the literary practices that are underwritten by modern literary theory and all the classroom practices that theory might authorize. He speaks of these operations, in fact, as if they were the molecular units or building blocks for what he calls "textual competence," and he distinguishes them under three headings, which we can (without much distortion of Scholes' theoretical framework) encapsulate as follows: (1) *reading*, addressing the question, What does it say? (2) *interpretation*, addressing the question, What does it mean? and (3) *criticism*, addressing the question, What is its value? or So what? (21–24). He further notes that each of these mental operations of a reader also entails the production of text either in writing or in the mind of the reader. Thus in Scholes' memorable formulation, reading produces *text within text*; interpretation produces *text upon text*; and criticism produces *text against text* (24).

While Scholes' framework for thinking about textual competence may appear largely commonsensical and hardly different from the way many teachers intuitively think about their own instruction, it nevertheless offers us a useful paradigm for describing transactions with texts and for analyzing virtually all of our teaching practices and plans. Just as importantly, we can use Scholes' model of literary discourse to launch us on a more comprehensive inquiry into the kinds of thinking and intellectual processes that we are teaching by virtue of our instruction in literature and how these thinking processes link literary study to what may be even more fundamental educational goals and to all other academic disciplines.

Let us begin our more comprehensive inquiry by looking at the activities of reading, interpretation, and criticism as they connect to one another and are actually employed by readers in the course of interrogating and discussing literary texts in classrooms or in other contexts. Although it is not the case that readers necessarily engage in all three activities with every literary encounter or engage in all three modes of thinking in a strictly linear process (readers will sometimes register an immediate critical judgment or presume an interpretation before all the facts that might produce it are collected), it does appear to be the case (as our discussion of the Pat Mora poem demonstrated) that reading, interpretation, and criticism represent a hierarchy of nested intellectual activities, and that they bear a particular kind of logical relationship one to the other. That is to say, the way one interprets a text depends to a very large degree upon what the text says—what the textual facts are—and the way one criticizes or evaluates it depends to a very large degree upon how one interprets it.

More specifically, the relationship between reading, interpretation, and criticism is usually and to a very significant degree (if not entirely) a relationship based on evidentiary reasoning. The critical claim of some readers that Pat Mora's poem was intellectually reductive and guilty of ethnic stereotyping in its representation of the Anglo women was found to be a partially invalid critical statement not because readers disagreed with it, but because it was contradicted by compelling interpretive evidence that the "careful women in crisp beige suits" are not necessarily Anglo women and, in fact, almost certainly include at least one woman among them who is Hispanic.

And that interpretative claim about the women is in turn based on a careful reading of the first lines of the poem, where the speaker says she lives in a doorway between two rooms, a statement that makes sense in the context of the poem only when it is subjected both to a metaphoric interpretation and to a plain-sense reading. That is, the statement derives its meaning in its poetic context by being interpreted as a metaphoric statement about cultural or psychological space rather than physical space. Yet the plain-sense language representing the organization of space discloses the relationship of the speaker to the two cultures that define her identity.

Our interpretations of texts, then, as we have seen, can be sustained only if they are supported by evidence located in the words of the text or in the world from which the text emerges. And our criticism of the text, which may be linked to our values and to other forms of extratextual knowledge (Scholes refers to the discourse of criticism as "text against text," meaning that every critical perspective is informed by values, expectations, and ideological perspectives that themselves constitute a text that is juxtaposed against the text under scrutiny), still depends for its plausibility on an interpretation that is itself plausible in its reasoning from evidence. It is no accident, then, that the most fine-grained ethnographic study available of an exemplary advanced placement literature class in a high school found that the most important cultural practice and key to full membership in the intellectual community of that classroom was the practice identified in the study and in that classroom as "making a case" (Rex 1997; Rex and McEachen 1999).

Let us now look again at Scholes' triad of literary skills or ways of thinking in the reading of literature and ask if there are counterparts to the cognitive operations that define reading, interpretation, and criticism in the mental operations that are essential in other academic disciplines or intellectual enterprises aside from literary study. What such an inquiry reveals is that the teaching of literature does, in fact, teach students a pattern or discipline for thinking that is applicable to every field of study and probably every complex human endeavor, and that can serve as a description of critical thinking in virtually every context. Thus, if we translate reading, interpretation, and criticism into their counterparts in every other field, we'll see that the question defining reading, "What does it say?" translates in all other fields into the question, "What are the facts?" The question defining interpretation, "What does it mean?" translates to the question, "What inferences can be drawn from the facts?" And the question of criticism or value, the question of "So what?" translates into such questions as, "What applications does it suggest?" and "What theory does it generate or challenge?"

Consider a scientist in the laboratory or field. She begins with making observations, collecting data, and recording facts. From those facts she derives some principles or conclusions in the form of generalizations about how a phenomenon works. From such conclusions or generalizations come practical applications or new or revised theories.

Or consider a detective at a crime scene. He first collects the facts, the raw data that might or might not become clues. Then he examines the data to see what leads will serve as clues, and he makes inferences about the identity of the perpetrator of the crime. On the basis of these inferences he will then have to determine what applications or actions are appropriate—whether to make an arrest or seek an indictment, for example.

What we can fairly conclude, in other words, is that in teaching the operations of mind that are fundamental to the study of literature, we are also teaching and providing students with regular practice in a process of evidentiary reasoning that is the basis for effective intellectual work in any academic field or profession they might enter, and that also defines critical thinking in every enterprise of business, civic, or private life.

Step 5: Drawing Conclusions from the Experiment—Essential Principles to Guide and Sustain the Teaching and Learning of Literature (15–20 minutes)

The experiment I have conducted here as a model for instruction in literature can be interpreted to yield three principles or propositions about the teaching and learning of literature that I want to propose for their pedagogical and political value to classroom teachers. They are principles to be kept in mind in planning and conducting literary instruction and in defending the discipline of literary study itself in a political and educational culture that often threatens to minimize or dismiss its importance.

> 1. Reading is a process of constructing meaning or composing a text, exactly like writing. The reading of any difficult text will entail drafting and revision (largely in the reader's head) and will frequently begin with what amounts to a zero draft. Just as writing may be defined as rewriting, so is any reading worth doing essentially a process of rereading.

Scholes (1985) and a number of reading theorists (see Tierney and Pearson 1983 and the summary of research and theory in Chapter 1 of Olson 2003), along with more radical postmodern theorists like Barthes (1975), have together made what by now amounts to an unassailable case for looking at reading and writing not so much as reciprocal activities but as parallel ones, both entailing the construction of a meaning. What a reader sees on a written page are black marks, to which he gives a meaning as he constructs in his head some idea or set of ideas, which then can be said to represent or reconstitute what had been written.

I want to push this idea further by noting that the meanings constructed through reading are also composed exactly as written work is composed and through a process that entails rough drafts and revisions as much as any task of difficult writing would. In fact, for its heuristic value, I would offer the paradoxical proposition that reading is more like writing than writing is. Consider how often we have seen our students in composition revise their papers and make them worse. But in reading, revision never fails to be productive in yielding additional insight or the recognition of new problems—the confusion that represents an advance in understanding.

Experienced readers know that their first vision of a text may be entirely misdirected or so minimal as to appear worthless (consider the way most readers initially apprehend the Thoreau passage introduced in the previous chapter). But they also know that such a reading is merely a zero draft, a starting place for a series of rereadings that will gradually yield an increasingly more adequate and illuminating sense of a meaning that they are constructing to reconstitute the text in front of them. Inexperienced readers may regard all encounters with difficult texts to be worthless, because they have never progressed beyond the inchoate and apparently pointless zero draft represented by their first reading. Thus, based on their experience, they will declare quite accurately that for them the reading of poetry (or most other challenging texts) is an utterly worthless enterprise.

> 2. Reading is, and needs to be in classrooms, a social process, completed in conversation. Students will learn literature best and find many of their best opportunities for learning to become more competent, more intellectually productive, and more autonomous readers of literature through frequent work in groups with peers.

This principle, whose validity became at least partially self-evident in our workshop, is supported by a long history of classroom experience and by a sizeable body of research and theory (see for example, Nystrand and Gamaron 1991; Smith 1994; Pradl 1996; Schoenbach et al. 1999). Conversation following reading is, of course, almost a natural event or as natural as any ordinary civilized custom feels. Whenever we are witnesses to aesthetic or natural phenomena that take our breath away or that move us or touch us powerfully, we tend to want to share the experience with others, partly to confirm our own experience, partly to relive it by recounting it and hearing it recounted by others, and partly to gain the broader perspective that comes from such sharing. Most people I know would prefer to go the movies or the theater or an art gallery with someone else rather than alone, not just to have somebody to hold hands with, but to have a partner for a dialogue about the experience that is shared and that may be different for each of the parties. So it is with books, which is why so many readers belong to book clubs and love to encounter someone else who has just read the same book they have.

Wayne Booth, in *The Company We Keep* (1988, 70–77), has demonstrated that this process of talking with others about our literary experiences and making literary judgments is essential to the making of literary knowledge, and he has further dignified the process by identifying it as a socially constructed form of reasoning that he calls "coduction." Coduction differs from the more rigid and interior processes of induction and deduction in two principal ways: first, in the way in which it derives from conversation or a kind of collaborative discourse or negotiation conducted with other readers, and second, in the way it yields knowledge that is always provisional, insofar as literary opinions and judgments are always rooted in comparisons with previous literary experiences and change as our experience grows richer and more varied over time.

The importance of conversation to the making of literary knowledge through coduction would alone make a powerful argument for providing students with frequent conversational opportunities among themselves, preferably in small groups, where participation can be more frequent and intensive and where the kind of conversation needed for genuine negotiation about meaning and value will not be suppressed by the derivative and nonprovisional kinds of literary opinions that are characteristically delivered through large lectures and the official curriculum. An equally important and persuasive reason to have students talk to each other about their reading, however, has to do with the nature of texts and the limited attention of readers. Literary texts are filled with data. Novels contain whole worlds. Good poems have more going on in them than any single reader is likely to notice without years of attention to the same few lines.[3] The virtue of having students (or any readers) talk to each other in groups is that they can help each other notice what is worthy of notice and thereby apprehend works of literature more fully (as well as from multiple perspectives) than they might otherwise.

Two additional purposes—purposes that seem to me most important of all and that go far to address the problem that is the focus of this workshop—are also served by having students work in groups and talk about their reading experience. One has to do with the fact that most teachers of literature will acknowledge that they did not become truly skilled and powerful readers of difficult literary works until they found themselves faced with the task of teaching such texts, including many that they had not been taught in college. Having to teach a text forces an interpretively dependent English major to become an interpretively autonomous English teacher.

In my introduction to this volume I tell of a moment early in my teaching career when I experienced what for me was a shocking recognition that the roles and responsibilities falling to teachers and students in conventional literature classrooms provided most of the opportunities for learning to the teachers rather than to their students. I realized in the midst of my own teaching one day that as long as I was the one who had the responsibility of preparing for my teaching prior to each class by solving the most difficult interpretive and conceptual problems that might trouble my students as readers of the texts I had assigned, then I was the one who was doing most of the learning in my English class. My role seemed to be to present my students with the fruit of my intellectual labor so that they would then know it and record it in their notebooks. The role undertaken by my students, then, was largely not to be persons who performed acts of learning themselves, but to serve as witnesses and recorders of my learning.

I was struck at that moment in class by what I came to think of as the ironic paradox of teaching: the fact that the intellectual work undertaken by teachers in the teaching-learning relationship presented richer opportunities for learning to the teacher than anything the teacher might do in the course of teaching his students.

And a few years later I presented a lecture focused on that irony under the title "On the Advancement of Learning Through the Abolition of Teaching." The problem, insofar as I understood it at that time, appeared to me to have its only solution in the resolution of teachers who cared about their students' learning to refuse to teach or to find ways whereby the conventional roles of teachers and students could be somehow reversed.

Having students work in groups helping each other solve the textual and conceptual problems that difficult texts pose for them turns out to be the most practical way available to put students into something like one of the roles that teachers usually occupy, a role where much of the task of figuring out the problems that teachers are expected to solve now reverts to the students to solve for one another and in collaboration with one another. Insofar as the work that takes place in groups represents more of a collaboration than it does a reversal of the roles of teacher and student, so much the better. It is, in fact, a better model of teaching than the traditional model. That is because in such collaborative relationships, everybody gets to be the teacher and everybody gets to be the learner, according to her needs and strengths moment to moment. Students get to work with one another, in other words, in what Vygotsky (1962, 1978) calls the "zone of proximal development," where they are able to do together more than any of them can do by themselves, and through that process grow toward greater autonomy and independence (also see Lave and Wenger 1991).

Group work on problem texts is also crucial to the learning that needs to take place in literature classes because of what it contributes to the construction of a particular kind of classroom community and classroom culture and for the sort of ethos it fosters for intellectual work within such a culture. Working in groups on interpretive problems helps to build a classroom culture that honors the process of noticing and acknowledging difficulties in understanding texts. It dismantles the intellectually counterproductive culture of most classrooms where answers are valued and confusion avoided. In a classroom where intellectual problems and confusion are honored as rich occasions for learning, students and teachers will be more inclined to confront and even seek rather than avoid the textual and conceptual problems that offer the richest opportunities for learning.

Moreover, and perhaps most importantly, in a classroom that cultivates a disposition to uncover and examine problems in learning and understanding, students learn to look more honestly and critically at the state of their own understanding, to make distinctions between what they do and don't understand, and to note qualitative differences in the kinds of understandings they themselves possess. Every experienced teacher of students in secondary schools or of undergraduate students early in their college years knows that if you ask students who have completed their reading of a difficult literary work what questions they have about it, there will often be no response. All teachers know how the drill goes. "What questions do you have? Seeing none, may I assume that you understand everything? No? Well, do you understand anything? No? Is there no word or phrase you understand? Are you saying that in reading this entire short story, you understood not one sentence about what was happening in it?"

From that point, perhaps, some dialogue may begin. But getting students to tell you about the state of their knowledge appears to be a major obstacle to getting them started in the direction of solving any of the problems that may be obstructing their understanding of what they have read. The less competent the students, the more likely they are to have no questions, as if, paradoxically, only the strongest readers don't understand what they have read, while the weakest readers have the fewest problems. The reality, of course, is that one of the principal characteristics of weak readers that accounts for their weakness is their disinclination and lack of experience with, and therefore their apparent incapacity to monitor their understanding as they read or talk about the ways in which they do and don't understand what they have read. Reading specialists and learning theorists use the term *metacognition*, thinking about one's thinking, to talk about such monitoring and such discourse (see Kirby and Kuykendall 1991, 40–41; Schoenbach et al. 1999; and Olson 2003, Chapter 14).

No characteristic seems to me to better differentiate the strongest readers from the weakest among students in late adolescence than this capacity for metacognition, for paying attention to the state of one's understanding while reading so one can catch problems and solve them as they arise, and for being able to describe the state of one's understanding so that problems can be identified and explored for solutions. All of the stories I recounted in the previous chapter about the culture of school as it is conventionally conducted demonstrate how such a culture conspires against the development of such metacognitive skills. Introducing regular group work on difficult texts in a classroom that foregrounds and honors difficulties, confusion, and intellectual problems is the best way I know to change the conventional culture of instruction.

> 3. Literary reading and literary study, as they are ordinarily sponsored in rigorously conducted English classes, teach students an intellectual discipline that defines critical thinking in every field and fosters academic success in every subject of study.

I am here repeating a conclusion I offered only a moment ago, but I want to offer it again now as a proposition that English teachers need to keep in mind as the best defense available against the various sorts of educational "reforms" that would substitute practical or utilitarian reading for literary texts in the required English curriculum. If there is any doubt about the need to defend literary study against those who would replace it with more "practical" disciplines, consider the case of a major state university and a statewide community college system a few years ago that jointly recommended that all community colleges in the state teach critical thinking as an essential component of the freshman-level English courses required for transfer from the community college system to campuses of the university. The result of this recommendation was that (with a few exceptions) community colleges throughout the state removed literature from the freshman English curriculum and replaced it with various forms of instruction in critical thinking. Such instruction was doomed to failure, of course, as long as it was not linked to the actual study of some discipline where critical thinking is authentically employed. Ironically, of course, critical thinking is almost always authentically employed, as we have seen, in the teaching of literature, which was being systematically abandoned.

Threats to literature instruction are nevertheless relatively rare in higher education, except in composition programs that sometimes remove literary study for fear that it will overtake and marginalize the study of rhetoric, or in the interest of asserting the value of composition across all disciplines. Otherwise the privileged status of literature is generally protected, in spite of the movement in many English departments to transform literary study to cultural studies or textual studies, which mainly entails a sort of colonial expansion of the sphere of literary study rather than its demise. But in the world of K–12 education a number of recent movements and proposals have emerged to constitute clear and present dangers for the future of literary study.

In the highly politicized arena of public elementary and secondary education the opposition to literature has emerged largely from two quarters and in two forms. First, it has emerged from some precincts of the school-to-work movement and from other practical-minded reformers who want secondary schools to educate students primarily for employment. Their argument has been that literature is a curricular frill of merely aesthetic interest to an elite group of academics and should therefore not be entirely removed from the secondary school curriculum, but relegated to the status of an academic elective. Required English courses should in the meantime direct their attention to the marketable and survival skills of reading such informational texts as warranties, instructions, textbooks, and newspapers.

Opposition to literature has also emerged as a minor theme in the politics of reading, where some zealots of the basic skills movement have found literary texts unsuitable to the systematic teaching of skills and a distracting temptation for teachers and students who would rather enjoy a story aesthetically than use it for a reading lesson. Their argument amounts to a perverse sort of Gresham's Law argument that literature—since it has the power to interest and engage students emotionally and intellectually—will always chase the more needed instruction in basic reading skills out of the curriculum. Literature should therefore be banned. A related argument, whose presuppositions are just as unwarranted as its conclusions, holds that non-literary texts, unlike literature, can't mean whatever you want them to mean and are therefore more suitable to a skills-based method of reading instruction (rather like typing instruction) focused on accuracy, speed, and correctness.

The chapters that follow will include experiments in literary reading and interpretation that will dismantle and correct most of the mistaken assumptions held by the critics of literary study about what literary study entails and about how meaning in literature is construed and validated. Unfortunately, no one except teachers of literature is likely to attend to such evidence. In the meantime, we can probably make our best case for the utilitarian importance of literary study by demonstrating how the processes of reading, interpreting, and criticizing literary texts teach and call for the exercise of evidentiary reasoning and the practice of critical thinking skills that are required for successful intellectual work in every field of study and academic discipline.

Notes

1. I hesitate to speak of literary independence, because I don't want to promote what Valentine Cunningham (2002, Chapter 2) calls the "myth of the independent reader," the idea that there can be a truly solo reader whose reading practices are untainted by theory, tradition, instruction, and a wider literary community.

2. The exercise I describe here and a number of variations on it that I use in my teaching and workshops originated in earlier activities I had been experimenting with for some years in my classes, but it also owes crucial elements of its present structure to a lesson Tom Newkirk (1984) describes in his now classic essay "Looking for Trouble: A Way to Unmask Our Readings."

3. I am indebted to Professor Gerald Graff of the University of Illinois, Chicago, for offering this observation as a participant in one of my workshops.

3

Which Interpretation Is the Right One?
A Workshop on Literary Meaning

The problem I want to address in this chapter and workshop is the problem of differing and contradictory interpretations and the ways they challenge instruction and raise questions about the validity of the interpretative enterprise in classrooms. To describe my aims in terms of more practical results for students and teachers, I want in this chapter and workshop to provide an opportunity to interrogate and correct two common and closely related misperceptions that students bring with them to my classes. The first is the widely held idea that there is only one authoritative and best interpretation for most literary texts, what Susan Hynds (1991) calls "the myth of the one correct response." That is the response or interpretation taught by teachers and presumably authorized by the scholarly community and represented in such reliable sources as lectures or essays by eminent literary scholars or study guides (presumably written under the authority of respectable professors) like Cliffs Notes. The other, equally common in recent years, is the opposite belief, which many students and some respected scholars think to be the logical alternative to the first position (cf. E. D. Hirsch 1967, Chapter 1; Fish 1980; and Derrida as explicated in Scholes 1989, Chapter 2). It is the position that if there is no single or authoritative interpretation for a literary text, then the discipline of literary study is one in which any and all interpretations have equal authority. Or, as many students put the case, a poem (or any other literary work) can mean anything you want it to mean.[1]

The Workshop

With no further introduction, except the observation that the workshop I am about to present can usually be completed within the compass of an ordinary fifty-minute class period and is best presented with no introduction at all, let's proceed to the workshop, which I would describe in my syllabus or in talking about it for students merely as an experiment in interpretation. The poem to be used here and passed out at the beginning of the workshop is Theodore Roethke's widely anthologized "My Papa's Waltz," a poem that I have seen in literature texts for all grades from ninth through college. The poem was first published in a Hearst magazine in 1942 and next appeared in 1948 in the second collection of Roethke's poems, called *The Lost Son and Other Poems by Theodore Roethke*. By the mid-fifties, it was already showing up in college anthologies of poetry.

My Papa's Waltz

The whiskey on your breath
Could make a small boy dizzy;
But I hung on like death:
Such waltzing was not easy.

We romped until the pans
Slid from the kitchen shelf;
My mother's countenance
Could not unfrown itself.

The hand that held my wrist
Was battered on one knuckle;
At every step you missed
My right ear scraped a buckle.

You beat time on my head
With a palm caked hard by dirt,
Then waltzed me off to bed
Still clinging to your shirt.
  —*Theodore Roethke (1908–1963)*

Activities

READING AND WRITING

T: Please read the poem by Theodore Roethke (which some of you may have read before) a couple of times to make sure you have read it fairly well, and then do two things with it. Identify any lines you are still having trouble understanding and write out your question or questions about them, and then pick the line you regard as the most important line in the poem. Copy out that line in your log and write a paragraph on why you think it's the most important line.

Commentary: The assignment to select the most important line, which I adopted from workshops conducted by David Bleich, is almost a fail-safe way to foster useful discussions of a text among students. But any way of initiating a discussion of the poem will be satis-factory here, as long as it encourages enough interpretive discussion to enable students to see how they and the different members of the group are interpreting the poem. The prob-lem with simply asking students to write a brief response to the poem is that such responses often mask interpretive differences.

SHARING IN GROUPS OF FOUR

T: Now move into groups of four, making sure your groups are as diverse as pos-sible—in gender, ethnicity, region of origin, age, and whatever else you can think of. In your groups your task will be simply, first, to share any problems you had with specific words or lines and clear them up as quickly as possible. Then share (which is to say, read aloud to your group) the line you picked as most impor-tant and what you wrote about why it is the most important line. Then talk about differences and similarities in your reading.

Commentary: I always try to make my groups as diverse as possible for this exercise on the outside chance that sociocultural perspectives will play a role in what sorts of read-ings emerge in discussion of this poem. What I am looking for are different readings or disagreement about this poem in every group, not agreement. So I do whatever I can in advance to foster disagreement and, finally, as will be evident below, I directly ask for it. But not until students have had a chance to take positions and begin arguing for them. I also insist that students in their groups read aloud what they have written, rather than merely talk about it.

T: (About 10 minutes into the exercise) Ladies and gentlemen, please forgive me for interrupting. I have been walking around the room listening to your con-versations, and I can see you are quite engaged and still working. I would like to ask you to monitor your own thinking at this point and, especially if everybody in your group seems to be reading the poem in the same way and you have been silent or reluctant to disagree, yet feeling some reservations, ask yourself if you really agree. If you don't, please speak up. Please make your private reservations, doubts, or disagreement known to your group members now.

REPORTING OUT

T: Are there any groups that found themselves in complete agreement in their interpretations of this poem? I see that only one group found itself of one mind. Can someone from one of the groups where there was disagreement character-ize, very briefly, the nature of the disagreement in your group?

S1: Well, they all thought that when the father and son were dancing, it was some kind of act of violence or something, and I didn't think so.

S2: We didn't all say it was violent, but we felt that there was a lot of cruelty in it.

S3: Some of us thought it was violent.

S4: I thought the child in the poem was a little girl. They all thought it was a boy.

S5: "It says 'the whiskey on your breath could make a small boy dizzy.'"

S4: The child in the poem could still be a girl. She says "boy" to show how strong the whiskey breath was.

S6: But the author's name is Theodore. So he's a man. And the poem is a memory from the child's point of view.

S4: But that doesn't mean the speaker in the poem is a man. The poem has a persona.

T: That's right. We don't know for sure, do we? But it sounded to me as I went around the room that most of you assumed the child was male. Does it really make a difference anyway?

S4: It made a difference to me, because I identified with the child and maybe that's why I assumed it was a girl. I used to dance with my father that way.

T: Well, do most of you feel that the poem leaves a gap there, not requiring us to identify the child as necessarily male or female? Poems leave gaps that readers have to fill in (Iser 1974, 274–94). Like, how old is this child? The poem constrains our imaginations but doesn't tell us exactly, does it? Could the child be fourteen or fifteen? No? Why not?

S5: He has to be waist-high on the father—to scrape his ear on the belt. So he can't be three or four either.

T: So what are you imagining? What age is the child you visualize in the poem? Older than, say, five? Could he be six? No? Maybe? Seven? Some of you imagine seven. Eight? OK. Twelve? No? Ten? Is that the outer limit? Somewhere between five and ten? But you can't say exactly and we'll all fill in the gap through our own experience. What color is the child's hair? What sort of clothing is he wearing? What's his color or ethnicity? I assume you are visualizing a child, making your own movie in your head, and it's slightly different for each of you, though quite similar insofar as it is consistent with the facts of the poem or maybe what you know about Roethke. So is the gender of the child also a gap in the poem that you can fill in your own way? Some of you apparently think it is. And isn't it pretty much the same poem whether the child is a boy or girl?

S6: I don't see how it could possibly be a girl.

T: Well, if you feel strongly about this issue (as some of you apparently do), you may be interested in knowing that in the first draft of the poem (which is housed in the University of Washington library and may be seen online at <*www.bedfordstmartins.com/virtualit/cultural.html*>), you can see that Roethke had initially written "girl" and then crossed it out and wrote in "boy" in the line that says "make a small boy dizzy," though I'm not sure how that fact might influence your reading or your feeling about the poem.

S4: See? It could be a girl. That's really interesting!

S5: No, it shows that he intended it to be a boy and he made a definite choice.

T: I thought you might have different interpretations of that interpretive evidence, too. But let's get back to the major grounds for debate. Could someone characterize the different readings in any group that found itself divided? How would you name the different sides people took?

S7: In our group, some of us thought that when the dad beat time on the boy's head, it meant that he was beating the boy, but the other people said that it was a loving gesture.

T: How about if we hold up for a minute on details and just try to give a characterization, sort of a label for the different readings that emerged in your groups?

S8: OK. Some of us thought it was a happy poem and some thought it was tragic.

S9: Well, not tragic, but sad.

S3: Not just sad, either. It's violent.

S4: Most people thought it was about abuse. But I thought it was a sweet memory.

S10: Or bittersweet.

T: So I'm hearing at least two main and competing readings. For convenience, can we for the moment call one the "abusive" reading and the other the "happy" reading? All right. So let's see how it breaks down by numbers. How many of you thought that this poem was a poem about abuse or at least a poem with serious abusive elements in it? That looks to be maybe three-quarters of the group. OK. How many of you found it basically a happy memory, a memory recalled fondly of an event that was, when it happened, largely a happy event? A handful of you—maybe 20 percent of the group. How many of you are reading the poem in some third way? All right—a couple. Aren't we missing some voters here?

S11: I started out thinking it was happy, but then in the discussion was persuaded that it was about abuse. And now I can't make up my mind. Maybe it's both.

S10: I think the poem has both elements in it. It's basically happy, but it's bittersweet, you know, because the dad is an alcoholic, but this is probably the best attention the kid can get.

S3: How can that be best if the dad is beating him?

T: You're reading the poem as the dad inflicting a beating?

S3: Isn't that what the waltz is?

T: How many of you are reading it that way: the waltz as a metaphor for a beating? Seven. That's what I've been getting lately for that reading, sometimes more. So it looks like we have what amounts to three or four readings of the poem in this room: first, the reading that takes the poem as basically a happy memory of a cherished moment with the speaker's father, and then the reading that finds the poem to be about the abuse of the child at the hands of the father. And there are two versions of this second reading: one that reads the dance as a metaphor for a beating—a reading that turns the whole poem into something like an allegory—and the reading that the majority seem to be advancing, taking the dance as a real event, but seeing the entire event as one that constitutes a form of abuse in a relationship and family that is, as they say, dysfunctional. Is that fair to say? And then there is the reading that sees the events as remembered fondly by the speaker, but nevertheless having some elements that were bitter, but still overall a fond memory? Yes? No? You're not so sure. Can we stick with the two major or superordinate readings for a while (since they seem to contain the other readings and are held by almost all of you) and examine the evidence that leads you to one claim or the other, that is, to read the poem as a largely positive and happy memory or to read it as somehow about child abuse? Who wants to present the evidence for the majority reading, that this is a poem that is in some fundamental way about abuse? OK, Sarah, let's hear it.

S2: First of all, the father is drunk.

S12: We don't know that.

S2: His whiskey breath "could make a small boy dizzy." So you can bet he's had enough to be pretty loaded himself.

T: Let's let Sarah finish.

S2: Well, the poem is filled with evidence: the boy gets hurt from the dance—his ear scrapes the dad's belt with every step; the dad beats on the boy's head. That can't be pleasant. The father's knuckle is already scraped as if he'd been fighting in a bar on the way home. So he's at least a rough, violent person.

S3: It could be scraped from beating on the boy.

S2: It could.

T: Anything else?

S13: The mother can't stop frowning. She is upset by what she sees.

T: Right. Do we know why she is upset?

S11: Because the house is shaking so much that the dishes are about to fall off the shelf.

S1: That doesn't mean that the child is being abused. She may be upset the way mothers often are at ordinary male roughhousing. It's too rough for her, but the boy and his father like it.

T: That's plausible.

S4: If the child is a girl, the mother could be jealous.

T: Oh yes! That's an interesting interpretive twist. Terrific. But what other evidence can we find on the abusive side?

S14: The father's hands are caked with dirt. So he is some kind of laborer.

T: And what do you make of that?

S14: Well, maybe that means something . . .

T: You mean laborers or men who work with their hands are more likely to be alcoholics and child abusers than other people—say, middle-class folks like yourselves? Are we hearing some class prejudice here?

ALL: (Titters and murmurs.)

T: OK. I'll give you some good reasons later why—aside from its basis in class prejudice—you might not want to consider the dirt on the father's hands as evidence either way. What other evidence can we find to support the abusive reading?

S7: Well, the boy holds on like death and he is waltzed off to bed at the end, still clinging to his father's shirt.

S1: Where do you see abuse in that?

S7: It shows that the child, like all children of alcoholics, is terrified, but still holds on for dear life to get whatever kind of contact and affection he can. It's a sad picture, not a happy one.

T: OK. Good. Let's now switch to the other side. Where is the evidence that it's a happy poem? Sean?

S12: First of all, he calls the poem "My Papa's Waltz," which sounds affectionate and names a dance. And he could have referred to his father as his old man. *Papa* is a loving term.

S15: It's a happy memory because dancing with your father is a wonderful thing to do, even if his breath smells like whiskey. Look. I'm sorry to sound upset, but I don't see why people want to ruin this poem. It's like digging up gossip on somebody who is basically a good person and trying to make him look bad. The mother frowns because that's what mothers do when they see horseplay. "Oh, my dishes! My furniture!" It's not serious.

S12: I agree. He says that they romped and he says that at the end, the boy still didn't want to go to bed. He continues to cling to his father's shirt.

T: You read that line as evidence that it's a happy poem? But Sarah's group read the same line as evidence that it's a poem about abuse.

S14: Well, it's not!

T: OK. Anything else?

S11: The waltzing is not easy.

S6: Isn't that evidence that the dancing is abusive?

S5: It could show how much the boy liked dancing with his dad. He kept at it even when it was difficult.

S10: That's why I read the poem as bittersweet. It has all of these elements of abuse in it, yet the boy cherishes the opportunity to be close to his dad and works hard to keep the closeness going.

S16: But the father is drunk and even if the boy wants what he can get from him, it doesn't change the bottom line that the father is drunk and an alcoholic and on the edge of being out of control. And whenever that is what's happening, that's abuse for the child who has to live with it. And that's what the mother sees and is also afraid of.

S17: We don't know that the father is an alcoholic or that he gets drunk very often. Maybe that's the only time he loosens up enough to play with his kid. That's not abuse. Maybe it's more abusive when he's not drinking and ignores his child.

S18: Right! I can't believe what you guys are saying about this poem! Didn't any of you ever dance with your dad the way it's described in the poem? I did as a little kid. And nothing that happens in this poem is in any way abusive. What's abusive is what you are doing to this poem!

T: There's a strong reading! Thanks, Eric.

S16: Are you on his side? Let Eric tell us, if he thinks it's not about abuse, why the poem has all those words and descriptions that show abuse: beating, scraping his ear, whiskey on his breath, dizzy, mother frowning, battered knuckle, hung on like death! Come on!

T: Apparently we could go on with this argument for some time longer and maybe also hear from those of you who have not spoken up. But I think we've heard most of the evidence to be found in the poem from both sides. And not only does that evidence seem inconclusive, but some of the same evidence gets cited in favor of opposite positions. I hope that by now, even if you are as certain as you can be about the validity of your own position, you can also see the logic or the reasonableness (and possibly the passion) of the position being argued by those who disagree with you. That is, I suspect that given the evidence you've heard on both sides, you can intellectually respect the position of your classmates on the other side from yours, even if you "know" that they are wrong.

All right. How can we adjudicate between these two competing interpretations of the poem or validate any of the variant interpretations? Where can we go, besides to the poem itself, for additional evidence?

S8: You could ask the author, if he were still alive.

T: I think that's what most people would say, especially people outside of the literary community. It seems commonsensical. And I know somebody who did just that and I'll tell you about it later.

MANY STUDENTS: No! Tell us now! It's not fair if you know! (And so on.)

T: I'm sorry I mentioned it so soon. OK. I'll tell you what I know that someone claims to have gotten from Roethke himself.

A couple of years ago I conducted a workshop much like this one for the Illinois Association of Teachers of English, and in the middle of it a teacher in the group raised her hand and said that she had once asked Roethke about this poem. I asked her to hold on to her information until near the end of the workshop and then tell us what he had said. So at the proper time, she told us that she had read the poem in the mid-fifties and began to teach it, and had always felt that the poem was ambiguous or ambivalent in its tone. Then in about 1960, she met Roethke at an NCTE conference, where he was giving a reading, and asked him about his intentions in the poem. He told her to look at the last lines of his poem, because a poet always shows you what he is after with a poem in its last lines. And what are the last lines? "Then waltzed me off to bed / Still clinging to your shirt." Unfortunately, those are lines that in this room both sides have cited as evidence for their opposite positions!

S1: But when he said that, he must have thought it would show the reader how the poem was about a warm and loving experience. Because that's what any normal person in 1960 would think about those lines.

ALL: (Many voices with laughter and objections.)

T: That's my prejudice too, I admit.

Reflections, Meditations, and Explications: Debriefing and Extending the Workshop

Commentary: What follows is a series of discourses, discussions, or mini-essays on a number of issues—theoretical, practical, and historical—arising from the workshop experience. These discussions, which serve to reflect on and extend the more experimental segments of the workshop, are reconstructions of what I usually say in actual workshops with students or with teachers. However, I am taking the additional liberty offered by the absence of time constraints and the advantages of written composition to elaborate these discourses more extensively than I would in an oral presentation. For the sake of space, moreover, I am deleting the clarifying and challenging questions and statements that students and teachers typically contribute to what will appear on these pages as unrelieved monologue. Finally I want to note that as these discourses focus increasingly on theoretical and professional matters, they increasingly addresses themselves to teachers rather than to students.

Discussion 1: On Questions of Poetic Identity, Persona, and Biographical Evidence

Let us now look at other kinds of evidence to see what we might find to help us adjudicate between competing readings of the Roethke poem. For one thing, we are sophisticated enough to know that, although poems are written by their authors, they are spoken by speakers, who are what we call the *persona*. The author of a poem might be a modern woman, but the speaker in a poem she writes could be a medieval duke.

(Poems are constructed and they are fiction. They are not or need not be confessional.) We even have evidence that in composing this poem, which may feel to us highly autobiographical, Roethke entertained the idea, at least for a while, of having it spoken by a female persona.

(On the other hand, if we didn't identify the speakers of many lyric poems with their authors, we wouldn't be very interested in the poems.) Consider a poem like Ben Jonson's elegy on the death of his first child ("On His First Son"). Most readers find that a powerful poem and would do so no matter who wrote it. But part of its power for us resides in our sense of its sincerity, our sense that the voice of the poem is a real one and belongs to someone who has experienced this loss in actuality. And, of course, in this poem the name of the poet and the dead child appear in the body of the poem as well.

For another example, think about George Herbert's religious meditations. If we didn't believe that these poems were the sincere expressions of the rhythms of his own spiritual life, we wouldn't find them nearly as compelling or important, aside from their metrical and imagistic virtuosity, even though there is abundant evidence that they were revised significantly to remove some of the personal dimensions of the poems and make them more public documents—more expressions of typical spiritual life or exemplary spiritual life. But part of their power for us lies in our taking them seriously as representations of the spiritual experience of George Herbert, the living person who was Orator at Cambridge, who relinquished the opportunity to hold powerful public positions in order to become a country parson, and so on.

My point is that no matter how sophisticated we are as readers, we are inclined—and wisely so—to identify lyric poems with their authors, unless we have some reason to separate them. And here it might be salutary for us to realize that the very idea of a persona for a first-person poem or for the entire genre of lyric poems was largely an invention of the New Critics in the mid-twentieth century. The term *persona* was used throughout most of literary history, beginning with Plato and Aristotle, to distinguish the voice of created or fictional characters within poems from the authentic voice of the poet speaking for himself or herself. In drama those other voices were and still are referred to as *dramatis personae*. But until well into the twentieth century, it was generally assumed that when the poet spoke in a poem in his own person—rather than in something like a dramatic monologue with a clearly invented character—it was the poet speaking (see *persona* in Preminger et al. 1993, *The New Princeton Encyclopedia of Poetry and Poetics*). In fact, the *Oxford English Dictionary* (Compact Edition, 1971), probably reflecting late nineteenth-century poetics, defines the term *lyric* as "now used for the name of short poems . . . expressing the poet's own thought and sentiments."

It was the New Critics in the twentieth century who, in their opposition to biographical readings of poems and their insistence on the poem as a created artifact distinct from the poet and her intention, introduced the idea that even in lyric poems the speaker can't be equated with the poet. And one measure of the pervasive influence of New Criticism on literary education is the fact that virtually all English teachers I encounter continue to insist on talking about speakers in all poems as the persona and to enforce that practice among their students. Fortunately, they know better as readers and frequently ignore their academic practice when they encounter and talk about most lyric poems they care about.

But before we go too far in abandoning the idea of a persona, let me point out that many lyric poems of the Renaissance—especially love poems that appear to be written directly from the heart—are, as the critic and poet J. V. Cunningham (1966, 162) used to observe, written less by a man than by a tradition. That is, what the poem does and says is to a very large extent conventional and imitative of similar poems in the Petrarchan or classical traditions. And that surely raises questions about how much the speaker of the poem is the individual who is the author or the author in his role as poet and as the figure a poet is expected to cut in the culture. More-over, many modern theorists would insist that all poems in every age are necessarily written by a confluence of cultural forces and antecedent voices, and the very idea of a single author for a text is something of a fiction.

Still, we are inclined, and I think reasonably so, to read most lyric poems as per-sonal utterances, and I think most modern poets would not discourage that inclina-tion. And in Roethke's case and in the case of this particular poem, we seem to be especially invited to do so. Although the poem was originally published in 1942, Roethke included it in a 1948 volume of collected poems called *The Lost Son*, where it appeared as one of fourteen poems in an opening sequence of transparently auto-biographical poems referred to by his biographers and critics as "the greenhouse poems," including the now widely anthologized short poem "Child on Top of a Green-house," about how a boy climbs up on the roof of a greenhouse in a nursery and up-sets all the adults who see him up there spread out on the glass. And here I should mention that Roethke was raised around greenhouses because his father and grand-father were florists who worked in their own greenhouse next to their home in Saginaw, Michigan. That might explain why the father in "My Papa's Waltz" would have hands caked hard by dirt. Finally, as if to quell any lingering doubt about the autobiographical origins of the poem, Roethke included a headnote for the poem in one of the early published versions of it, saying (as nearly as I can remember, since I can no longer find the volume where I saw it) the following: "My father used to dance with me sometimes when he came in from work: ta tum, ta tum, ta tum"—surely a happy-sounding note.

Now, I don't know if Roethke's father was an alcoholic. But Roethke himself was a famously hard drinker. Might that suggest that his father probably was or that it's a reasonable guess that he was? And does that support one reading over another? On the other hand, I was doing this very workshop for a college English department some years ago, where the English department chair told me afterward that while he liked how I worked with the poem, he also knew how Roethke intended the poem to have been read. He had been a doctoral student at the University of Washington in about 1960, where Roethke taught in the English department. And he had heard Roethke read the poem on several occasions and he always read it in a lilting voice as if singing a song or chanting in waltz time. It was, said my colleague, clearly a poem of joy or one registering a happy memory for Roethke. But if that seems a definitive answer, you should know that I have another friend who is himself a distinguished poet and who also knew Roethke. He told me that he had heard Roethke read this poem in a gruff and rough-sounding voice as if reciting a list of capital crimes to a prisoner about to be shot.

Discussion 2: A Teacher's History of the Reception of Roethke's "My Papa's Waltz"

Let me now recount to you the history of the reception of Roethke's poem among readers like yourselves, based on my experience of having taught the poem over a period of two generations, or about forty years. I don't remember the first time I taught the poem, but I know that I taught it in various classes throughout the sixties, and I distinctly remember discussions of the poem in a college freshman English class I taught in about 1962 or 1963, when I was a TA, and later in an introduction to poetry course that I taught as a professor in about 1966. I would guess that in the two and a half decades from 1960 up to about 1985, I taught the poem fifteen or twenty times in university freshman English classes or introductory literature courses like the one I presently teach. In all that time—that is, in the twenty-five-year period between 1960 and 1985—no student in my memory ever said anything in class discussion or in a piece of writing or in private to me about this poem having anything to do with abuse, with dysfunctional families, with alcoholism, or with violence.[2]

The first time I remember hearing the word or idea of abuse applied to this poem was in 1985, when I had been invited to be on a panel of University of California English professors at a late summer conference on new theories and approaches to the teaching of literature, sponsored by an association of English department faculty at California Community Colleges. As it turned out, I was unable to attend the conference and regretted it very much because the featured speakers for the conference included several theorists and practitioners I admired very much. But, alas, I had made a prior commitment and couldn't accept the invitation.

However, only a week or so after the conference, I ran into a colleague who taught at our local community college, a colleague who was my exact contemporary, who seemed to me highly knowledgeable on professional issues, and who had a wide reputation as an outstanding teacher. As it turned out, he had attended the conference and was delighted to tell me about it, insofar as that was possible with the two us standing in the middle of the aisle of a hardware store. But he did tell me some of the highlights of what was clearly an informative and provocative conference, and he told me specifically of a talk given by Nancy Comley of Queens College in New York City in which she spoke of how her students interpreted Roethke's poem "My Papa's Waltz." Her students—an ethnically diverse group of urban students, mostly from working-class and middle-class homes—took that poem, my colleague informed me in a tone signifying derision, to be a poem about child abuse. And to make matters worse, he noted, she—the professor, the distinguished scholar—thought that was a legitimate reading. Then he added, confident that I, his exact contemporary, would share his sense of outrage: "Do you see how crazy these modern critics have become!"

I confess that I nodded in agreement, while thinking that I needed to get home to reread the poem, because it seemed to me offhand that it might indeed be about abuse or that a strong reading could be offered based on the claim that it was about abuse. As I have said, at that time I had never heard a critic or student offer such a reading, but then at that time I hadn't had an opportunity to teach the poem for several years. I was determined to teach it again, however, at the first available opportunity, which came that very fall in a lower-division English course I had volunteered to teach on composition and literature. I taught the poem early in the quarter and found that many of my students produced the same readings as Nancy Comley's students. And I have had similar results with every group of students as well as with every group of teachers I have worked with in the years since.

On that first occasion, actually, the class split nearly down the middle on the abuse question. Thereafter, I have taught the poem virtually every year to some group of undergraduate students and have regularly conducted workshops like this one with preservice and inservice teachers as well. From 1985 until about 1990, the number of readers who read the poem as a poem about abuse grew every year, until by 1990–91 it was typically about 85 percent. Then it began to drop for a few years, back to a more nearly even split by about 1996. In recent years it has risen again, so that, by the turn of the century, it was typically 75 percent, and now in the year 2002, I again characteristically find 80 or 85 percent of the readers in a class or workshop insisting that the poem is about abuse.[3] And to support their reading—which, mind you, was almost unheard of twenty years ago—I have been told by my colleague Joe Trimmer of Ball State University in Indiana that a billboard and brochures in Indianapolis advertising the services of a shelter for abused women and children show this poem as a background text. If our students want to find more corroborating testimony, they can go to the Internet, where they will find "My Papa's Waltz" by Theodore Roethke indexed on several Internet search engines under the topics of child abuse and alcoholism.

In the meantime, many accomplished readers, especially readers of my generation and older, still tend to read the poem as basically a warm and loving memorial (an ode) to the poet's father and to his own past. Quite typically, one of the most widely used and most respected college anthologies of literature (Kennedy and Gioia 2000, 526) treats the idea that the poem may be about the father's abusiveness as a reading that misses the tone of the poem and ignores its humorous side.

So what happened? How can we account for the fact that no student in my classes before 1985 ever made a case for or even pointed me in the direction of the reading that so many contemporary students and most of their teachers seem to regard as the preferred or even normative reading of this poem? The answer, of course, is that before the mid-eighties, ideas about abuse and dysfunctional families and discussions of alcoholism in one's family were not part of the public discourse. They became a part of that discourse with the explosion of twelve-step programs in middle-class communities in the decade of the eighties and with the public revelations in the eighties and nineties of the substance abuse problems of celebrities and their family members. There also appears to have been a concerted effort on the part of mental health workers, government agencies, and the women's movement during the past decade to build public awareness about child abuse and various other forms of family violence, particularly against women and children. The effect of such a change in public discourse is that virtually all Americans—and surely all literate middle-class Americans—are alert to signs of abuse and suspicious about any hint of violence, especially where there is evidence of alcohol use.

Nor do I think we can assume, knowing what we now know about the hidden side of American middle-class family life, that there were no students in my classes in the decades of the sixties and seventies who read Roethke's poem as a poem about abuse. But to make a case for such a reading in those years would have required speaking from personal experience of what was at that time still unspeakable. It may also be the case that the students most likely to read abuse in the poem were—as the children of alcoholics themselves—also those most inclined to dismiss their own perceptions as distorted and unworthy of calling to anyone's attention. By the mid-eighties, however, the entire country was speaking of what had once been unmentionable, and it was possible and almost inevitable to know of such matters without having had any comparable experience in one's own life. Moreover, to speak of such experiences in one's own life—to unmask what had been a source of shame—was now widely seen as personally restorative and a method of overcoming shame. What we can say, then, is that a change in the culture made a particular reading available that had not been culturally available before (cf. Mellor, O'Neill, Patterson 1992).

Discussion 3: Sources of Interpretive Authority

The attractiveness and popularity of what appears to be the dominant current reading of Roethke's poem does not, of course, make it correct. But then what would make any reading more correct than another, unless we establish, as E. D. Hirsch urged us to do in 1967 in *Validity in Interpretation*, some basis for authorizing or validating readings? Hirsch has argued that authorial intention is the most credible and trustworthy source of authority and must therefore serve as the basis for determining interpretive validity, especially in cases where competing interpretive claims are being advanced. But even if there were unequivocal evidence about how Roethke may have read his poem at the time he wrote it, the limited value of that evidence as a guide to our current reading is suggested by imagining what Roethke might say if he were to return from the grave to reread his own poem from the perspective of what he might now know.

It seems hardly far-fetched, in fact, to imagine him saying what many middle-aged adults of my acquaintance have said about their childhood experience: something like, "I always thought I had a happy childhood, but now that I look back on it, I realize I was abused." Picture Roethke making an appearance in a classroom full of students studying his poem and saying: "When I wrote this poem, I thought I was celebrating a moment of closeness between myself and my father. But now that I look back on it—given all that I have become aware of in recent years having to do with alcoholism and family dysfunction—I can't regard it as such a fond and humorous memory anymore. And I must have sensed the problem even then or I wouldn't have used so many words and images hinting at a violent subtext for the more overtly happy surface action."(Such a reading, in noticing textual contradictions of which the writer was unaware at the time of composition, might even be said to constitute a deconstructionist reading, a reading that discovers ways in which the text subverts or deconstructs its own pretensions to a dominant tone and coherent discernible meaning.)

In the case of this poem then, as I suspect might be true for many texts, it's not hard for us to imagine circumstances under which(the writer might embrace an interpretation of his text that was not part of his own original conscious intention in writing his text, creating thereby a kind of new authorial intention retroactively declared and a convincing case for a deconstructionist reading.)In any event, while I confess that like most readers of my generation I am personally convinced that Roethke's poem ought to be read as a warm and generally fond memory of a moment of closeness with his father, I don't believe that the available evidence would allow me as a teacher to insist on my own reading as more authoritatively correct or more reasonable than the alternative readings offered by a new generation of readers.

Discussion 4: An Apology *for* the Interpretation of Poetry: In Defense of Literary Study as a Disciplined Enterprise

If we are unable to settle on a single authoritative and fixed meaning for this poem and presumably for other poems, does it follow, as many students will happily insist, that one of the advantages of studying literature over other subjects is that there are no right answers and that a poem can mean anything a reader wants it to mean? And is it also fair or reasonable to conclude—as have a number of outspoken critics of exemplary instruments for assessing literary reading (see Blau 1994a and 2001)—that if teachers of literature are unable to authorize a single and fixed interpretation as the only correct answer to the question, "What does this poem mean?" then those teachers can't possibly be respectable practitioners of their discipline, or else the discipline is itself an intellectual sham? Literary study can hardly be worthy of respect as an intellectual discipline, the argument goes, if it is, in fact, what many students think it is: which is to say, if it lacks, first, a reliable body of knowledge about the meanings of the texts that are the objects of its study and, second, a well-established procedure or set of disciplinary standards for distinguishing between valid and specious claims about the central questions and objects of disciplinary study. In other words, if we can't produce a single and fixed interpretation of a poem, like Roethke's "My Papa's Waltz," and if we regard any interpretation a reader offers to be as valid as any other, then something is seriously lacking in our professional skill or in our profession.

To answer such critics of our teaching (and of our best assessment) practices and of our profession, we need to unpack and correct some of the presuppositions that make their line of argument appear reasonable. We may also need to clarify for ourselves just how it is that our practice is, in fact, governed by established disciplinary procedures that provide standards for distinguishing between valid and invalid interpretive claims.

First, that we have entertained several different and sometimes opposite interpretations of the same poem hardly suggests that a poem can mean anything a reader might claim it means. Is it merely an accident that nobody interpreted the poem as a representation of a sporting event or a high school prom or a religious experience? In fact, the varied and competing interpretations of the poem show a very high degree of agreement about what the poem says and even what it means, with the areas of disagreement quite narrowly constrained. In other words, our disagreement operates within a very narrow range of possible meanings and suggests that we have already agreed on a great deal about the meaning of the poem. Many things that might be said, perhaps by less competent readers of this poem, neither were said nor would have been acceptable as valid if they had been said (cf. Fish 1980, 342–45).

Second, every reading offered and counted as a viable reading was supported by evidence to warrant it. In other words, the discourse of interpretation proceeds according to the rules of evidentiary reasoning, and the adequacy and persuasiveness of such reasoning serves as the standard by which all interpretations are evaluated. Thus, when one student wanted to picture the child in the poem as a girl, the rules of evidence were called into play to evaluate that interpretive claim. And while the weight of the evidence suggested that the figure in the poem was a boy, it had to be allowed that the evidence is inferential and that the poem—not identifying the child explicitly as male—leaves a gap, albeit a small one, in the narrative, which a reader might fill in a way that is imaginatively satisfying for the reader. However, the conversation also made it clear that to read the child as female required an imaginative leap into that small gap that ran counter to the preponderance of inferential evidence. Therefore, the reading was allowed, even if somewhat begrudgingly. To disallow it entirely, however, would be to violate the rules of evidentiary reasoning, which authorize and limit all readings.

That some pieces of evidence were counted as evidence by readers arguing for opposite interpretations might suggest that the process of interpretation is simply a matter of using evidence in any way one might choose to support one's argument. In fact, it merely shows us that textual evidence is itself subject to interpretation. That is, insofar as the evidence cited is itself textual, it is a text to be interpreted. However, it also demonstrates the epistemological phenomenon and logical problem of the hermeneutic circle. We depend on evidence or facts that constitute evidence to produce an interpretation, but we also interpret the facts or the evidence available in the light of the interpretation that we anticipate or have hypothesized. Thus, readers who see the poem as describing an abusive event read the child's clinging to the father's shirt as evidence that the child was abused and holding on for dear life, while those who read the poem as a warm and appreciative memory construe the child's clinging as evidence of his wanting to remain in the company of the father.

While that process of circular thinking might appear to call into question the validity of the evidentiary reasoning that produces interpretations, it is hardly different from the process of scientific reasoning that is the widely accepted model for advancing knowledge in the direction of truth. Scientific reasoning and inquiry, as Michael Polanyi (1966) has demonstrated, would seem, in fact, to be another version of the hermeneutic circle, depending upon the tacit dimension of knowing, whereby a scientist must first intuit research findings or new discoveries that are to be made in order to recognize a finding or discovery when it is finally available for recognition. That would seem to be a version of the common experience of shoppers who say, "I can't tell you what I want, but I'll know what it is when I find it." Whatever enables them to know what it is when they find it is their tacit knowledge of what it is before they find it.

It would seem to be the case, moreover, that all of the interpretive difficulties and epistemological uncertainties that render the discipline of literary study suspect to critics who expect more authoritative answers and more reliable procedures from a respectable academic discipline apply with no more perilous force to literary study than they do to other fields of study and certainly to all the other human sciences or professions. For example, if the difficulty of establishing a trustworthy and somehow authoritative interpretation of Roethke's poem seems to be a problem deriving from the status of the poem as a literary work, consider how the interpretive process would proceed if the facts represented in the poem were drawn from a real event (as they presumably were) that was witnessed by a group of social workers peering through various windows of the house where the events transpired.

Imagine them witnessing the narrated events—the boy dancing with his dad, the scraping of the child's ear, the smell of whiskey (or some visual evidence of the father's intoxicated state), the mother frowning, and so on. And then imagine those social workers meeting to compare notes about what they saw and what they made of it. Could they agree about whether they had witnessed an incident of abuse or one of parental love? What would make such an incident easier to interpret in real life than in a literary artifact? In fact, isn't it frequently the case that parents are arrested or suspected of child abuse on the basis of evidence that social workers and courts later determine gives insufficient grounds for labeling as abuse? So the source of uncertainty in Roethke's poem may not be any feature of the poem as a literary artifact at all, but a function of the ambiguity that resides in our culture and in our understanding and legal definitions about what constitutes abuse, even when we may be witnessing it.

If this seems a special case and one that avoids the issue of the usual interpretive uncertainties and competing meaning claims to which literary texts are subject, consider what field of human endeavor is less subject to interpretive uncertainties and competing claims about meaning and intention and so on. Surely not the institution of marriage or courtship. Who among us has not had some disagreement in the past day or week or month with a loved one over what we meant when we said or did this or that, and what we intended, and why we said or did thus and so, if we intended some other meaning, and how we must have unconsciously intended to send the very message that we are now disavowing?

Better yet, if literary discourse seems particularly susceptible to multiple interpretations and ultimate uncertainty in attempts to adjudicate between competing claims about meaning, consider the discourse that is regularly produced with the sole intention of preventing any disputes about meaning, intention, or interpretation—the one species of discourse where specialists are paid and paid handsomely to produce documents that cannot be subject to multiple, competing, or uncertain interpretations. I am speaking, of course, about legal discourse and the specialized skill of lawyers to write contracts and laws that will exactly represent the intention of their signatories at the time they are written and forever after. And what happens as soon as the contracted business is completed or as soon as a law impedes somebody's financial or civic interests? The answer is obvious. The parties to the contract are in court arguing over what the language of the contract actually requires of the various parties, or the justices of a state or federal court are at work on what they spend most of their time doing: trying to figure out what a particular law as written—written, mind you, so there could be no more than one way to interpret it—actually means or whether it is in conflict with other state or federal statutes (or constitutions), whose meanings are also subject to continuing and unending debate.

And when, after months or years of debate and thousands of pages of interpretive writing are devoted to a question of meaning and it is finally settled to the satisfaction of the court, it is usually settled by a majority of the justices voting in a particular way, with a minority still convinced of a different conclusion or several different conclusions. And even then, the majority decision is only a provisional one and is subject to reversal by a higher court or by the same court some years later, as we have seen in cases where the U.S. Supreme Court renders decisions that reverse Supreme Court decisions of earlier generations, precisely for the same reason I have conjectured that Roethke might change his mind about what his own poem means: cultural changes render our understanding of concepts like privacy, equal opportunity, equal treatment under the law, and child abuse different from what they were in generations past.

Why, then, should we expect greater interpretive stability and certainty from linguistic structures we call literature and the discourse of literary study—a study of fictional worlds designed to instruct and entertain us—than we expect from the discourse of the legal profession or from that of social workers, diplomats, psychologists, physicians, or husbands and wives, upon whose utterances and interpretations the health and happiness of real, not fictional, human beings may daily depend? The reality is that human beings live in a sea of texts, where our survival and happiness depend on our ability to read the language that, as Thoreau observed, "all things and events speak without metaphor," as well as the verbal language of human utterance and written texts. In such a universe of meaning, teachers of literature are privileged to

[handwritten margin note:] activity for readers to see interpretation aspect of lit: argue court cases, or Bill of Rights issues

be able to work in a field of signification where the stakes may be relatively low, but their instruction salvational. In the example they set of interpretive attention, awareness of nuance, the weighing of evidence, and alertness to problems in interpretive authority, English teachers may serve as the most reliable guides and models for all persons, whose private, civic, and professional lives (whether they want it this way or not) require constant negotiation with texts whose meanings are finally no less indeterminate or subject to multiple interpretation than any novel or poem in our literary canon.

Notes

1. Stanley Fish, in a classic essay ("What Makes An Interpretation Acceptable," 1980), argues that a more sophisticated version of this state of affairs has always obtained, but only insofar as it describes the range of possible interpretations that are authorized by an interpretative community, which in the case of literary interpretation refers to the community of literary scholars and critics who teach in universities and control the conferences and journals where literary interpretations are published and presented. In the view of many students, that simply means that a poem (or any other literary work) can mean anything you want it to mean, but that some teachers will lower your grade if you don't agree with them.

2. I do not mean to claim that no reader until the 1980s had seen abusive elements in the poem. John Ciardi (1959, 1003) speaks of the poem as one which "despite its seeming lightness . . . is a poem of terror." And the teacher I met in Illinois had seen some kind of ambivalence in the poem as early as 1960. But it was not a reading I had encountered among my students or that was generally noticed by teachers. And neither Ciardi nor the astute teacher from Illinois would have gone so far as to claim that the event narrated in the poem—as ambivalent as it may appear—constitutes a version of abuse. The first published account I am aware of (thanks to Candida Gillis) where explicit mention is made of readers reading Roethke's poem as a poem about abuse is in an article by Celeste Resh in the Spring 1987 issue of the journal of the Michigan Council of Teachers of English.

3. Why the number of people reading abuse in the poem has gone down and then up again in the groups I have surveyed since 1990 mystifies me. Nor can my counts be easily dismissed as statistical accidents. I survey at least four or five groups of students and teachers each year and get consistent percentages year by year.

4

The Problem of Background Knowledge
A Workshop on Intertextual Literacy

Purpose and Method of Presentation

In this chapter I want to explore the problem of background knowledge, or what I am calling "intertextual literacy," and the role it plays in the teaching and reading of literature. The concept I address as intertextual literacy is hardly different from what E. D. Hirsch (1987) calls "cultural literacy," and I hesitate to use a new term where an old one might do as well. Unfortunately, Hirsch's term is heavily laden by a politics of literacy and a controversial pedagogy that for many teachers obscures the legitimate and important insights he has brought to the attention of teachers of literature. So I have appropriated a term from postmodern theory and recombined it in a fashion that seems to me apposite and more compatible than Hirsch's familiar term with the project and practices of this chapter and book.

My procedure here will be to begin with a narrative or dramatization of a workshop I regularly engage in with students in literature classes, where they will be reading a great many pre-twentieth-century literary works and where much of the language and many of the references they encounter will be unfamiliar to them. It is also a workshop I regularly present for preservice and inservice teachers of English, who will be teaching noncontemporary and classic literary works in secondary schools and colleges. This particular workshop consists of a series of experiments I conduct with my students to illuminate for them how much their reading is assisted by their cultural knowledge or knowledge of texts residing behind texts, or can be impeded by the absence of such knowledge. Each experiment is also followed by or punctuated with some extended discourse in the form of a mini-lesson for students or a mini-essay for teachers on issues raised by the experiment. The point of the entire workshop, as

I hope will become clear, is not to convince students of their ignorance but to persuade them of their capacity to negotiate meaning and acquire increasing linguistic and cultural competence as they operate within a culturally alien text, and in the meantime to be patient with themselves as they feel uncomprehending and make the mistakes that are inevitable for all travelers in foreign lands where they are first beginning to use the language.

The Workshop

Experiment #1: How We Use Our Cultural Knowledge to Read

T: Let us begin this workshop with a poem on your handout called "Pitcher" by Robert Francis. Please read it through once or twice and then we'll talk about it.

Pitcher

His art is eccentricity, his aim
How not to hit the mark he seems to aim at,

His passion how to avoid the obvious,
His technique how to vary the avoidance.

The others throw to be comprehended. He
Throws to be a moment misunderstood.

Yet not too much. Not errant, arrant, wild.
But every seeming aberration willed.

Not to, yet still, still to communicate
Making the batter understand too late.

—*Robert Francis*

T: Let's first make sure that everybody understands the poem. Please turn to a neighbor and ask any questions you might have about this poem and try to get them answered. After you've had a few minutes to talk, please report out to the entire group about any problems you and your partner couldn't resolve.

S1: Is this poem about more than it seems to be about?

T: Well, what is it that it seems to be about?

Several students: Baseball.

T: How do you know?

S2: There's a pitcher. He throws. There's a batter. And it describes how a pitcher works to fool the batter.

T: And if you didn't already know about baseball—if you were an English speaker from some part of the world (if any should exist) where they don't know about baseball, how would you have read this poem?

S3: You might think it's about making pancakes with a pitcher you pour from, and the batter would be the pancake batter. But you couldn't put it all together. It wouldn't make sense.

S4: I thought that the pitcher was a ceramic jug on my first look at the poem.

T: Sure, why not? But when it didn't make sense you had to reread. And you could then make sense of the poem because you had the requisite cultural knowledge in your familiarity with baseball. Without it, the poem is virtually meaningless to you.

S1: But is it really about baseball?

T: OK. What about something other than baseball? Are some of you trying to say that the poem isn't about baseball?

S5: That's right. I think it's about being a salesman, a person who makes a pitch. Or maybe it's about filmmaking or art.

T: That's an interesting reading. So then the pitcher isn't a baseball pitcher and the batter isn't a baseball player?

S5: Well, maybe they are, but that's not what the poem is about.

T: So explain this. Is it or isn't it about baseball?

S1: You know exactly what we mean! On the surface it's about baseball, but it's also about something else.

T: OK. How many of you think it's about something else? Fewer than half of you. How many of you think it's about selling or art? Nobody else? What then?

S6: I think it could be about anything where there is skill and sort of secret knowledge of a craft or something like that.

S7: I think it's about acting. It's a perfect description of what an actor does.

S1: I think it's about writing poetry.

T: About writing poetry only or about poetry itself or what?

S1: OK. It seems to be about what the poet does in a poem. So I guess it's about the writer and the poem, and maybe what a reader needs to know.

T: How many of you can buy that? Oh, most of you now think it's about more than baseball? How come? What happened?

S3: Well, as soon as she said it was about poetry, it all fit together. Like the picture of the witch and the young woman. First you see it one way, then you see it another.

T: Does everybody see it now as about poetry?

S7: I still see it as more about acting. But I can see why people are saying it's about poetry.

T: What do you see in the poem that suggests it's about poetry?

S1: All the words about writing or reading: *comprehended, communicate, misunderstand.* That's not baseball talk.

T: That's good. Notice that the first two stanzas are a bit mysterious, but then in the middle just as you realize with "throw" that it's probably about baseball, you start to get ambiguous language about language—with "comprehend" and "misunderstood." Then in the end, with the "batter," you know it's about baseball, but you also get the words *comprehend* and *communicate.* But you wouldn't recognize that it could be about poetry either, would you, if you weren't also already familiar with how poetry works?

S8: How can you be sure it's about poetry? It says "pitcher" and "batter," but it never says "poet" or "poetry."

S3: Once you see it, you can't avoid connecting it to poetry. Too much fits just right. It can't be an accident.

T: Are you all pretty much persuaded now? Should I also mention that I happened to see the poem listed recently in a book of poems about poetry? But what made the editor of that book confident enough to include it? I think the answer is that the logic of the poem and its language almost demand that we read the pitching as a metaphor for what a poet also does. Yet we have to acknowledge that our reading remains a matter of drawing inferences from evidence. So while our reading may be a highly plausible one, it can't be said to represent what amounts to a brute fact. It's a highly plausible deduction, not a certainty. Even E. D. Hirsch, whose critical project is devoted to developing an interpretive practice that will ensure validity in interpretation, points out that validity isn't the same thing as certainty and that in the sphere of interpretation, "certainty is always unattainable" (1967, 164).

S9: I believe you when you say it's about poetry, and I can really see it for myself now. But I didn't see it at all before. Does that mean I have to depend on expert readers of poetry to show me what poems really mean? I thought I understood that poem. And then, bam! you hit me with a hidden meaning. It makes me feel like I'm not a good reader of poetry.

T: I don't think your missing the metaphoric meaning of this poem is a sign that you aren't a good reader. I think it could happen to any reader. And I think sometimes you'll be the one to notice what another good reader has missed. Let me tell you a story about this poem.

Several years ago I wrote a chapter on reading and writing poetry for a high school English textbook, and I put this poem in the text as one I thought students would connect to. But an editor took it out and replaced it with a sappy nature poem of the kind that makes students—especially boys—hate poetry but that she thought more appropriate because it was more conventionally poetic. I was upset by the change and went to the editor-in-chief at the publishing house to urge the restoration of the Francis poem. She read the baseball poem over and agreed that it was a good poem and that it would be a shame to lose it from a chapter on how to read and write poetry, because the poem was also about how poetry worked. I looked at the poem again and said, of course, how could I have missed that? And how did you notice it? She said, I just saw it. She was no English professor, though she was a very smart woman and a good reader and happened to have an M.A. in English. But my point is that it didn't take highly specialized or technical knowledge for her to come up with that reading, and I don't think my not seeing it until she pointed it out means that I'm a poor reader (though I confess that I feel embarrassed about missing it). Yet, for her to be able to see it and for me to be able to see it once she did point it out—and for all of you to see it—does require that we know something about how baseball games and poetry both operate. And perhaps one of the lessons the poem can also teach us is to watch carefully for the change-up pitch, for what we don't expect or what doesn't quite fit—in this case, the language of communication where we might expect the language of sport.

Experiment #2: How Gaps in Everyday Knowledge Can Impede Reading

T: Let's now look at another poem, also a modern one. It's one I remember feeling shocked by the first time I read it, when I was a sophomore in college. And I still feel some of that shock each time I read it. It's by Randall Jarrell, an influential poet, teacher, and editor, who was himself one of the leading exponents of the New Criticism. Please read it a couple of times and identify any lines you don't understand or any other problems you have with the poem.

The Death of the Ball Turret Gunner

From my mother's sleep I fell into the State,
And I hunched in its belly till my wet fur froze.
Six miles from earth, loosed from its dream of life,
I woke to black flak and the nightmare fighters.
When I died, they washed me out of the turret with a hose.

—*Randall Jarrell (1914–1965)*

T: Well, what do you make of this one?

S10: I love it.

S4: I can't make any sense of it.

S3: I can't tell if it's about an animal or a person or what's happening.

T: I'm not surprised. To how many of you does this poem make almost no sense at all? Let me see hands. That's most of you. So what are your questions? And maybe the few of you who can make sense of this poem will provide some answers.

S11: What's a ball turret gunner?

S12: You have to know about B17s, the flying fortresses.

S13: What are those?

83

S12: The kind of bombers they flew in World War II, and the turret was the plastic dome or bubble in the belly where a machine gun was mounted.

S10: The guy in the turret was the most vulnerable man on the plane and most important, because his gun could keep off the fighter planes attacking from below. And he was the only one who could see them. But there was nothing to protect him from machine gun fire or flak, except a plastic bubble. You want to hear about this?

T: Sure, Jeff. Please, go ahead.

S10: Well, the guy who was stationed in the turret was basically cut off from the rest of the crew during flight time. He couldn't get out of the turret without their help and they couldn't really get to him while they were doing their jobs, especially under battle conditions. So on some missions the ball turret gunner would be stuck in the turret all curled up and nearly freezing for twelve hours or more, and under attack for maybe four hours continuously. There are stories about gunners getting shot near the beginning of a flight and nobody could get to them and they'd bleed to death all by themselves for hours. It was a tough assignment.

Commentary: At about this point I usually do a crude chalkboard drawing of a WWII bomber, showing its ball turret, or I ask a workshop participant to do such a drawing. I have never conducted this workshop, by the way, for teachers or for students, where I didn't have at least one participant (invariably a man) who knew about WWII bombers and ball turrets. And usually, as in this case, there are a couple.

S14: What's flak?

S15: It's shrapnel, pieces of metal that fly out of hand grenades or artillery shells when they explode.

S10: The idea of antiaircraft fire from the ground wasn't to score direct hits on planes, though they would have liked to, but to explode shells at an altitude that would send out jagged pieces of metal to punch holes in a plane's skin and injure the crew and damage the plane.

T: Don't many of you still use the term *flak*, as in "Don't give me any flak"? No? Most of you have never heard it? So what can we say about what you have to know to read this poem?

S10: You have to love movies about the Second World War.

S12: Or be old enough to remember.

T: Right. You have to know mainly what a ball turret gunner was, which, when I was introduced to this poem in college in the mid-fifties, wasn't a problem for any of us.

S6: Why does he say from his mother's sleep he fell into the state? What's that mean?

T: They are difficult lines, aren't they? Anybody?

S12: I'll take a crack at it. He's saying that he and the whole country were asleep before the war. I guess his mother is his real mother but also his country—sort of motherland. And he's saying that almost without realizing it, he went from a sleeping state (*state* is the right word here, isn't it?) into a state of war (another state), in uniform, in the air force, in a plane, and so now he is in the state and he is also sort of back in the womb, curled up fetuslike in the belly of the bomber.

T: I think that's a very good reading. And how much does it depend on specialized knowledge or a particular cultural experience?

S12: Not much, except you need to know about the war a little and what it means maybe to be drafted or something about how young men go off from home to fight in wars. It's not specialized knowledge, but it's not what everybody knows anymore, so it's not common knowledge, either. But it used to be.

S4: What about how his wet fur froze? Is he being described as an animal?

T: What about that?

S15: He's like a frozen animal in the turret. And the leather jackets of the air force guys had fur collars. And I think they were called "flak jackets."

T: Good. Anything else about this poem? If not, let's move on to another poem, one that may be more or less accessible for you than the last two. But we'll see.

Experiment #3: The Texts Behind Texts: Pretexts and Prereading

T: Here is a poem some of you may have seen or taught before, called "The Parable of the Old Man and the Young." Please read it once or twice and then let's have somebody else read it aloud, and then I'll read it aloud another time.

The Parable of the Old Man and the Young
So Abram rose, and clave the wood, and went,
And took the fire with him, and a knife.
And as they sojourned both of them together,
Isaac the first-born spake and said, My father,
Behold the preparations, fire and iron,
But where the lamb for this burnt offering?
Then Abram bound the youth with belts and straps,
And builded parapets and trenches there,
And stretched forth the knife to slay his son.
When lo! an angel called him out of heaven,
Saying, Lay not thy hand upon the lad,
Neither do anything to him. Behold,
A ram, caught in a thicket by its horns;
Offer the Ram of Pride instead of him.
But the old man would not so, but slew his son,
And half the seed of Europe, one by one.
—*Wilfred Owen (1893–1918)*

85

T: Your oohs and aahs to the oral readings tell me that many of you find this a very powerful poem. But I assume that even after three or four readings, some of you merely find it puzzling. How many of you don't have much of a response to the poem, except puzzlement over what it's talking about? That's about a third of you. How many of you feel you know precisely what this poem is talking about, almost in every line? That's maybe 20 percent of you. What about the rest of you?

S3: I understand the general drift of the poem, but I'm not feeling very confident about it.

S6: I think I understand it, but I wouldn't say I understand every line or know precisely what it's talking about.

T: OK, what is it you need to know—what text do you need to know to get how this poem works structurally and in its narrative? What do you have to recognize here?

SEVERAL STUDENTS: The Bible story, the story of Abraham and Isaac.

T: And how does the story in the poem connect to the story in Genesis of Abraham and Isaac?

S12: It's a retelling of the story from Genesis.

T: Just a retelling?

S12: I think it's pretty much word for word.

S1: But with a different ending.

T: Right. It retells the Genesis account but then in the final couplet that made so many of you ah or moan or whatever you did, it puts a reverse twist on the ending. But how many of you didn't happen to recognize the pretext for this text, either because you didn't remember the story of how God tested Abraham's faith and obedience or because you simply don't know the story? That is relatively few of you. With a class of typical high school or college students—at least in my part of the country—you may find that half have never heard the story and may not have any idea about who Abraham and Isaac are. In my undergraduate classes I bring along a one-page handout with a copy of the relevant Bible verses (Genesis 22) printed on it and give it out and ask students to read it, both to see what they missed and to see how easy it is, relatively speaking, to acquire what is missing in their backgrounds.

Commentary: An alternative approach I sometimes employ to demonstrate the relevance of background knowledge is to bring to class a handout with the Genesis verses on it and a couple of other Wilfred Owen poems. I'll then give that handout to half the class and ask them to read it before we begin to discuss "The Parable." Then in working on the poem, we'll notice and discuss the advantage that half the class had in reading this poem. In any event, I eventually give all the students in the class a copy of the relevant verses from Genesis.

T: What else do you have to know in advance in order to read this poem?

S12: You have to know about World War I.

S8: How do you know it's World War I?

S16: It was trench warfare and it was in Europe.

T: How many of you recognized it as a poem about the First World War? That's about a third of you. How many of you didn't know or still don't think it's about the First World War? That's about half of you.

S8: There were other wars in Europe where they built trenches. And "parapets" suggests some earlier war.

T: Let me ask the question this way: How many of you are absolutely certain that this poem is about World War I, and were sure about it very soon after you looked at the poem, even before you had read it carefully? At least a dozen of you. Why are you so sure?

S17: Because it's by Wilfred Owen.

T: And what do you know about Wilfred Owen?

S12: That he died on the day of the Armistice.

S17: That he wrote poems about World War I.

S18: I didn't know who Wilfred Owen was, but I could see the poet's dates and surmise pretty quickly that it was almost certainly about World War I. I mean, he was twenty-five years old when he died, if the dates are accurate, and he died in 1918, so what other war could it have been?

S19: He could have been writing about war in general.

T: That's a possibility. But you could infer from the dates and additional evidence in the poem that it was probably about World War I. Still, I'll bet that the folks who had previously read some of Owen's poems, yet had never seen this one before (and none of you had seen it before, it seems), knew what this poem was about with a kind of certainty and immediacy that others lacked. Because if you've read Wilfred Owen before, you probably know that all he wrote about, at least as far as most of us are aware, was the First World War—dramatic and graphic poems about the misery and suffering experienced by soldiers in war, choking from mustard gas, and so on, like "Dulce Et Decorum Est." Remember now? In fact, those who have read Owen before and remembered it (as some of you are now remembering, I see) knew what this poem was about even before they read it. You knew as soon as you saw his name attached to it. But you might not have been aware of how you came to your own knowledge about what war the poem referred to as you proceeded to read and interpret the poem and talk about it with others.

On Demystifying Skilled Reading

This phenomenon of the preread text, the text that is, as it were, already read before it is read by virtue of a reader's prior knowledge, is an important one for students and especially for teachers of literature to recognize. One of the unfortunate consequences of literary study for many students is that it convinces them that they are not good readers of literature and will never be able to perform the interpretive miracles they watch their teachers perform. Yet unless one of the goals of literature courses is to promote a conviction of inadequacy among students who enroll in them, it is important that teachers understand and demystify for students what they (the teachers) do or know that allows them to read and interpret texts so skillfully.

One of the ways we as teachers impress our students and possibly deceive ourselves about our literary skill has to do with this phenomenon of the already-read text. That is, we frequently seem to be under the impression and we certainly give our students the impression that our understanding or interpretation of a text derives from our careful analysis of the text and from our skill in figuring out nonobvious meanings, when in fact, our interpretation derives from prior knowledge that we didn't make our students aware of because we may not have been aware of it ourselves. I'm not talking about the kind of pretension that inexperienced and insecure teachers are sometimes guilty of when they teach what they know a text is supposed to mean based on their old notes from a college course or a consultation with Cliff. I'm talking about what experienced and highly competent teachers of literature can do inadvertently whenever they notice that their students are reading less intelligently than they are and they fail to examine the sources of their own more thoughtful or sensitive readings.

A teacher teaching Wilfred Owen's poem, for example, may actually think that her assumption that the poem is about World War I is based on evidence provided within the text that she, as a sensitive reader, picked up and her students missed. Such a teacher needs to recognize what actually enabled her to read the poem so sensitively, so that she might provide instruction to replicate her knowledge for her students. In this case it would be by having her students read one or two other Wilfred Owen poems before coming to the less explicit war poem, which is fittingly called a parable. Similarly, teachers need to let students know that some readers can interpret the otherwise puzzling parable not because they have engaged in some complicated interpretive procedure, but because they happen to know the text that lies behind the text of the poem in the story of Abraham and Isaac. And rather than lecture students on the background for that poem, implying again that the required background can only be achieved with years of study, a teacher who wants to share her knowledge rather than impress students with it will have students read a printed version (King James, ideally, since that is the version quoted in the poem) of Genesis 22, which is only a half-page in length, adding only enough commentary, perhaps, to contextualize this strange but easily understood incident within the larger narrative of the Genesis story.

Let me recount another example of how teachers need to examine the sources of their own knowledge in order to avoid giving students a false sense of the interpretive power of English teachers. Some years ago I was teaching an introduction to poetry class for prospective English majors, most of them sophomores and freshmen. I had the students working in groups in response to an assignment I give in almost every introductory literature class, which I call the Goldilocks Assignment. It requires that students read through their poetry anthology at home and select three poems to write about in their reading logs and identify for discussion in class: one poem that they judge to be too hard, one that they think too easy, and one that is for them just right. It turned out that several students individually and then several groups of students had settled on Sylvia Plath's poem "Lady Lazarus" as their too-hard poem and were working on that poem in groups in my class.

As I circulated around the room monitoring the work of the various groups, I noticed that none of the three or four groups working on the Plath poem had been able to recognize what the poem was about, though they had managed to come up with plausible interpretations of some individual lines that I thought to be very difficult. I thought then and still think now that the poem is a very difficult one with several lines that I have never been able to understand. What is not difficult about the poem, however, is its apparent generative occasion and its references to the best-known fact of Plath's personal life. Without giving you the whole poem, let me just quote some key lines to give you some sense of what I mean about the poem's transparent autobiographical character. The poem begins: "I have done it again. / One year in every ten / I manage it—." Later it says: "This is number three . . . The first time it happened / I was ten. / It was an accident. / The second time I meant / To last it out and not come back at all." And still later: "Dying / Is an art, like everything else. / I do it exceptionally well."

Now, with no more than these few lines from the poem, many readers who have never read the poem or have no memory of it will know what the poem is about just as I did. That part is easy for us. And as I moved about the room noticing that my students had no clue about the central events being narrated in the poem, I wondered why they failed to see in the poem what seemed so transparent to me. They seemed to be perceptive readers in many ways, and every group seemed to know (and a footnote in the text reminded them) that Lazarus was a figure who came back from the dead. But not one group had mentioned in my hearing anything suggesting what to me seemed the most obvious fact about what the poem recounted, a fact I am withholding here so that readers who know it can realize they know it and think about why, while readers who don't know it can recognize their feeling that they are in the dark and in the uncomfortable position of inferior readers because of their failure to draw an interpretive inference that I have labeled as obvious, and that even now seems so obvious to me (and surely to many others of you) that it is difficult to believe that any reasonably proficient reader of college age could possibly miss seeing what this poem is about. In fairness to my students I should also note that the lines I have cited as compelling evidence of what the poem is about do not appear in a cluster in the poem, but punctuate a poem of some one hundred lines of very difficult verse, so they do not leap out at a reader in their thematic unity, but are likely to be noticed and aggregated only by a mind that is, in a sense, as I'll explain, already prepared for them.

Fortunately, on that occasion in my class, I had the presence of mind to avoid simply telling my students what these key lines referred to and instead asked the following question, which was a genuine question for me at the time: How come I was reading the poem as a poem about suicide or a suicide attempt, when none of the students in the class seemed to be finding any references in the poem to such an act? I want to emphasize, again, that I asked the question honestly, with no answer in mind. My students, bless them, jumped to the challenge and asked me what evidence I had that the poem included any references to suicide. I cited the title and the lines about her being an artist of death, having done it three times, and intending not to come back at all. For many students, simply noticing the thematic connections between the lines I have mentioned was evidence enough. Others asked, reasonably I think, how I knew that the speaker hadn't had some near-death experiences from illnesses or accidents, or that the references weren't entirely metaphorical, not connected at all to a physical death or near death, or that they weren't about the deaths of people close to her, making her feel that she had died or wanted to die? What evidence could I find that made suicide a more plausible and compelling inference than some other drama of the human soul?

Since no other interpretation of the lines seemed even remotely possible to me compared with the certain and obvious interpretation I had offered, I had to ask myself about the source of my certitude, and the answer was suddenly as obvious to me as it must now be to anyone familiar with Plath's biography, but not to anyone who knows Plath only through this one poem, "Lady Lazarus," without any biographical note to accompany it. We know that the speaker's references to Lazarus, her expertise in dying, and the repeated doing of something from which she meant the second time not to come back all refer to suicide attempts because the principal fact that we know about Plath's life is that it was filled, from childhood until her eventually successful suicide at age 31, with a series of suicide attempts. That fact became well-known to the public after Plath's suicide in 1963 and the posthumous publication of her thinly disguised autobiographical novel, *The Bell Jar*.

I asked my students how many of them had heard of Plath or knew anything about her. The answer: not one. No wonder, then, that no reader except me would interpret the lines that seemed so obviously about her suicide attempts as about such attempts. And my students pointed out quite wisely that such a reading would probably have been largely unavailable except to Plath's own inner circle of friends at the time she wrote the poem, which was, of course, before she finally did kill herself and before her history of suicide attempts became public knowledge. Whether it was ever read by anyone except her close friends before publication is doubtful, however, since it never actually appeared in print until it was posthumously published in 1965.

My point in recounting this story is to demonstrate the importance on that occasion of my wise decision (not one I have always made, I confess) not to tell my students how I was reading the poem (and thereby correcting their mistaken or inadequate readings), but to problematize for me and them the fact that we were reading the poem differently. That is, I made the interpretive work of our classroom not the work of coming to see how the best and most authoritative reading of the poem is the correct reading (which happened, as usual, to be mine), but the work of accounting for how it is that members of the class were reading the poem differently.

That shift in focus allowed my students and me to discover that my capacity to construct a more coherent and satisfying reading of this difficult poem (insofar as I could do that) derived not from my specialized training in the occult art of literary interpretation, but from the accident of my knowing (as most literate persons of my generation would likely know) one or two facts about an author's biography. It happens, in fact, that I have never read *The Bell Jar* myself. But there was no way I could avoid knowing about what the book recounted, when so many of my peers in the mid-sixties, when the book came out, were reading it.

I hope I am not belaboring the point, but I want to emphasize the danger and opportunity that English classes offer for convincing students not of their capacity and potential as readers, but of their intellectual insufficiency. The ethical issue here is not that teachers have a responsibility to build student confidence (they do, but not by promoting a specious or false confidence), but that they have a responsibility not to misrepresent the kind or quality of knowledge that students may lack and teachers may possess.

An Example of Literary Miseducation

A classic example of how teachers sometimes misrepresent the gap in knowledge between themselves and their students may be found in the way I have seen teaching assistants in college freshman English courses teach one of the most widely taught texts of such courses, Swift's satiric essay of 1729, "A Modest Proposal." The usual approach to teaching this essay is to have students read it without warning them (and most freshman English textbooks conveniently conspire in this surprise) that it is a satire and that it must be read ironically rather than literally. Then the essay is discussed in class under the direction of the teacher, with the teacher eventually pointing out that no such proposal could possibly be offered or taken in earnest. The teacher would then prove his point to the still doubting students by elucidating the many places in the text where Swift reveals, through his frequent denials of having any self-interest in his apparently civic-minded plan and a number of humorously exaggerated details, that he is being satiric rather than serious in his proposal to rescue the impoverished Irish by having them sell their young children to butchers as tender meat for more prosperous people—and especially for the exploitative British business classes—to eat. Both the method and manner of instruction commonly employed in such classes communicate the idea—an idea I have often heard stated explicitly by teachers in conversation—that skilled and sensitive readers will recognize the proposal as satiric immediately and also be able to detect the abundant evidence of satire in the text, while those who take the proposal as a serious one are somehow less skilled readers, if not intellectual clods.

Yet much of the pedagogical exercise I have described entails a misrepresentation of the interpretive skill of the teacher and of the presumed illiteracy and ignorance of the students. For, in a post-Holocaust era, why shouldn't student readers assume that a proposal to butcher and eat the children of the poorest Irish peasants would be offered and taken in earnest by a ruling British colonial government? Why is it more outrageous or impossible to conceive of the commodification of children as meat in the eighteenth century than as lampshades and experimental animals in the twentieth? Would Nazi documents outlining procedures for collecting the gold teeth or using the skins of millions of dead Jews seem any less outrageous to readers in the years before the Holocaust than the wild proposal advanced by Jonathan Swift? And if such proposals in recent history are known to have been made in earnest and acted upon as the official policy of an established government, why should readers who know nothing of the source of what may be an even less barbaric proposal from the eighteenth century assume that it was offered as satire?

Nor is it the case that the teachers (always graduate students in my experience) who presumed themselves such superior readers to their students actually employed their superior interpretive powers to determine that Swift's proposal was a satire. Rather, they knew it was a satire only because it was presented to them by their professors and literary history as satire. And how did literary historians or the document's earliest readers establish that it was a satire? Only because (as the distinguished modern critic Hugh Kenner was fond of pointing out) it was attributed to England's greatest satirist, Jonathan Swift, who was also the dean of St. Patrick's Cathedral in Dublin.

In other words, we have here another instance in which intertextual literacy, or knowledge of prior texts and background information, is crucial to producing an accurate reading of a literary work, but is also the exclusive possession of teachers and not of their students. Yet this privileged knowledge is not recognized by the teachers themselves as the knowledge that they need to transmit or otherwise replicate in their students so that their students may function as competent readers. It rather becomes the instrument for a mode of mystifying instruction that positions the teachers as readers who are capable of extraordinary interpretive insight, while their students appear to be (and see themselves as) insensitive and unperceptive clods, wholly dependent upon their teachers for all but rudimentary interpretative observations.

Experiment #4: Building Literary Confidence and Respect Through Conversation Across Four Centuries

Let me now present an exercise or experiment in intertextual literacy or prior knowledge that will demonstrate to students the importance of possessing the cultural knowledge presumed by a text (and its author) at the same time that it demonstrates respect for what students themselves know and can read as literate persons.

This exercise begins with asking students to read the following short poem by a Kentucky poet, Bobbie Copeland:

For Valerie

Yesterday, stopped at the traffic light,
this old lady comes over to the bike,
says, "Could you direct me to the Y?"
I tried, but couldn't remember street names;
so she puts on the extra helmet
and fifteen minutes later we were there.

Something in the way she held me,
tight about the waist; I knew it was you,
forty years from now—a red scarf
and blue jeans—catching a ride.

—*Bobbie Copeland*

The poem hardly requires much commentary. Virtually all students of high school or college age can understand it as a narrative and as an expression of generous and loving feeling. Many readers find it a moving and elegantly effective little poem.

The experiment I conduct with this poem begins with the following instructions:

1. For this experiment, please find a partner and when you have done so agree on which of you will be A and which B.
2. If you are A, you are yourself. If you are B, you are Sir Phillip Sidney. That means that you were born in 1553 and died, much too young, in 1586. You are the author of one of the most widely appreciated and most influential sonnet sequences in the history of the English language (*Astrophil and Stella*) and the author of a prose romance (*The Arcadia*) that is seen by some as the forerunner of the English novel. You are also the author of one of the earliest and most influential works of literary criticism in the English language ("The Apology for Poetry"). You are, in other words, one of the greatest writers in English literary history and one of the best readers and critics of your time. You are also a consummate gentleman and were regarded in your day and for generations afterward as the model courtier, military man, and man of letters. You are a contemporary of Shakespeare, Spenser, and Marlowe, but you died earlier than any of them in 1586, heroically, at age 33, of an infection from an arrow wound in your thigh, suffered in a military action where you removed your own leg armor because your counterpart on the other side appeared on the field without his leg armor.
3. Your assignment in pairs (A and B) is now to read the poem "For Valerie," by Bobbie Copeland, doing the best job you can, given the identity you have been assigned, offering to each other, whenever possible, whatever help may be

93

needed. Remember who you are as you engage in this exercise and do the best you can, given who you are and what skills and knowledge you can bring to the task of understanding this poem.

The results, of course, are amusing and informative, as students see just what problems one of the most literate men in the history of the English language now experiences in reading a poem that any present-day teenager can readily understand, and how much more competent they themselves are as readers of this poem than the great sixteenth-century poet and critic.

Prodded to explain the difference between the partners as readers, students will quickly point to the number of simple terms or references that were mystifying to the learned Sir Phillip and to the places where a sharp-witted Sir Phillip may have been able to penetrate the text with surprising linguistic insight, but still with an effort not required of a modern reader. The point should be obvious but still warrants explicit articulation. Sir Phillip Sidney may be one of the most learned and literate readers in the history of English literature, but he can't read a fairly simple modern poem very competently when that poem is packed with references he doesn't know, given that he died in 1586. Yet what he doesn't know that keeps him from understanding Bobbie Copeland's poem isn't highly technical information or knowledge possessed only by philosophers and literary theorists and scientists. It is information that any living person standing in the street or even prone in the gutter would know. People who never went beyond third grade in school, who were themselves entirely illiterate, would know what the learned Sir Phillip Sidney doesn't know but would need to know to understand this poem. And what Sir Phillip wouldn't and couldn't know represents ways in which our culture—including our daily practices and ordinary objects for use—is different from his or has changed over the past four hundred years.

And what is true for Sir Phillip trying to read a text of our time and culture is true for us trying to read a text of Sir Phillip's time and culture, which is also Shakespeare's and Donne's and Marlowe's. Many of the references and everyday terms used in the 1580s and 1590s (and therefore in Shakespeare's plays) will be unfamiliar to us. Again, most of what we don't know will not represent the specialized knowledge of philosophers and scientists (in fact, the language and references of science, theology and philosophy have tended to survive the ages and find uses in our own time), but knowledge that would be the ordinary possession of ordinary people—of farmers, blacksmiths, beggars, and children. Shakespeare's plays, we need to remember, were apparently easily understood and wildly popular among the groundlings, a crowd of people most of whom were probably illiterate and poor—the folks who at a public entertainment could not afford to buy a ticket that would give them a seat.

The point of this exercise, then, is not simply to recognize that any time we read a text that derives from a culture or period different from our own, there will be many gaps in our understanding representing the ways that the world has changed or cultures differ. It is also to see that what we are missing is not a sign of any insufficiency in our interpretive skill or intelligence. We may be as gifted and as learned as Sir

Phillip Sidney, and we will still not know much that a ten-year-old child knows in a culture separated from ours by two hundred or four hundred years or sometimes even fifty years.

Most of what we need to know, however, can be picked up as we become more familiar with the culture through our experience of reading texts of the culture, just as we would pick up the same kind of knowledge by spending some days or weeks in the world from which the texts derive. One of the virtues of literature is that it takes us into a world not our own and gives us the opportunity to live in that world as travelers do, who if they remain alert and interested and do not isolate themselves in their hotel room or among foreigners like themselves will soon find that they are learning the language and customs of the country enough to get what they need and understand what is going on around them. In the meantime, guidebooks and glossaries prepared for us by more experienced travelers can also help.

The skills we need to enjoy our travel in a foreign country, however, are not primarily the skills that allow us to consult our guidebooks. If we keep our noses in such reference works, we will hardly live the life we want to experience. Rather, they are the skills and qualities of mind that enable us to try to talk with the natives, even if it is difficult, to take our chances with new tastes and sensations, and to have patience with ourselves (and a good sense of humor) as we make the mistakes that any immigrant or newcomer is likely to make.

In the meantime, as I hope all of the experiments and examples presented here will demonstrate, our job as English teachers is not to convince our students that we are in possession of some unattainable knowledge that makes it easy for us to navigate in textual waters that are perilous for them, but to help them acquire, insofar as possible within the scope of our own course, the same background knowledge and intertextual experience that confer on us much of our advantage and competence as readers. In the case of a poem like Wilfred Owen's "Parable of the Old Man and the Young," for example, it behooves us not to teach such a poem at all (unless we wish to use it for the sort of experiment I have described) until we have provided our students with the prior reading experiences that enable us to read the poem much more easily—in this case merely a few verses from the Bible and one or two additional and more accessible poems by Owen himself.

I will not pretend that it is always possible in our classes to have students first complete the kind of background reading they need to do for competent reading of the core texts we wish to teach—not if we are ever to get to those texts themselves. And the problem becomes especially, if ironically, difficult to address when it is also the case, as it so often is, that the core texts are the very texts that are crucial to a student's intertextual literacy. But I hope I have made at least a plausible argument here for a syllabus and for curriculum planning that reflect some thinking about our responsibility for promoting intertextual literacy, at least in the order of our assignments and through some limited preparatory reading, rather than by depending exclusively on teacher lectures and footnotes. I also hope I have made a case for how important it is for us to monitor our own teaching practices to ensure that our instruction does not exaggerate the gap between what we are able to do and what our students are able to do as readers and interpreters of the texts we assign. And one way we can do that, as I have shown, is to demonstrate to students just what sort of background knowledge they are lacking and how it reflects neither on their skill as interpreters nor on the intelligence they exhibit as participants in their own cultural life.

5

Where Do Interpretations Come From?

What Is Interpretation?

This chapter is about the discourse of interpretation—the conversation and writing about literature that define much of the activity of most literature classes in middle school, high school, and college. It is also the discourse that characterizes much of the writing in professional journals about literature and much of the conversation and formal presentations that take place at professional conferences of teachers of English, as well as in such settings as book clubs and literary groups, and so on. Robert Scholes, in *Semiotics and Interpretation* (1982, chapter 1), says that the fundamental and defining act for the field of literary studies and for all the humanities is that of producing interpretive discourse. To a very large extent, then, the function of a literary education appears to be to enable students to talk and write about literature in ways that mark them as literate persons and members of an academic or literary community. And this means being able to participate in and contribute to a discourse that is largely interpretive.[1]

Not all school discourse about literature is interpretive. In the early grades and to some extent in the later grades and even in college, attention needs to be paid to what we usually think of as reading (see Chapter 2), which would include decoding or recognizing words and comprehending the plain sense of a text—the dimension of reading that answers the simple question, What does it say? That remains a challenging question for students at all levels of education when the texts being taught present linguistic difficulties that can puzzle students who might seem to be highly competent readers of more accessible texts.

For example, in my Introduction to Renaissance Literature course at my university, I find it necessary, before we attend to problems of interpretation, to help students apprehend the plain sense of a text like *The Faerie Queene*, which uses language that was already considered archaic in the 1580s, when it was written. And to help my students read that difficult text, I find myself using a number of pedagogical strategies that are versions of what elementary teachers do to help their students make sense of what they read. Thus, as part of a typical class session, I will often select a passage of perhaps a dozen stanzas and ask students to work together in pairs or groups of three, reading the passage aloud to each other, pausing at any point where any of them feels even slightly confused or puzzled about the meaning of the text, and collaboratively trying to resolve whatever difficulties the text presents to them. Then as a whole class we hear reports on the problems encountered and solved and focus on the portions of the text that remain problematic for individuals and groups of students.

The difference between reading and interpretation (as the exercise I have just described always reveals) is frequently not clear or easy to demonstrate. The problem of determining or describing or addressing that difference has been the subject of considerable literary, philosophical, and pedagogical debate from at least the Middle Ages to the present moment, when the issue has also become implicated in the politics of literacy at every level of governance (see Blau 1994a). To say that reading addresses literal meaning and interpretation addresses inferential, metaphorical, or ironic meaning might not satisfy all the participants in the current debates, but it may point in the direction of a commonsense distinction that most readers will recognize. When we speak of reading literature (in American and most European schools and universities, at least),[2] it may be possible for all mature readers to agree that literary texts can be said to yield two kinds of meaning that are fairly distinguishable in the kinds of statements readers are likely to make about what they read.

Readers from the earliest grades will be regarded as literate if in their reading of a literary work, they recognize and can talk about meaning at a level that addresses what happens within the work—what characters do and say and what events take place under what circumstances. But starting by about fourth grade, teachers begin to expect children to talk about another kind of meaning produced by or found in the first set of meanings. In elementary classrooms this additional kind of meaning is often referred to as the moral or lesson that a story or fable is said to yield. And it is often introduced to students first through fables or tales or myths that make their lessons obvious if not explicit.

As readers and literary texts become more sophisticated, the lessons literary works are said to yield become less obvious, more complex, and more difficult to articulate or even agree upon. But their recognition and discourse about such meanings become increasingly important in conversation and writing about literature. Given samples of student writing about literature, teachers at every grade will invariably agree that students whose writing about a literary work goes beyond the brute facts of a text to address issues of meaning that the text evokes indirectly (as distinct from what is represented or dramatized directly) are more competent readers than those who merely retell the story, and that competence in producing such interpretive readings is a principal aim of a program of literacy instruction in school (Woodward and Halbrook 1999; Blau 2001).

Looking for models of the highest achievement in literacy for fourth-grade children, a group of eight experienced elementary teachers who had been identified as experts by their peers selected precisely this sort of a demonstration of reading competence from among hundreds of samples of student writing about reading. In one particular writing sample selected as exemplary, the student retold a story she had read about a child who collects fireflies in a jar one summer night and takes the jar to her room when she goes to bed. Noticing that the blinking of the fireflies becomes dimmer and dimmer as the night passes, the sleepless child in the story gets up in the middle of the night and, through the open window above her bed, releases the fireflies into the night sky. The reader then went on to speak about how the little girl in the story learned what happens when we try to use living things for our own entertainment and not respect nature as we find it. That addition, that elaboration of meaning beyond the facts directly represented by the story, is interpretive discourse.

In talking with teachers of literature at every level about the kind of meaning that is addressed by interpretive discourse, I have found that we do not have available to us a serviceable and widely shared vocabulary for referring to the dimension of meaning we want to indicate. The distinctions of Medieval and Renaissance exegesis, with their literal, allegorical, moral, and anagogic levels of meaning are no longer apposite for our culture and are surely inadequate to the classroom problems encountered in reading and teaching (in spite of Northrop Frye's [1950, 1957] attempt to reconstitute them for modern readers). Many contemporary students and some teachers will speak of interpretation as addressed to the meanings that reside "between the lines," and I recently read a manuscript in which a high school English teacher referred, as many students do, to "hidden meanings" as the focus of an English teacher's textual attention. Terms referring to what is hidden or absent do have the merit of representing a kind of commonsense perception about how interpretation addresses meanings that are not directly asserted by literary texts, as did the observation of the elementary reading teacher I met some years ago, who in response to my friendly observation that we were in the same business claimed to the contrary that she taught students to read what a story said, while I taught them to read what it didn't say.

The defect of such descriptions of literary meaning is that they all reflect the mystification that many students experience in hearing the interpretive discourse of their teachers. Yet even that sense of mystery has a certain kind of historical authority in linking interpretation to the discipline of hermeneutics, the art or science of interpretation, whose name is associated with the Greek deity Hermes, the bringer of messages from the gods, who is in turn associated with revealing what is hidden. It also links interpretation to the esoteric art of interpreting dreams, an art possessed by Joseph in the Bible as a divine gift, rather than a competency that may be acquired by all ordinary mortals. And a divine gift it must seem to the many students who experience the art of interpretation in classrooms almost exclusively as witnesses to the mysterious interpretive operations performed by their teachers and by other authorities in sourcebooks.

Other common locutions identify interpretation with the production of meanings that are "broader," "wider," "more universal," or "deeper," again suggesting something like levels of meaning, but also obscuring as much as they reveal about the relationship between one kind of meaning and another. Nor, as far as I can tell, is there much help to be found conceptually or terminologically in the discourse of modern critical theory or contemporary hermeneutics, where, as Vincent Leitch (2001) says, leading theorists have proposed "completely different models" of reading in relation to interpretation, and "the problematic of reading/interpretation continues to be a major preoccupation in the field of theory and criticism" (2–3). Moreover, with some rare exceptions, the problem as it is treated by critics and theorists is usually contextualized within historical discussions or as part of a technical discourse that is virtually inaccessible to teachers who are not already participants in the advanced conversations taking place in the community of academic theorists (see Touponce 1991).

For our purposes, I think we can clarify our conceptions and our language for distinguishing between the spheres of meaning addressed by reading and interpretation—at least in literary discourse—if we construct a model of literary meaning that (with some indebtedness to Todorov 1978/1990) posits two axes of meaning, which we can call the *representational* axis and the *evocative* axis, showing the representational axis as an unbroken horizontal line and the evocative axis as a dotted or broken vertical one.

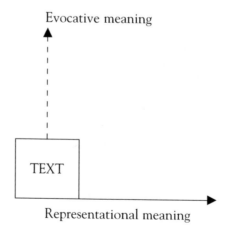

Figure 5.1

The horizontal line directs us to what a literary work shows and tells us directly, while the vertical, broken line refers to meanings that are not actually represented by the work but released by, derived from, or evoked by what is represented in actions, events, images, and so on. Discourse that addresses itself to *evocative* meaning is what I want to focus on in this chapter.

The Problem

One of the great sticking points in the development of writers and surely the most vexing challenge that secondary and college teachers worry about in the teaching of writing is the challenge of getting students to move beyond what amounts to descriptive and narrative writing, or the acts of recording and reporting, to what we generally regard as the cognitively and socially more demanding discourses of exposition and argumentation (see, for example, Moffett 1968, 14–59; Blau 1983; Hammond 1991; Harris 1997, 97–116).

In literature classes this problem translates to the challenge of moving students beyond writing mere plot summaries to a discourse that is more analytical and interpretive. Teachers and study guides for high school and college literature courses typically devote much of their instructional attention to providing students with organizational formulas, literary terms, and examples of how to produce an acceptable piece of what is often called "critical writing." Recently, teachers who have become specialists in how to prepare students for academic writing and particularly for writing on Advanced Placement examinations in English have developed empirically based descriptions of successful literary essays and ratio formulas and techniques for color-coding sentences in essays, so that students will be able to see when they have achieved the requisite ratio of interpretive discourse or *commentary* to mere *plot summary*. Papers that meet the expectations of evaluators of such writing, it is claimed, almost always have a predictable shape and invariably include a significantly higher ratio of commentary sentences to plot summary sentences (Schaefer 1995; Olson 2003, 223–25).

My own dissatisfaction with the analytic and interpretive writing of my freshman and sophomore literature students, however, and the problem addressed by the workshop I shall present in this chapter, does not derive from my students' failure to produce enough commentary relative to plot summary or from their failure to have mastered the conventional form for a literary essay. It's rather that even when they produce well-organized literary essays with adequate quantities of commentary, those essays (like many of the commentaries they offer in class discussions) often constitute a species of discourse that seems to me pseudoliterate or possibly counterliterate. I'm talking about readings that treat texts as objects requiring mechanical analysis rather than as invitations to genuine human illumination and pleasure. Faced with a text identified as literature, these students appear to enact a parodic and misapprehended version of the New Criticism of the 1950s or 1960s (see Blau 1994b) and

101

behave as if they are obliged to hunt for symbols, predictably describe the operations of literary devices, engage in perfunctory discussions of prescribed universal themes, or gratuitously compare and contrast characters, rather than address any of the issues that might illuminate a text for a reader who cares about it or account for why a text might be important or interesting or even offensive to real readers.

One possibility, of course, is that their required reading of the assigned texts has deadened rather than quickened their thinking. But we have some evidence (Marshall, Smagorinsky, and Smith 1995, Chapter 1) that at least some students who produce perfunctory literary responses in classrooms (or no responses at all) may in fact be engaged in their reading and able to talk about it outside of an academic context. When they are asked to talk about a text in class, however, they act like witnesses to a crime who are afraid of being personally involved or have been warned by a judge to stick to the facts and not draw any inferences or reach any conclusions of their own. They generally suspect that they are supposed to do more than provide a mere plot summary, but they seem not to know what else there is to say in an academic context that isn't either plot summary or else the predictable pseudoacademic observations encouraged by study guides and, unfortunately, by some typical school assignments (see Rosenblatt 1968/1938, 285–86).

This is the pseudoliterary or antiliterary discourse that Robert Scholes (1999) described in a recent essay commiserating with high school teachers about the commodification of literature through standardized testing and its marginalization in a generally anti-intellectual culture. Scholes urges teachers to rescue literature from test makers and from student indifference by helping students see how it speaks to them as human beings rather than as test takers and technical analysts. And the first step toward that goal, for many teachers, he says, is to drop those writing assignments that focus on technical features of literary works. By asking students as they read to look for and analyze such elements as irony, theme, symbol, tone, and so on, he says, we erect a screen or alternate text "that stands between the literature students read and their own humanity" (35).

Nor should we deceive ourselves even for a minute to think that such topics and writing assignments are generated only by secondary school teachers for the literary miseducation of high school students. Surely similarly empty technical exercises are assigned with some frequency in college and university classrooms (cf. Graff 1985, 76–79), where instructors may want students to practice using the terms and techniques of analysis associated with a New Critical "close reading," or with more recent critical approaches like semiotics and structuralism that also feature a technical vocabulary and lend themselves to the pseudoanalysis that consists of the naming and explaining of parts. In letters and at public readings of her own stories, Flannery O'Connor famously complained about how such instruction made her stories less rather than more accessible to student readers, once telling an audience of college teachers and their students that "in most English classes the short story has become a kind of literary specimen to be dissected. Every time a story of mine appears in a

Freshman anthology I have a vision of it, with its little organs laid open, like a frog in a bottle" (cited by Stanford 1999, 367).

What bothers many of us about what I am calling mechanistic readings, I believe, is not that they interrogate or analyze a text according to procedures identified with a school of criticism we don't like, but that they appear to produce the analysis for no genuine intellectual reason at all, except to satisfy an externally posed assignment. Thus, students searching for paper topics will often settle on a comparison-contrast essay not because such an exercise might reveal something worth knowing about the text or texts they are writing about, but because the comparison-contrast topos is one that has been taught to them in their English class as a method for producing required literary papers for English teachers.

So what may be most unsettling to us about the merely mechanical gestures of literary analysis produced by our students is that they turn our hope for an opportunity for engaged inquiry and discovery within the literary community of our classroom into a discourse that makes painfully visible the students' disengagement and alienation from the text addressed and from the task of literary analysis itself. They are, in other words, evidence of our failure as teachers. They are evidence, at least (perhaps despite our best efforts), that the students who produce them have not yet become engaged by the texts or the literary, ethical, or psychological issues posed for readers by those texts. Or, just as likely, they are evidence that many students, when asked to interpret or comment on a literary work as an academic assignment, tend to cancel out their own native intelligence and capacity to make sense of or read events they encounter in their own lives in favor of interpretive moves they have been taught in school and that they assume are required of them when faced by the verbal icons of literary texts.

I devised the workshop I am about to re-create here in the interest of demystifying literature and desanctifying acts of critical or interpretive discourse so as to activate the native sense-making powers of students and demonstrate to them where more authentic interpretations come from. I can recommend this workshop with some confidence as one that students (and their teachers) will enjoy and find instructive, but as I'll explain shortly, it didn't have the exact instructive impact I had hoped for it. On the other hand, it produced insights and questions about the process of interpretation and the sources of interpretation that may be more important than the more simplistic pedagogical results I was shooting for.

The Workshop: Where Do Interpretations Come From?

What I will be presenting below is a dramatized narrative (based on notes, videotapes, and memory) of the workshop as I have conducted it for my own students in my own classes and with English teachers at professional conferences. I begin here with a reconstruction of the first time I conducted this workshop as an experiment with my students in an undergraduate intro to literature course, where I opened the workshop with two versions of a story about events that had transpired that morning. Since those stories remain so useful for the purposes of this workshop, I have continued to tell them within a frame narrative of what happened the first time I told them, when they could be told truthfully about what had happened that very morning. In other words, in my current workshops I begin by telling the story of what happened in my class with the stories I told the first time I conducted this workshop. And that's what I'll do here. I should add that for the purposes of this book I have allowed myself to elaborate on and explore theoretical ideas more fully than I would under the inevitable constraints of time and attention that operate in a classroom or in an inservice program. When I discipline myself not to indulge in extensive theoretical speculations (though some are necessary and constitute the point of the exercise), I find that I need sixty to seventy-five minutes for the completion of this workshop.

Preparatory Instructions and Discussion

T: I want to work today on the problem of interpreting stories. We have been interpreting stories in class and asking about the validity of those interpretations, what sorts of evidence we find to support various interpretations, whether an author may have or may not have intended a story to be interpreted a particular way, and whether an author's intention is determinable or relevant as a criterion for evaluating an interpretation. I want now to explore the nature of interpretation further by examining stories about which we are ourselves authorities—the stories we ourselves tell to our friends and family members, including stories of which we are the authors and those we transmit as members of a group, like a family. You know, the kinds of stories that members of a family tell at Thanksgiving, like when everybody recalls the time Aunt Sally got so angry at Uncle Jack that she dropped a ladle of gravy in his lap.

First, let us observe that we all do tell stories and tell them, if not every day, then frequently and certainly on special occasions like when we gather with family at a holiday dinner table or meet with old friends after a long separation. Stories are what fuel much of our conversations with people we are coming to know as friends or partners. We may even think of much of our life history as a series of stories we tell to ourselves and to others in order to make sense of who we are and what and where we have come from.

So let me now begin with my own story about today—something that happened this morning. This is the story of my coming to class today. I live at the top of the mountain overlooking the town and the campus. My house is at an altitude of twenty-five hundred feet. If I walk up the road in front of my house just a couple of hundred yards, I can look directly down on the campus and (on a clear day) see the building that houses my office. It takes me about twenty minutes to drive from my house to the campus parking lot, which isn't very long, considering that I drive from one climate zone to another. But I still need to make sure I leave in time to make that drive and get from the parking lot to class on time. Today I was delayed by snow and snow damage from yesterday's snowfall in the mountains, so I was worried that I'd be late. But as you see, I managed to get here on time. So here I am, and that's my story. How do you like my story?

STUDENTS: (Many show looks of puzzlement and disdain.)

S1: It's OK.

T: Is it a good story?

S2: Well, it's not much of a story.

T: Why not?

S2: It has no conflict.

S3: It's kind of a boring story.

T: What are you inclined to say when you hear a story like that?

SEVERAL STUDENTS: So what?

T: That's right. It's the kind of story to which one wants to say, "So what?" which is a way of saying to me that my story isn't really a story at all. It has no point. And that suggests that all stories have a point or we aren't likely to accord them the dignity of calling them stories. And to say that a story has a point is the same thing as saying that it has a meaning and is therefore subject to an interpretation. The fact that we don't bother to make our interpretations of most stories explicit doesn't mean that we don't know how to interpret them. If we didn't know how, then we'd look puzzled or say, "So what?" or "What's your point?"

Let me try another story, this one a more complete account of what happened today. As I said, I live in the mountains above the university at an elevation of twenty-five hundred feet. It's often ten or fifteen degrees colder where I live than it is down here near the ocean. Here you live in Southern California. Where I live—only about ten miles away—it's sometimes more like Colorado. And yesterday afternoon and evening we had a snowstorm in the mountains. The snow level dropped to about fifteen hundred feet. I'm sure you all saw the snow on the mountains this morning. At my house we had ten inches of snow, heavy wet snow that stuck to the branches of the oak trees and weighed them down, so that huge branches were falling down everywhere. These trees have no experience with snow. They haven't grown up having their weak branches gradually pruned by snowstorms. So this one snowfall—the biggest snowfall in anybody's memory in these mountains—simply bent the branches of mature oak trees until they broke, and it knocked down some whole trees. My wife and I walked around in the snowstorm yesterday and listened to the crack of the branches as they broke and the swishing sound they made as they fell and then the thud as they hit the ground. It was probably stupid to be walking around our property with all the branches falling down around us. Fortunately none fell on the house, though one did fall on my wife's car and damaged the hood.

Anyway, at breakfast this morning I told my wife that I needed to get started early in case the snow should delay my getting to school on time. My wife said,

"Forget it; you can't go to school today. The road is probably closed, and even if it isn't, it's too slippery and dangerous to drive. Besides, there are huge limbs down across our driveway, so you probably can't even get off our own property."

I said that I was going, that I wasn't about to miss class because of a snowstorm on the mountain. She said it was probably not possible—the road was, no doubt, impassable—and if it were possible, it would be foolish and dangerous to try. I said I'd call my colleague, Lois, who lives about two miles from our house and one thousand feet lower in elevation and whose husband goes down the road early every morning to have breakfast with their granddaughters. If Bob made it down the mountain, so could I. So I called Lois and she told me that Bob had made it safely down the mountain on the old back road and that while it was slippery and dangerous at some spots, it was passable. So I told my wife I was going and that I'd also use the old back road down the mountain. She objected, noting that I still had to traverse at least two miles of road, probably covered by snow and fallen limbs, to get to the road that Bob had used.

But I decided I was going. So I got out the chain saw and used it to clear the big limbs from our driveway and then got in the car and made my way carefully over the snowy and limb-strewn road from my house down to the old mountain road, which was fairly clear all the way down the mountain. And as you can see, I'm here and our class didn't have to be cancelled. So what do you think of that story?

S1: It's a better story.

T: Why?

S2: It has a lot of description and detail.

T: That's true. I hadn't thought of that as a major difference, but it may be significant. It does feel more like a constructed narrative—a planned discourse, while the other was almost just a comment. Still, is that the major difference?

S3: Well, your second story seems to have a point.

T: You mean you aren't inclined to say "So what?" to this one? What point do you see it making?

S3: That you are devoted to your work and weren't going to let anything make you miss your class.

S4: That you live in a wild climate and with some danger and excitement. And you like it.

S5: That you like to teach and would risk your life to be with your students.

S6: That your wife loves you.

T: Where do you see that in the story?

S7: She worries about you.

S8: She was trying to keep you from getting hurt.

T: That's interesting. I didn't see it that way. I read it as an instance in which my wife expressed insufficient respect for my work. I saw it as interference and nagging, rather than an expression of love. But your interpretation seems entirely plausible to me and even more convincing than my own. So I think I'll call my wife later this morning and apologize to her for my ungenerous and childish reading of her concern for my safety. Still, whatever her reasons for discouraging me, the fact that she discourages me isn't central to the meaning of this story, is it?

S7: It's one of the obstacles you have to overcome to get to class.

T: That's a good way to frame it.

But the point is, ladies and gentlemen, that all of the interpretative statements you have offered seem plausible and intelligent to me, including the one that contradicted the way I had thought about the meaning of at least one detail of my story before sharing it with you. And I believe I have come to see my own story better and more clearly than I did before—to understand it better now as a consequence of interpretations given to me by my auditors or readers that I had not intended in the telling of my story. Can I now say that your interpretation is wrong because it doesn't comport with my intention? Of course not. So here is an instance in which we get a dramatic piece of evidence supporting the idea of the *intentional fallacy* (Wimsatt and Beardsley 1954), one of the foundational principles of the New Criticism, that a writer's intention—contrary to commonplace ideas about meaning—is not reliable as a source of authority in determining the meaning of a text. And we also see how a story can be subject to multiple interpretations, all of which are plausible.

In fact, research on what happens in conversations when people tell stories (Polanyi 1979, 1985) shows us that there is often a process of negotiation that takes place in the form of interrupting comments and responses between the storyteller and her conversational partners through which they reach a kind of shared agreement about the meaning of the story, which may be different from the meaning that the narrator had in mind in initiating the story or seemed to be leading to with the story. It also appears as if storytellers often begin stories with no more than a feeling that some event or experience is worthy of a story even though the storyteller doesn't know exactly what the story means. Then the meaning of the story is discovered in the telling of it.

But most importantly, perhaps, for purposes of this exercise, we see how a story that does not evoke a "So what?" response—which is to say, if it is worthy of the name *story*—has a point (or possibly several points) and is subject to interpretation, even if we see no need to make our interpretation explicit. My point is that we are always telling and hearing stories and always interpreting them, and we have not needed a specialized course in school to enable us to interpret the stories we hear. And my evidence that we do know how to interpret them in a way that is satisfactory to us is that we don't usually say to the storyteller, "So what?" or "What's your point?" We don't ask because we already know, even if we aren't quite prepared to make our tacit knowledge explicit in language.

Activities

1. To test my claims about stories and our interpretative powers, I would now like you to think about the stories you tell in your family or tell when you get together with old friends. Or think about the stories you tell when you are first dating someone who might become a serious long-term partner for you. Think about your early dates with such a person. Isn't it the case that much of your conversation—for both of you—consists of stories that tell who you are and where you come from? Think about some of those stories, the ones you yourself tell or the ones that are regularly told at family gatherings, and make a list of two or three of the most interesting ones. As you make your list, try to give them titles that might forecast what they are about. Try to get down at least two or three titles. We'll take just a couple of minutes for this. If you can't think of a good story, try thinking first about some categories for stories or common sources for the stories we tell or places from which we often derive our stories: vacation stories, pet stories, first-time stories (first kiss, first date, first day on the job, initiation stories), car stories, accident and illness stories, getting-in-trouble stories, scar stories, wedding and graduation stories, embarrassing moment stories, stories about lessons we learned, revenge or punishment stories.

   Now that you have identified two or three stories by their titles, let's hear some of the titles, just to get an idea of what these stories are about and perhaps remind other folks of stories they sometimes tell but have momentarily forgotten. We'll go around the room and have you tell us the titles of one or two of your favorite stories and maybe give us a sentence about them, if the titles aren't self-explanatory. Or pass, if you haven't yet thought of a story you might tell. OK? Let's hear some.

   "Forgetting My Party"

   "My Grandma, the Bootlegger"

   "Topless in Baja" (too embarrassing to tell in a large group)

   "Jasper Bites Aunt Suzie on the Behind"

   "The Accidental Interview" (about how I got my job)

   "Down and Out in Westwood" (about a summer when I lost my job)

   "The Eating Machine" (about my dog, a lab)

   "Skiing and Freezing in Hell"

   "The Bra and the Fishing Pole"

   "Camping with Scorpions"

   "Living with Cats"

   "The Recycled Gifts"

"Hunting on a Beaver Dam in Winter" (about a time I almost froze to death)

2. Now take another minute—in case the titles you heard reminded you of other stories of your own—to see if there are additional stories you might want to add to your list. Then look at your list and select the most interesting of these stories and make a few notes about it to help you remember it. This is the story you are going to tell to two partners.

3. Now, in groups of three, taking turns, tell your story to your partners. After each story is told, take a few minutes for the partners, one at a time, to offer their interpretation of your story. If you are the auditor of a story, consider how or why it is a story to which you don't say, "So what?" Remember that if you don't feel inclined to say, "So what?" (and do say it, if that's really what your response is), you must have a sense of a meaning for the story. So try to tell the storyteller how you see his or her story as meaningful, as having a point. Articulate briefly your interpretation of the story. If you are the storyteller, just listen to the way your partners interpret your story. Don't argue with them, though you might want to correct any misunderstandings you notice about the facts you related. You'll be able to talk about your different interpretations later.

4. When you have all told your stories and have heard how your partners interpreted them, spend a few minutes discussing how you feel about the interpretations you heard or about the difficulty of interpreting a story. Consider how some stories were difficult to interpret and how some stories invited different interpretations. Talk to each other about how accurately you feel your story was interpreted. How differently did your partners interpret your story from the way you would interpret it? How do you account for the differences? Think about how you knew how to interpret the stories you heard. Where did your ideas about how to interpret them come from, aside from the stories themselves?

    Let me elaborate on that question. What do you know or what experience have you had that enabled you to produce the interpretations you offered? Would any seven-year-old child be able to produce interpretations like yours? If not, why not? What do you know that a child wouldn't know that enabled you to construct the interpretations you produced? Talk in your groups about these questions for a while and then take a few minutes to write about them and about other questions that arise for you about interpreting stories.

5. Now let's hear some of the stories told in your groups and some of the interpretations offered. Let each group pick at least one of the stories they were told and let us all hear that story as told by the original storyteller. Then let's hear how the partners interpreted it, and maybe we'll offer some alternative interpretations.

Examples of Student Stories and Responses

Here are two typical student stories, actually told aloud in class, but in two different classes in two different years of the same introductory literature course.

Lori's Story

Lori's group volunteered her to tell her story about visiting the campus with her boyfriend:

> Before I transferred here from my community college at home, I drove up last spring with my boyfriend to check out the place, you know, and look for an apartment in Isla Vista [a student beach community adjacent to campus, consisting mostly of apartment buildings and fraternity houses] for the fall. We came up on a weekend when a lot of parties were happening and our friends took us around to the parties and to visit people in different apartment buildings. And everywhere we visited they offered us drinks. My boyfriend really got into the party scene and at one of the parties joined in a drinking contest with some other guys, so he was really wasted before the night was over. I mean, we had to carry him up the stairs when we came back to my girlfriend's apartment, where we were staying. He didn't throw up or anything, but he wasn't really conscious by the time we got him to bed. But then in the middle of the night, he got up to pee and was disoriented and didn't know where he was or where the bathroom was or anything. So he went into the other room where I was sleeping and opened up my suitcase and peed in it. And then he went back to bed.

Of course the story produced much laughter in the class, though it left me wondering how anyone could come up with an interpretation for it. What could it mean, except that maybe she's got the wrong boyfriend? But I didn't say that. I asked the members of Lori's group how they interpreted her story. Amy, speaking for her group, offered this:

> We read it as a male pissing story. You know how little boys are always peeing off porches and having peeing contests for distance. And then as they get older they seem obsessed with peeing in the snow and making initials, and hitting things in the toilet. Their peeing is sort of like shooting guns or like the way dogs and wolves mark out territory and show who is in control. So we read this story as an example of a male behaving like an animal, as so many males do, by marking his girlfriend as his property before she moved away from home to attend college.

The class roared with laughter. I was delighted and impressed by the wit of the interpretation and asked Lori what she thought of it. She said she thought it might be a good analysis of what her boyfriend had done. But it didn't do him any good, she added. She broke up with that boyfriend shortly after moving to campus. "Good for you," I thought.

NICOLE'S STORY

In most classes I try to listen in on some stories as they are being told in the groups. But my presence often has an unmistakably dampening effect on the stories and responses, so I have to do my best to eavesdrop unobtrusively. Nicole's story is one I heard at first by eavesdropping. But I got so interested that I actually pulled my chair into the group before Nicole had finished. She was so engaged in telling her story that she hardly noticed. It was also a group with three very confident students in it, so I had a reasonable hope that my presence wouldn't inhibit any of them. After class, I asked Nicole to retell her story for me into a tape recorder. It took her a couple of weeks to get around to it, and I'm afraid it wasn't as good in that retelling. So this version is drawn partly from the tape but enhanced with what I remember from what I heard in class, where she told it first in her small group and then again for the entire class.

> When I was at home this past summer from college, I really couldn't wait to get back to school. It was difficult to be home with my parents. Being with them is like a constant battle between what they want to know about and what my sister and I want to keep to ourselves. This past vacation, a month before I was supposed to return to school, I decided to spend the weekend with my friend Amanda, whose family has a house near the beach. She had been inviting me all summer and I thought it would be fun to spend one of the last weekends of my summer vacation there. When I told my sister, Kirsten, how I was going to spend that weekend, she asked if she could come along. She is two years older than I am, but she was friends with Amanda, too, and I thought it would be fun for all of us. So we planned to go together and my parents didn't have any objection. They liked it better that we would be driving together for the two-hour trip.
>
> But once we are in the car on our way to Amanda's, Kirsten tells me that she isn't really going to go with me for the weekend. She's going to spend it with her boyfriend at his house, which is only about a forty-minute drive from where Amanda lives. Kirsten and her boyfriend go to the same college, and have been together for almost two years, but my parents don't approve of him, so Kirsten didn't get to see him much in the summer. Now she wanted to spend the weekend with him and to let my parents think she was with me at Amanda's.
>
> So when we got near Amanda's I took Kirsten to a shopping mall, where her boyfriend was going to pick her up, and I waited with her until he arrived. And before she got in the car with him, she took out a piece of paper and wrote his number on it, in case I needed to call her at his house. I put the number in the glove compartment so I wouldn't lose it.
>
> Well, the weekend was great and my parents never suspected anything when we first got home. But sometime in the next week my mother starts asking me and Kirsten all these questions about the weekend, really interrogating us about everything we did and who was with us and how we spent our time and stuff. My sister and I were cool about it and didn't say much. We said we went to the beach and went shopping and went to a movie, and things like that. My sister and I had already

worked it out about everything that I had done that weekend including the movie, which she hadn't ever seen. I had told her all about everything, just in case my parents went into one of their private eye investigations with us, which they sometimes did when they had some reason to be suspicious.

And they did ask my sister about the movie when they got her alone one night after dinner. That really freaked us out because we couldn't figure out why they would be suspicious at all. Then one afternoon my mother sits me down at the kitchen table and asks me if my sister was really with me at Amanda's for the entire weekend or did she go to her boyfriend's. And I go, Of course she was with me. So my Mom pulls out the slip of paper with Kirsten's boyfriend's phone number on it and asks me how come his number was in the glove compartment of the car. I nearly choked. I had forgotten that I had put it there and never took it out. And how did she even know it was his number? But I stayed cool and said, How would I know why his number was in the glove compartment? Maybe she wanted to remember it and wrote it down sometime and put it in the glove compartment. How would I know?

Well, since Kirsten and I both stuck with our stories, my parents couldn't do anything. They would never call Amanda or her parents or anything to check up on us. That would be too humiliating for them, and Amanda knew how to back up our story anyway. They could only try to get one of the two of us to break down. And neither of us was going to do that. But they didn't stop trying. Not that they directly accused us of lying or acted angry at us. They just tried to wheedle it out of us, by hinting around about the importance of honesty in a family and how we needed to trust each other and things like that—trying to make us feel guilty about deceiving them. But we didn't feel guilty at all. We felt angry about how they were trying to manipulate us and neither of us could wait until it was time to go back to school again.

Finally it was time for Kirsten to go back. Her school started a week before we started here. So my parents decided to take us out to dinner the night before Kirsten was to return to her college for her senior year, and we were supposed to have a nice farewell family dinner. Well, it was a nightmare. It wasn't so much what they said, but the silence over what they weren't asking and what they were waiting for us to tell them. All through dinner they dropped hints about clearing the air before our family went off to different places, but mostly they didn't talk about what was on their minds. But we could feel it. You could cut it with a knife. And it drove us crazy. But there was no way either of us would ever tell them what they wanted to hear. I couldn't wait to get away from that table and couldn't wait to get back to college a week later, and I'm not looking forward to going home for the next vacation either.

By the time Nicole finished, I was already seated in the group, breathless to know how the students would interpret this tale that would be of enormous interest to any parent who had been through the experience of having kids go away to college and come home for vacations. Laurel offered her interpretation first:

I think this story is about how sisters stick together against their parents. My sister and I are the same way. We have always protected each other against my parents. We never told on each other (once we were older, anyway) and would always be willing to lie to them to protect the other or to back up each other's stories. They would try to break us down, but could never do it and would never do it. We'll stick by each other till our dying day.

Matt was next:

I sort of agree with Laurel. But to me this story isn't just about sisters sticking together against their parents. It's about how all children have to plot and rebel against their parents. I hear it as a story about the war between the generations. It's about how parents are always trying to control all their children and children have to do what they have to do to grow up and parents really can't do anything about it. If you want to lie to your parents and do what they don't approve of, you can do it and almost everybody does do it some of the time. You have to, if you're normal. And there isn't anything your parents can do about it. And if you're not a screwed-up person or a heavy-duty druggie or anything like that, it's a good thing. Because you need to take control over your own life in order to become independent and to become an adult. I actually hope my children will lie to me that way. Even though I know it might be painful for me as a parent and that it can sometimes be uncomfortable for the kids too.

I wasn't about to withhold my interpretation, which like Matt's and Laurel's was also colored by the lens of my personal experience—but in my case as a parent who had seen three children through college (two of them daughters who had been in college at the same time):

I like Matt's and Laurel's interpretations and would agree with them, while also offering an additional way to look at the story. I'm inclined to read it more from the point of view of the parents as a story about the frustrations of raising kids during their college years. I see the parents as fighting one of the last losing skirmishes in a hopeless battle for control of kids whom they can no longer control. When your kids go off to college, you lose almost all control over them. Your kids still need you to pay the bills and to be parents to them in many ways, but you can't control what they do day by day and at night, when they live away from home as emancipated adults, even if they are still only eighteen or nineteen. You don't know and can't know where they are at night, or if they come home, or whom they may be spending the night with, especially in this world where students tend to live in apartments and not in dorms, where parents at least used to have resident advisors and such to act in their behalf.

Then your kids come home for vacation and live under your roof and you are again responsible for them and feel entitled to enforce rules that would properly apply to a child living under the roof of his or her parents' home. But your kids have already been away to college and are used to having their freedom and aren't going to suddenly live as if they are not the self-regulated adults they have been all year at college. And as a parent you are caught in between two world orders. You feel responsible for what your kids do, living under your roof, and you have standards of behavior you want to enforce. But you know that your kids are used to living their own lives and you trust that they have been doing so successfully at college. So you don't want to squash their independence. And yet you can't relinquish your responsibilities. Hence the awkward position of Nicole's parents, who want to issue rules but don't want to do so overtly. So they are left in the limbo of having to request—though they can't demand—that everybody be open and honest about what they do and with whom. And Nicole's parents have the additional problem of not approving of the sister's boyfriend. So they are even less inclined to accept her spending the weekend with him than if she had spent it with a prospective husband they liked.

And what about Nicole? How did she feel about the interpretations she heard? She agreed with them all and found mine to be the one that seemed to have the most explanatory power and offer the most illumination for her story in ways she had never thought of before. That brings us to some of the problems and critical issues raised by this exercise.

Discussion: Debriefing the Workshop

I expect the discussion following the set of activities described above to yield a number of insights (as well as some new problems) for students. First, it usually shows students (or most of them) that they are experienced interpreters of stories and that interpretation is not an activity that necessarily requires specialized training in English classes. Second, they see that their interpretations did not tend to focus on literary devices, and that what they did have to say was generally more important to say and more respectful of the story as an engaging narrative than any schooled observations they might have mechanically offered about literary devices. Third, and here we begin to approach the problems that the exercise also uncovers, they begin to recognize how difficult it often is to produce a plausible interpretation of a story, even when they feel confident of the worthiness of the discourse as a story.

Some students, demonstrating that the workshop achieved for them precisely the opposite effect it was intended to have, have claimed in my workshops that they could not produce any interpretive statements at all about a story they heard, even though they felt they understood and appreciated the story as a story. Their experience in the workshop suggested, contrary to my expectations, that they lacked the resources or background that might have enabled them to move beyond merely impressionistic responses of the kind expressed in remarks like "That's a really funny story," or "I like that story," or "That's a good story." A few students have insisted, as every teacher who has taught a literature class might expect, that a story was just funny and didn't have any other meaning or that stories you like shouldn't have to be interpreted.

A promising way to help such students and illuminate the interpretive process for all students (aside from listening to and inviting the whole class to offer interpretations of the problematic stories) is to conduct an inquiry in class (at the end of the workshop or in the class session following the workshop) on the question of where interpretations come from. How did the students who produced interpretations do so? What knowledge or experience allowed them to produce some sentences that may be said to be interpretative, and what did they do or think to help them arrive at the interpretations they eventually produced?

Such an inquiry might begin in the workshop I have just described with questions about how individuals came to the interpretive statements they offered about my story of coming to class on the morning after the snowstorm. Most students (like most other people) have no idea, of course, how they perform intellectual tasks that they appear to be able to perform competently. In fact, the students who seem to have the clearest ideas about how interpretations are (or ought to be) produced are often those who are unable to produce anything of interpretive value in the workshop, but will readily testify that interpretation involves certain formulaic procedures taught to them in school about identifying literary elements (see Mike Rose [1984] on blocked writers).

Some probing questions and careful reflection on the interpretations students actually produce in a storytelling workshop can begin to help them describe something about the thinking process they engage in when constructing interpretations of the stories they hear. When my students said that my story about coming to class after the snowstorm was a story about how seriously I take my teaching responsibilities or that it was a story about how my wife loves me (even though that seems an incidental fact of the story and not its point), they were reasoning inferentially, deriving their statements not directly from the events narrated or the words spoken in my narrative, but indirectly through a kind of intellectual leap based on their thoughtful reflection on or analysis of the available evidence.

As figure 5.1 on page 100 indicates, the meanings that are represented by interpretive discourse are not represented directly by the words of a story or by the sequence of events narrated, but bear a relationship of meaning to the text that we can say is more indirectly evoked or inferentially produced on the basis of what is directly represented in words or narrated events. Insofar as there is some sort of a translation, it is a translation of particular textual facts into statements that are not textually represented (what the text doesn't say), but that operate on a more abstract or general level ("You like to teach and would risk your life to be with your students," or in the case of Nicole's story, "This is a story about the war between the generations") than anything represented directly by the text. Moreover, the facts that are being interpreted are, as we have seen, also generally subject to alternative and multiple interpretations, all of which may be plausible. The process of translation or the interpretive act is therefore also creative, with each interpretive claim amounting to something like the construction of a hypothesis or theory that might then be confirmed, disconfirmed, or refined in response to additional evidence or analysis.

And what did it take for my students to engage in such hypothesis making? If we focus on what is analytically obvious yet frequently unmentioned in accounts of academic competencies, we can say that it required, first, that they pay close, thoughtful attention to the story. Second, it required that they actively participate—that they engage themselves in the intellectual work and take the risk of offering an interpretive hypothesis that they might then have to defend through evidentiary reasoning or possibly revise in response to new evidence or counterarguments. Students un-willing to pay sufficient attention to the details of a story or unwilling to do the some-times difficult and intellectually risky work of thinking through the reasonableness of possible explanations or interpretations for the actions and events represented in a story will probably not be able to produce plausible interpretive comments. This is not because they don't know how or don't have the necessary cultural knowledge or literary skills, but because they won't focus attentively on the story and do the nec-essary thoughtful work. To a very large extent, then, their skill may be said to reside in their will (see Blau 1981 and Chapter 10). Nor are they likely to learn how to exercise their will to produce a satisfying interpretation in the face of frustrating in-terpretive difficulties when teachers prematurely take over the task of providing authoritative interpretations for their students (see Chapter 1).

Now, for the Rest of the Story: Some Less Comfortable Findings

The account I have just presented of how interpretations are constructed and what intellectual and personal demands are made by the task of interpreting literary or other texts seems to me largely accurate and probably pedagogically useful, as far as it goes. I also believe that the workshop I have described can reveal much about the act of interpretation to many students while helping some of them to become more confi-dent and willing participants in the discourse of the literature class. Nevertheless, as in many arenas where we are tempted to analyze a problem in human behavior in terms of oversimplified ethical or moral choices, the limited interpretive skill of many students can't always be understood as correctable with admonitions to think harder or pay closer attention or exercise more intellectual courage. There may be other obstacles for students to overcome aside from an infected will. In fact, the storytelling workshop, as I have described it here and have usually experienced it, almost always yields—aside from usefully satisfying insights on what interpretation entails and what attentional resources it calls for—some discomforting intimations about the difficul-ties of the interpretive process for many students, along with some promising hypoth-eses about why some interpretations (and some stories) may seem so much richer and more illuminating than others.

Let's begin this more advanced and more uncomfortable phase of our inquiry by returning to two of the stories told in the workshop described above and some of the interpretations they elicited. I think most readers would agree with my judgment that the story told by Nicole about the war she and her sister seemed to be waging with their parents is a more interesting and significant story than my anecdote about over-coming some snowstorm obstacles in order to get to work one day. What can we say to describe the difference?

For one thing, Nicole's story is about a troubling and abiding problem encoun-tered in many families within the culture in which the story is set and told. The prob-lem or conflict it highlights is dramatized as an entirely local event, embedded in the culture of Southern California at the turn of the twenty-first century; yet, as some of its interpreters suggest, it also tells a story that would resonate for readers across generations and regions across America and in many other parts of the globe. Compared with Nicole's story, mine is insignificant, a trivial anecdote about overcoming some minor difficulties to meet my responsibilities. It yields no insights into the nature of work or relationships (though my likely misreading of my own story and the subplot of arguments about work may be a more interesting story than my story itself) or the culture in which the action takes place. It hardly delights us as a narrative and it offers us almost no instruction.

Notice, too, the differences between the interpretations elicited by the two stories. My anecdote was said to show that I wasn't going to let anything stop me from getting to work—a readily available inference (based on a few narrative facts) about the motive of one character at one moment in time. Nicole's story was said to show us something important about the politics and psychology of family life across time and place. Her story has a kind of transpersonal resonance that mine lacks, an applicability to a wider range of experience.

That wider applicability is partly a function of the fact that my story was probably experienced by its auditors (my students) to be—in spite of its relative triviality—one worthy of my telling by virtue of the fact that it is based on what Livia Polanyi (1979, 1985) calls "personally interesting material." That is, my story is likely to be received as a narratable story or a story that is worthy of being told in a conversation (where a socially competent speaker, by virtue of taking an extended conversational turn, assumes an obligation to be interesting) with persons who know me personally and are therefore interested in almost any story about an experience that I find interesting to me. Nicole's story, on the other hand, is based on what Polanyi would designate "culturally interesting material." This type of story is interesting to auditors who may not be at all interested in the narrator personally, but whose interest in the narrator's story is based on the fact that they share with the narrator values, experiences and beliefs that define membership in a culture. These two kinds of stories (i.e., culturally interesting and personally interesting) occupy the two poles of Polanyi's system for classifying conversational stories, between which fall stories based on what she calls "socially interesting material," or narrative material of interest to auditors by virtue of their identity as members of some social group, according to their school affiliation, ethnicity, occupation, sports passion, and so on.

But as culturally interesting as Nicole's story may be, it doesn't require (as Laurel's interpretation about how sisters stick together demonstrates) that its readers interpret it in a way that recognizes it as culturally significant. In fact, it is probably the case that Nicole, in telling her story, regarded it as merely socially interesting, which is to say, interesting only to peers whose experience as college students would make them sympathetic and engaged auditors. Nevertheless, Nicole's story contains a narrative richness—including psychological subtlety, ethical complexity, and primal conflicts—that invites the sorts of sophisticated, culturally interesting interpretations that

Matt and I both offered, though even those interpretations, we should notice, derived from perspectives that were based on our own personal experience and present social location (as a college student/child or as a parent who had raised such children).

To offer the sorts of rich, culturally interesting interpretations that Matt and I offered, however, we had to do more work intellectually than was needed for interpreters to draw a fairly simple inference about how my actions in my snowstorm story suggested that I cared about my teaching. Our interpretations of Nicole's story required that we recognize in the narrated material large and enduring themes and issues that transcended the details of the story. And that recognition and broader application appears to be a more demanding and complex intellectual task than the relatively simple task of inferencing that is adequate to interpret my story. That difference may have a good deal to do with the variances I have noted in the quality of student interpretations and especially in the interpretations offered by more and less mature students.

I want to explore this issue further by telling what I think is a telling story of my second experience with the storytelling workshop itself. What was unusual about the second time I conducted the workshop was that it just happened that, aside from myself, there were two other highly experienced readers in my classroom that day—my research assistant, Denise (a former teacher and a doctoral student in English education), and Zachary, a visiting scholar from another university who was observing a variety of classes on my campus in connection with his own research project on education in the humanities. When it came time for the students to share their stories and offer interpretations of them, Denise, Zachary, and I formed our own group, told our stories, and produced admirably insightful interpretations for each other. But many of the student interpretations we then heard (but by no means all) were disappointing, though their stories were not. What, we wondered, could account for the richness of our interpretations compared with the relative poverty (or in some instances the absence) of the student interpretations, when the stories told by the students were for the most part no less interesting or ripe for analysis than our own?

One explanation is that the differences represent differences in our experience. As experienced advanced students in the human sciences, those of us who are teachers have spent years in classrooms and professional conferences engaged in interpretive discourse. It's what we do for a living. English teachers are engaged in interpretive discourse for much of every class they teach, not to mention their experience as undergraduate and graduate students of literature. Interpreting human motives and behavior is also the daily business of every elementary and secondary teacher, who is engaged in interpretive discourse on a regular basis in such discursive activities as conferences with parents, writing report cards, and talking with colleagues about problem students. Our students are simply less experienced than we are in such discourse and therefore less skilled at producing interpretations of the stories they hear.

So Where *Do* Interpretations Come From? Rethinking the Implications of the Workshop

Another related way of describing the difference between our interpretive skills and those of our students is to observe that many interpretations, particularly interpretations of rich and interesting stories, appear to derive from some theory—either a theory of human motives and action or a theory of art or science. We teachers have more access to and experience with the theories that might inform an interpretation than our students do. We might even want to claim that it is the accumulation of such theories that defines what a formal education and even life experience (for a thoughtful person) are about.

Much of the time, when we produce an interpretation of a text (including a story or any event or passage in the text of the world), we do so by contextualizing it within the frame of some meta-text or generalization that occupies a discursive space at a higher level of abstraction than the story itself. So when we say that a story is about the difficulty parents find in relinquishing control of their children as their children become adults, we are re-presenting the story from the more abstract perspective of a generalization about the psychology of parenthood or the politics of the family. Students who find it difficult to produce such analytical or interpretative statements—which seem most needed for the interpretation of complex and profoundly significant stories—may lack the life experience and/or the discourse experience that would otherwise equip them with an adequate repertoire of generalizations or theories to draw upon for a more abstract perspective or frame through which to reexamine a narrative (which also explains why we so often feel obliged to provide students with interpretations of the complicated texts we assign).

I have spoken of life experiences and discourse experiences as both being sources of theories or general principles that may be used in interpreting texts, because much of what constitutes our theoretical knowledge or knowledge at a level more abstract than narrative or experience itself comes to us not from generalizations we draw from our own experience, but from generalizations that are drawn for us by a community as part of its culturally transmitted knowledge (in the form of aphorisms, for example, or folk wisdom) or from generalizations that represent the disciplinary knowledge of fields like psychology, economics, or sociology in their popular as well as their academic expressions. Thus, a narrative about somebody whose drive to amass wealth quickly leads him to make foolish investments that eventually bring him to the brink of bankruptcy might engender an interpretation that reframes the narrative in the Wall Street figurative expression about how money can be made by bulls and by bears, but not by pigs. And the expression might be applied by someone who knows relatively little about the economics of the stock market in technical terms, yet has participated sufficiently in the discourse of the investment community to have picked up a little piece of folk wisdom applicable to a particular story or kind of story.

That example may seem to suggest that interpretation may entail no more than the kind of simpleminded thematizing or moralizing that tends to reduce a literary

119

work to a single moral lesson captured in a single sentence. But that is merely the least sophisticated version and method for describing meaning on what I have called the *evocative axis* of textual meaning as distinct from the *representational*. One function of a literary education is surely to move students in their reading beyond simple childhood fables with simple aphoristic morals to more complex works of literature that demand more complex and elaborated interpretive analysis.

No doubt the literary education of most students does take them, however unsystematically, from less mature to more mature books in the course of their own intellectual and literary development and as a consequence of being in classrooms with teachers who provide students with both age-appropriate and challenging books. Recently, moreover, many college English departments and a few secondary school English programs and instructors have begun to introduce students (systematically or through the accident of a student's encounters with a variety of instructors) to a range of different theoretical frames for discerning and discussing literary meaning.

While instruction in one or more of the currently fashionable critical theories often invites students to engage in the uncritical and intellectually dubious enterprise of assuming critical postures that they are hardly prepared to dispute or question (see pp. 4–5 above), the strategy of introducing students to a range of alternative critical theories and practices can be an effective method, when employed by pedagogically sophisticated practitioners (see, for example, Appleman 2000; Carey-Webb 2001), for providing students with a broader and more sophisticated spectrum of theoretical positions from which to interpret and analyze texts than that with which they appear to be already supplied by their education and experience. Even a highly reductive version of a theoretical orientation like that of the cultural critics can provide students with a useful frame for turning what might otherwise be commonplace observations at the representational level into uncommonly interesting interpretive observations. Reading through such a frame, students would be encouraged to notice how much their understanding of the significance of textual facts and their capacity to fill in gaps in a text testify to a repertoire of cultural knowledge shared (or not shared) by a reader and writer. What they can make of the text at a representational level could then be linked to broader observations about their own situatedness as readers, about the cultural knowledge presupposed by a text, and possibly about the ways a text tacitly promotes ideological positions that some readers might want to resist (see McCormick, Waller, and Flower 1987; Mellor and Patterson 2001; Carey-Webb 2001).

However valuable a variety of critical theories or frameworks might be to students in their role as interpreters of texts, I feel compelled to observe that it wasn't the perspectives or practices of contemporary critical theorists that accounted for the rich interpretations my colleagues and I offered for each other's stories that day in my undergraduate literature course. Nor can such critical sophistication account for most of the rich interpretations I have heard in my workshops with elementary and secondary teachers (compared with the relatively more impoverished interpretations that are generally produced by a class of college freshmen or sophomores or what I imagine one might hear in a typical high school classroom). That is, the best resource for theories of human behavior and axioms by which to understand and evaluate human action appears to be life experience and the kind of general education one receives through a college education and a lifetime of reading and conversation with literate and well-educated people. As in many spheres of skilled activity, here too, there is no substitute for a lifetime.

Young people will, of course, enthusiastically grab hold of any theoretical frame that strikes them as true and exciting in its explanatory power. And they will employ it to interpret everything in their lives and then readily reinterpret the world for their parents and friends. The attraction of theory, Jim Moffett used to muse, is the illusion of power. With a theory we gain in control what we lose in accuracy. It is in the nature of youth to seek control and to be especially attracted to the illusion of power. And that attraction makes a good argument for the advantages of teaching critical theories to students who are inclined to embrace or use such theories, though we need always to remind them and ourselves of Flannery O'Connor's (1979) admonition to English teachers that "where feeling for a story is absent, theory will not provide it" (437).

Moreover, the attractions of theory should not cloud our memory of what we as teachers and lovers of literature have always regarded as the nearest and best substitute for a lifetime: literature itself. Through what other means except literature could avid readers of literature have learned more and learned earlier than they have about psychology, history, religion, philosophy, politics, or love and death? The best resource available to us for helping students develop their capacity to produce insightful and interesting interpretations of what they read (including the text of the world they encounter) is the literature they read independently and with the guidance of their teachers. This may also suggest the advantage (often ignored or disputed in our generally healthy concern for making sure that students construct their own readings) of having teachers share with their students—though not impose upon them—their own interpretations of texts, thereby modeling the process of interpretation and giving instruction at the same time in the theories and generalizations that make literary interpretations worthy of attention and discussion.

Notes

1. Writing assignments are sometimes labeled in ways that obscure their interpretive function; but most of the typical assignments that teachers give their students amount to requests for interpretive discourse. Whether students are producing reading logs, critical essays, essays of analysis, or research papers, the superordinate aim of such writing is usually to produce a discourse that will advance, synthesize, or problematize an interpretation of a literary work, addressing the question of what a text means or—to use John Ciardi's (1959) New Critical formulation—how it means. Even discourses whose avowed purpose is to evaluate literary works do so largely on the basis of what a work achieves as a structure of meaning (Richards 1929, 10).

2. Reading is, of course, a socially constructed practice, entailing different sorts of activity in different communities and cultural contexts. Thus, in some parts of the world—as in an earlier period of American educational history—readers demonstrate their literacy by reciting a text from memory or by answering factual questions about narrative facts, and what I am calling interpretation might be considered a disrespectful practice for a student or layperson (see Luke 1988, Myers 1996).

6

What's Worth Saying About a Literary Text?

The problem of what to write about in a paper on a literary work might appear to be finessed for students in literature courses where teachers provide students with writing assignments that specify topics or particular critical approaches. But for teachers who think that learning to write has to include learning how to find and choose a topic for oneself (Moffett 1981), the idea of teacher-selected topics in a literature course may feel inconsistent with the responsibility most English teachers accept to teach writing along with whatever else they teach. (Teacher-assigned topics for writing also invite students to see the activity of writing about literature as more of a test of whether they can produce what their teachers ask for than an occasion for engaging in any sort of independent exploration of textual meaning or literary response.) Besides, when teachers assign paper topics to students, the problem of what is worth writing about isn't solved; it's simply transferred from the writer to the teacher as assignment maker. So it doesn't surprise me in talking to teachers of literature around the country that they regard the problem of what is worth writing about as a serious one for themselves as well as for their students.[1]

Nor is this a new problem in educational or literary history. Quite aside from what the oldest among us remember about teaching practices in literature of the past half-century or more or what we can infer from surviving samples of student work from past generations, we have the testimony of every new generation of literary critics that the theories and practices of the generation of their teachers were misdirected and intellectually unproductive—a situation that leaves every generation of teachers having to continue the discredited practices of their own teachers or figure out for themselves how to translate new paradigms of literary theory and unfamiliar critical strategies into instructional practices and writing assignments for students (Graff 1985, 1987, and 2001/1986, 2065; Adams 1991; Sullivan 1994).

For the two generations of English teachers who are presently in classrooms, I want to present a workshop designed to help students discover topics and an approach to talking and writing about literature in a way that is consistent with contemporary theorizing, yet does not demand that students or their teachers first immerse themselves in contemporary theoretical discourse. I will present the exercises constituting this workshop much as I use them in my introduction to literature courses but more in the spirit in which I present them in workshops on the teaching of literature for preservice and inservice teachers of English, teachers whose own literary education frequently appears to have left them more intimidated by than conversant with theory, if they were exposed to it explicitly at all.

I should note that while I have been introducing these exercises as mainly concerned with how to help students find topics or approaches to writing literary essays, the title of this chapter intentionally speaks of what's worth *saying* about a literary work, acknowledging that the question of what to write about a work of literature is a version of a prior question about what one might say about it either as a teacher or a student in the discussions that typically take place in literature classes. My assumption in conducting this workshop and in my own teaching is that our way of talking about literature with our students in our classrooms becomes the model they use in their own talking and writing about literature. As a large body of ethnographic evidence has shown us (Green and Dixon 1993; Dixon, Frank, and Green 1999; Rex and McEachen 1999), our classrooms are communities in which a culture is co-constructed by teachers with their students, and that culture includes rules of discourse that in a literature class would govern such matters as what counts as a literary observation or statement, what sorts of questions or responses to literary texts are appropriate, and what is worth saying about a literary text (also see Fish 1980).

A culture, of course, also includes rules, tacit or explicit, about roles, rights, and responsibilities or about who is supposed to do what with whom under what conditions and with what outcomes (Dixon, Frank, and Green 1999). In the course of this workshop addressing the question of what is worth saying about a literary text, I hope it will become evident that I am also demonstrating how teachers can foster the development of a particular kind of culture in their classrooms—a culture where the roles, responsibilities, and rights of students are such that they become engaged participants in the literary activity of the classroom, and contributors to (rather than mere observers or consumers of) the way texts are discussed and construed in a community of readers and writers.

The Workshop: Constructing Readings in a Literary Community

Introduction

This exercise is designed to give students a strategy for thinking and talking about literary texts that will help them generate ideas for literary essays or papers, based on their own readings of a text. It is built on the premise that there are many ways to read every literary text and that one of the functions of literary study is not to find the one right reading, but to explore the different avenues that readers might want to take in interrogating and talking about a literary work (see Patterson 1992, 1993). We can all become better readers of almost any text by exploring the various readings to which it may be subject. By "readings" here, I mean interpretations or critical perspectives or what we can simply call ways of looking at and thinking about a literary work.

While every activity I will be demonstrating in this workshop is something I do with my own students in introductory literature courses at the university, some version of it is also used in classrooms at virtually every grade from elementary school through graduate school by the teachers I work with in the South Coast Writing Project, where most of these activities originated in experiments we collaboratively conducted in our Literature Institute for Teachers, initially funded by the National Endowment for the Humanities. Teachers reading this book can therefore feel confident that the activities demonstrated here can be adapted for use with their classes and students at almost any level of education.

Among the problems many teachers will have to solve in adapting these exercises is the problem of time and the difficulty of completing the full cycle of these exercises within the frame of an ordinary fifty-minute academic period. It has been my own good fortune for a number of years to teach classes that are seventy-five minutes long, and in that time I can conduct the complete workshop presented here. Ninety minutes would be even better, which is now the time allotted for many English classes in secondary schools working with a block schedule and is the amount of time I generally insist on for inservice workshops I conduct with teachers. If I had to conduct this workshop within the constraints of a fifty-minute class, I would spread it out over two class periods, breaking it at one of its obvious dividing points.

Activity #1: Reading Silently (5 minutes)

T: Let's begin by reading a story with the title "Any Minute Mom Should Come Blasting Through the Door," by David Ordan, from a collection of very short stories called *Sudden Fiction* (Shapard and Thomas 1986). This collection of stories by established and emerging American writers includes some seventy short, short stories, all of them between one and five pages in length. It is a wonderful resource for English teachers looking for short literary works that can be read and discussed within the compass of a single lesson in class. I should note, however [see commentary below], that I have selected this particular story deliberately for use in my workshops with teachers and with college-age students, and would have some reservations about using the story with students younger than nineteen or twenty. But it should not be hard to find other very short stories to use for the exercise I will demonstrate here. In any event, please read the story now and notice as you read it any lines that particularly resonate for you. These might be lines that amuse, offend, or surprise you or that you find memorable, elegant, or puzzling. Simply notice any lines that catch your attention in any way.

"Any Minute Mom Should Come Blasting Through the Door"
by David Ordan

Mom died in the middle of making me a sandwich. If I had known it was going to kill her, I never would have asked. It never killed her before to make me a sandwich, so why all of a sudden? My dad didn't understand it, either. But we don't talk about it too much. We don't talk about it too much at all. Sometimes we try. Sometimes it's just the two of us at dinner, and things are almost good.

But only sometimes.

Most of the time it's different. Most of the time I do things like forget to leave her place out at the table. And then we don't know what to do. Then we don't even try to talk. Three plates. Three glasses. The kitchen shines. A bright, shiny kitchen, Mom used to say. And there we are—my dad, her place, and me. And any minute Mom should come blasting through the door, all bundles and boxes, my big winter coat squaring her off at the shoulders and hips, her face smiling and wrinkled like a plant.

I should have known better.

I should have known about these things.

Come on, Mom, what do you say? Is it going to kill you to make me one sandwich? Is it really going to kill you? Remember how you used to play with me? Remember? And then I snuck up behind her chair, undid her curlers, and ran my fingers through her hair until she said all right already, what kind did I want? Then she stood up, turned to my dad, and opened her bathrobe so he could get a peek just to see if the old interest was still there. But I don't think it was. What? he said. He hasn't seen this before? Make the sandwich, he said. And he let his body melt like pudding into the easy chair.

That was it. That was the last thing he said to her. Mom turned up the TV, went into the kitchen, and the next thing we knew, she was calling out for help.

Well, my dad didn't know what was going on anymore than I did, so he got up from his chair, trudged across the room—making sure to scrape his feet on the carpet all the way so he could really shock her good this time—and that was it. Mom was dead on the floor of the kitchen, her bathrobe open at the waist.

And I thought, Well, there's Mom dead, what now? No one thinks about that. No one thinks about what happens after you find your mother dead like that, all over the kitchen floor. But I'm telling you, that's when the real fun starts. That's when you have to try mouth-to-mouth on her—on your mother, for God's sake—knowing that if she does come around she'll spit up in your face, because that's what happens, but praying for it, anyway, because if she doesn't, then it's all over. That's when you've got to call an ambulance and wait for them to throw a sheet over her head so they can take her away from you. That's when you've got to sit there and watch them put their hands all over her body and know they'll never believe you even tried to save her. That's when the neighbors see the flashing red light in your driveway and wonder what kind of rotten son you are that you couldn't save your mother. That's when you've got your whole life to live, and all it's going to be is one excuse after another for why you didn't save her. What do you do? We didn't know, so my dad poured her on the couch, and we waited. We waited and watched TV.

It was on.

But like I said, we don't talk about it too much. How can we? Mom was the talker. That's what she used to say. She used to say, "Boys, what would you do without me?" And here we are, without her. My dad and I wouldn't know how to talk to each other if you paid us, so we don't even try. Not much, anyway. What am I going to say? How's your love life? What's it like to sleep alone? He doesn't want that. He doesn't want that at all. He wants me out of the house. But he doesn't really want that, either, you know. What would he do then? Six rooms can be too many if you're not careful. I tell him this at dinner sometimes. I tell him how much he needs me. How much he cares. But he doesn't care. He cares about the kitchen, the robe, the things I did to try to save his wife. My hands. Her body. My lips. Her mouth.

"Tell me," he says, "is that really how you want to remember your mother?"

Commentary: This story serves exceptionally well for the crucial portion of this workshop, which will involve developing a variety of perspectives on or different readings for the story. But its sexual suggestiveness probably makes it inappropriate for use in most precollege classrooms. Any time it is used, moreover, one must be sensitive to the possibility that some readers may be mourning the recent death of a mother or some other relative and may not be able to deal with the story as a literary exercise. I have had a couple of teachers and one student leave the room when I worked on this story because they were overcome by their emotional response to the account of the mother's death— an account that many adult readers will find quite funny. I should also note that I am inclined to find another story for this exercise even in college classes where most students are freshmen. It's my experience that readers don't generally appreciate the humor of this story until they are close to twenty. Many seventeen- and eighteen-year-olds seem too attached to their mothers to read the narrated events with the kind of detachment that will allow them to experience the ironies of the story. One of the ironies of this story, given the problems and sensitivities I have just mentioned, is that its author, David Ordan, was only nineteen when he wrote it (Lish 1986). I withhold this fact from my students until near the end of our discussion.

Activity #2: Jump-in Reading (6 minutes)

T: Now let's reread the story out loud and do it in a manner called "jump-in reading." It's a practice that middle school teachers call "popcorn reading." But I would never do anything in my university classroom called popcorn reading, so I do it as jump-in. As the name suggests, with jump-in reading, readers jump in and read aloud for about a paragraph and then stop. And into the silence somebody else then jumps in. There is no hand raising or protocol for determining who reads. You just jump into the silence and read a short segment of the text and then stop when you get to the end of a paragraph or to some other natural stopping point. But it isn't called jump-around reading. So make sure you start at the beginning of the story, if you are the first reader, and that each subsequent reader jumps in where the previous reader stopped, so that we'll hear the entire story in its original form. Again, please notice any lines or phrases that resonate for you or strike you powerfully in any way.

Activity #3: Pointing (5 minutes)

T: I would now like us to try something that we can call "pointing," borrowing the term from Peter Elbow (1973, 85–86) for an activity that is also a variation on what Elbow calls "text rendering." Elbow, as you probably know, makes extensive use of small writing-response groups for students where they read and respond to each other's work-in-progress. But most students don't know how to respond except by offering each other criticism (often based on mistaken notions about good writing) and advice (often bad). So Peter carefully trains his students in how to respond, partly through his own example, but mainly through practice with a number of response techniques that he systematically introduces for the writing groups in his classroom (see Elbow and Belanoff 1989).

His emphasis in the first weeks of writing groups is on helping students do what they are most competent to do, which is to respond to each other's work as real readers who tell each other what happened to them as readers of each other's work and not what they think a writer ought to be doing or ought to have done. And one of the first methods of response he asks his students to employ is that of pointing. In pointing, you literally point to and read out loud (if you have the text in front of you) or else recall (from an oral reading) and repeat aloud from memory a line or phrase that struck you as memorable or especially powerful in a writer's work. The responsibility to point helps keep readers in a writing group attentive. And for the writers, hearing lines from their work read aloud is both encouraging and instructive. It shows them where their work is moving or impressing their readers and it gives them a sense of being heard, which itself is an inducement to keep on writing.

In the Literature Institute for Teachers that I directed in our Writing Project in the mid- and late eighties, we experimented with applying many techniques we had already refined for the teaching of writing to the teaching of literature. Our experiments with pointing in our Institute (assisted by a presentation by Sheryl Fontaine, at that time Elbow's colleague at the Bard Institute for Writing and Thinking) and subsequently in our classes at every level of schooling have shown us that it serves very different and valuable purposes as a strategy for instruction in the reading of literature (or anything else), when the writer is absent.

Here is how we do pointing when working with literature: We simply call aloud lines or phrases from the text that moved us, touched us, or resonated for us in any way. These might be lines that struck us as memorable, important, shocking, or especially interesting for any reason at all or for no reason we can name. We don't have to explain or justify our interest in a line. And we'll call out the lines in a fashion that Elbow calls "Quaker style." He uses that term to refer to the way Quakers conduct their prayer meetings. The congregation sits on chairs or benches silently in a circle, and as the spirit moves them, members call out their inspired thoughts or feelings or whatever else might come to them. So that's how we'll do it here, except that we won't wait for the spirit to shove us; we'll call out our lines at the merest spiritual nudge.

And we'll observe two additional rules in our procedure. The first rule is that nobody has the exclusive right to any line. So if someone calls out a line that you wanted to call out, you are free to call it out too, whenever you please. The second rule is that there is no limit to how many times a line can be called out, even by the same person. So if you are in love with a line, you are free to call it out many times or to use it as a kind of refrain during the proceedings. You might use it as an answering line to one particular line or to many lines. Or you might simply call it out whenever you are moved to do so. But, of course, you are free to call out any other lines as well. So let's start the pointing.

S1: "I should have known better."

S2: "Is it going to kill you to make me one sandwich? Is it really going to kill you?"

S3: "Mom was the talker. That's what she used to say."

S4: "She used to say, 'Boys, what would you do without me?' And here we are, without her."

S1: "I should have known better."

S5: "That's when you have to try mouth-to-mouth on her—on your mother, for God's sake—knowing that if she does come around she'll spit up in your face."

S6: "That's when you've got your whole life to live, and all it's going to be is one excuse after another for why you didn't save her."

T: "It never killed her before to make me a sandwich."

S7: "Then she stood up, turned to my dad, and opened her bathrobe so he could get a peek just to see if the old interest was still there."

S6: "But I don't think it was."

S8: "And he let his body melt like pudding into the easy chair."

S9: "So my dad poured her on the couch, and we waited. We waited and watched TV."

S10: "It was on."

S5: "If I had known it was going to kill her, I never would have asked."

S1: "I should have known better."

S11: "That's when you've got to sit there and watch them put their hands all over her body."

S1: "I should have known better."

S12: "Is that really how you want to remember your mother?"

S5: "My hands. Her body. My lips. Her mouth."

S13: "I snuck up behind her chair, undid her curlers, and ran my fingers through her hair."

S3: "Is that really how you want to remember your mother?"

S6: "Is it going to kill you to make me one sandwich? Is it really going to kill you?"

S2: "Make the sandwich, he said."

S1: "I should have known better."

S7: "Mom was dead on the floor of the kitchen, her bathrobe open at the waist."

S3: "Is that really how you want to remember your mother?"

S5: "My hands. Her body. My lips. Her mouth."

S1: "It never killed her before."

S14: "He wants me out of the house."

S15: "What am I going to say? How's your love life? What's it like to sleep alone?"

S16: "He got up from his chair, trudged across the room—making sure to scrape his feet on the carpet all the way so he could really shock her good this time—and that was it."

S5: "Mom was dead on the floor of the kitchen, her bathrobe open at the waist."

S17: "Her bathrobe open at the waist."

S6: "My hands. Her body. My lips. Her mouth."

S3: "Is that really how you want to remember your mother?"

S1: "I should have known better."

S12: "Remember your mother."

T: OK. I see this could go on for a long time, but I think you get the idea.

S3: We were just warming up.

T: I think you were already pretty warm. But I need to move us to the next activity.

Activity #4: Writing About a Line (10 minutes)

T: We have now had three experiences of the text: we've read it silently; we've heard it read aloud in a jump-in reading; and we've heard parts of it read again (some parts many times) in pointing. Now it's time to write about the story. And I'd like you to do that by selecting the line of the story that you find most important to its meaning or possibly most interesting or puzzling in the context of the story and discuss that line and explain its role in the story and why you find it so important or interesting or puzzling. This might be one of the lines you pointed to or heard somebody else point to, or some other line entirely. Just write the line at the top of your page and take off from there. I'll write with you, but I'll time our writing and allow only seven point five minutes for it. So this has to be freewriting (Elbow 1973) or quickwriting, without any attention to editing or elegance.

Commentary: I typically announce seven or seven and a half minutes as the allotted time for writing but usually allow the writing to continue for nine or ten minutes or more, especially if I sense that most of the participants are deeply engaged in composing or if I am so engaged in my own writing that I lose track of the time. The relatively short time limit is important for a couple of reasons, however. I say seven minutes as a way of emphasizing that this can't be an exercise in writing polished, edited prose. It has to be first-draft writing, or else we'd have to give more time than the constraints of a workshop would allow. Moreover, many students (and many English teachers) are so phobic about errors in their writing that any hint that they might be expected to produce correctly edited and elegant prose will become an obstruction to their thinking about the substantive issues. So I want to make it clear that we will be writing for such a short time that nothing is possible, if they are to complete the task, except rapid, uninterrupted writing, directly recording their thoughts.

I set approximately ten minutes as the upper limit for the exercise because—aside from the ordinary time constraints of a workshop—I believe (along with Gabriel Rico, from whose workshops almost twenty-five years ago I learned the virtues of ten-minute writing exercises) that ten minutes represents something like a unit of concentrated thought for most writers. It's been my experience and observation over the years of writing with teachers and students that most writers engaged by a topic will descend into deep concentration in their writing and thinking for about ten minutes before coming up for air and looking around, especially if they know that they won't get more than ten minutes (or think they will only get seven or eight). So, if you tell writers that they'll only have seven or eight minutes to write about a topic that captures their interest, you are likely to get their concentrated attention for up to about ten minutes. It's also been my experience that very good pieces of writing can get their start in ten-minute chunks of writing. Many experienced writers will confirm my own experience of writing what amounts to the gist of an entire essay in a ten-minute sitting and then spending the next year elaborating and refining what was in some sense fully present in the kernel produced with concentrated attention in ten minutes or less.

I also want to point out that I always write with the workshop participants as they write, whether the workshop is for teachers or for students. And I think it is important for any workshop leader or teacher to do the same. If nothing else, it models engaged participation. More importantly, it models the risk taking that all the participants will be asked to undertake. It also presents, when we share our work as we ask others to share, a model of the kind of writing that can be produced in response to the prompt. In classes it thereby allows the teacher, through her own example, to teach both about the text being studied and about writing. And, most importantly, in workshops with teachers it models what I hope they will do in their classrooms. I wouldn't feel honest writing with teachers, however, if I didn't also write with my students.

Finally, I feel obliged to comment on the topic I have assigned. It remains a problem for me and I do not wish to present its current form as anything but a provisional one. I am trying to find a way of eliciting writing that will uncover for the writer interesting critical and interpretive problems in the text. And I want to allow for the possibility that the writer will find some grounds for producing a resistant reading of the text—one that reads against the grain, taking a position that opposes or challenges the values inscribed in the text or implicitly fostered by it. So I want to encourage response, yet I want to avoid the merely associational and sometimes critically irrelevant discourse that an unconstrained invitation to respond is likely to elicit from some readers. I therefore typically ask students—as I do with a slight twist in this case—to select the line that they regard as the most important to the meaning of the story and write about why it is important. But that prompt stated so nakedly can sometimes suppress the critically important response that begins by finding a story offensive (as some women do, in this case, by virtue of its treatment of the mother) or suppress illuminating questions, or the kind of puzzlement some readers of this story experience about the relationship between the father and son and their possible sexual competitiveness.

The prompt I show here and am currently using with my students tries to negotiate the territory between a free response focused on the reader and a highly constrained response focused on the text. I suspect that the kind of response such an exercise will actually elicit in any classroom will reflect the culture of that classroom and the tacit rules for discourse about literature that have already developed in that particular classroom community. That might also explain why we'll often get the same responses from our students even after we have revised a prompt or why we'll get different kinds of responses in different years from our students to the same prompt.

Activity #5: Sharing in Writing Groups (10 minutes)

T: I see that we've actually written for almost nine minutes, so please bring your piece to a close now and find two other people with whom to share what you have written. Then read what you have written rather than tell about it. It is actually more efficient as a way of showing your thinking and more useful as a way of learning about your own strengths as a writer. So don't let anybody in your group get away without actually reading what he wrote, unless he can convince you that what he wrote was for himself alone and much too private to share with anyone except a shrink or a confessor. And please, for the sake of time, keep your groups to three persons, unless our numbers force us to have one or two groups of four. After you have heard each other's writing, please be prepared to report out on how similar or different your pieces were and what sorts of issues got raised about the story.

Activity #6: Reporting Out and Publishing (12 minutes)

T: Now that you have all heard each other's pieces, I'd like to hear from groups about what you found people writing about, how much agreement you noted in how different members of the group saw the story, and so on. I would also like us to hear some sample pieces, if some of you will volunteer to read them. Or you might want to volunteer a neighbor, if you heard a piece in your group that offered you a new or surprising or especially illuminating perspective on the story.

S15: We volunteer Sue! You have to hear this one.

Sue: OK. This story really got me going. I'll read my line first and then my response:

> *"Come on, Mom, what do you say? Is it going to kill you to make me one sandwich? Is it really going to kill you?"*

Yes it will and it does. But it really doesn't matter (except for the embarrassment and inconvenience it might cause) to the son and the father, for whom this woman, like most women in the eyes of men and boys (or should I say only boys, since that's what the mother calls both of them and that's what all men are, especially in relation to women, sports, and food): women (I was saying) as most men and boys think of them, are nothing more than food and sex machines. The boy will recover and find himself a girlfriend or wife to make his sandwiches. And the husband will, no doubt, find someone else to play jokes on and feed his face and warm his bed.

This story infuriates me with its treatment of the mother as some kind of slave to her men, someone they own as their own possession. Both of them, even after she is dead, seem more obsessed with the fact that her boobs are exposed to other people than they do with what happened to her as a person. If I didn't see that the author's name is

David, I'd assume it was written by a woman as a parody on how insensitive and stupid men can be in their treatment of women.

MANY OTHERS: (Much laughter and clapping.)

T: I will not take the risk of saying anything about that one, except thank you for a very powerful piece.

S11: Eileen also commented on men as boys.

EILEEN: Yes, I did. But it was as if each of us in our group wrote about the story from our own experience as a parent or a family member.

T: Can we hear an example?

EILEEN: I'll read mine:

> "'Boys, what would you do without me?' And here we are, without her. My dad and I wouldn't know how to talk to each other if you paid us . . ."

This story captures one of the puzzling facts about life in many families and about differences between men and women as parents and people. The mother in the family is the mediator between the father and son. They don't talk to each other except through her. She even appears to do their talking for them: "Mom was the talker." But what about these males she calls "boys." They were people occupying the same house but unable to communicate except through the mother. Without the mother they don't know what to say to each other and are awkward in their silence. And this seems to me the circumstance in many families.

But it's also about men. Men and boys find it difficult to talk with other males in any circumstances. Men want to do something with each other like paint a garage, go fishing, fix a car, play sports, or watch a ball game. Then they can do things without having to say anything, except what's necessary, like "pass the beer." Without an activity to define their relationship they become uncomfortable. And this is often a source of conflict between men and women, because men expect being together with a woman to mean doing something (sex and eating both score high as doing something) and women often want to do nothing except be together with their companion. That situation feels like a trap to most men.

T: So what do we have here? Another piece with a feminist inflection, but now with a focus on issues of gender and family dynamics. Does that seem to characterize it accurately? Thanks, Eileen. I'm struck again, as I always am in workshops like this, by how much eloquent and powerful writing can get produced in an eight- or ten-minute span. OK. Let's hear another.

S3: I think you should hear Roger's.

ROGER: I don't think I want to share this one.

S3: We all teach adolescents and we know exactly what you are talking about. It's good! Read it. We want to hear from a man, anyway.

ROGER: (Reluctantly) OK.

> *"And then I snuck up behind her chair, undid her curlers, and ran my fingers through her hair until she said all right already, what kind did I want?"*

I see this story as one about the arrogance of young men in relationship to their mothers. This boy teases and manipulates his mother to give him what he wants and she does it. He is certainly big enough to make his own sandwich, yet he insists that his mother do it for him.

It makes me a little angry to read this because I have a son of sixteen who is already much bigger than either his mother or myself, but he doesn't seem to know that he is almost grown up. Sometimes he'll pick his mother up—literally physically put his arms around her in a bear hug and pick her up—and walk around the house with her as if she were a pet. It seems to me disrespectful, and yet it's sort of loving, the way the boy in the story is. He loves his mother, but he doesn't know how to show respect for her properly. Unfortunately, she lets him get away with it. The father is ambivalent about it (as I suppose I am too). He tells the mother to make the sandwich, but in the end he seems to resent the boy for the treatment of the mother.

S19 AND S20: We think you need to hear Mark's response to the same line!

MARK: Sure. But I don't want Roger to think I'm psychoanalyzing his family.

ROGER: Be my guest.

MARK: OK.

> *"And then I snuck up behind her chair, undid her curlers, and ran my fingers through her hair . . ."*

What sort of behavior is this for a boy to engage in with his mother? It makes him sound more like a lover than a son. And that is the way he is with his mother in much of the Oedipal drama enacted in David Ordan's very very short story. Even as his mother lies on the floor dead and he fruitlessly administers mouth-to-mouth resuscitation, he sees her bathrobe open, exposing her naked body, and thinks about how the rescue team will put their hands all over his mother's body. Nor does the sexuality of the mother-son relationship go unnoticed by the father, who earlier in the story declines the mother's gesture of sexual interest in him, because he knows it is really meant for the son who witnesses it, the son whose coat she is wearing as a girlfriend wears a boyfriend's letter sweater. The father, significantly, merely melts like pudding in an easy chair.

After the mother's death, the Oedipal triangle is recognized by both the father and son in their inability to talk to one another, in the son's recognition that his father wants him out of the house, and most of all in the father's jealous question about the boy's last sight of the mother naked on the floor: "Is that really how you want to remember your mother?"

T: Ah, the Freudian reading. Thank you. You aren't likely to get such sophisticated responses from your students, but you'll get interesting ones. Unfortunately, many of you won't be able to use this particular story. But I'm sure you can find equally provocative ones. William Carlos Williams' "The Use of Force" is just about as short and very powerful. And another very short story that I know will yield varied and interesting responses is Kate Chopin's "Story of an Hour." Just make sure that your students read the text a couple of times to give them a better chance of not misunderstanding the ending. You can also use an excerpt from a novel you are teaching. Can we hear another? Thank you, Maureen.

MAUREEN: I'll give you one about guilt.

"That's when you've got your whole life to live, and all it's going to be is one excuse after another for why you didn't save her."

I read this story as a story about guilt. About the guilt that a son feels when his mother dies. He may have good reason for feeling guilty because she ironically died doing what he asked her to do. Additionally, he tries to save her but can't and feels, naturally, that if he knew better how to administer help he might have saved her. So he feels responsible for her death because he couldn't save her and because she actually died doing what he asked her to do and what she may not have wanted to do. But she did it anyway for him. And the husband feels guilty too. He is guilty about treating his wife so callously. About treating her cry for help as a joke and going to her, when she needed real help, with the intention of giving her a shock from static electricity. He may also feel guilty about treating her so indifferently when she acted sexy with him. Probably this was his pattern. He appears to love his wife, and the son appears to love his mother. They don't lack love. But like most people, they take the people they love for granted. So when that person dies, those who are left often feel guilt and remorse for all the ways that they failed to express their love and all the ways they were thoughtless or cruel.

T: Thanks very much. Another fascinating take on the story. Can we label this one the ethical or moralist reading—partly a psychological reading, but one focused on issues of responsibility and guilt? One more.

S10: We volunteer Jason.

JASON: I wrote about the same line that Sue wrote about.

T: Great. Let's hear it.

JASON: I also take up several points already mentioned by others.

> *"It never killed her before to make me a sandwich."*
>
> This story is really an extended verbal joke built around the hyperbolic question that the son asks his mother, which sets the events of this story in progress: "Is it going to kill you to make me one sandwich? Is it really going to kill you?" And the answer is yes, leaving the astonished son to muse, "It never killed her before to make me a sandwich." One can speculate on the origin of this story in the writer's own musing about the possibility of an ironic outcome for a situation where somebody uses the conventional hyperbolic question form that people use all the time to manipulate others. Is it going to kill you to do this or that for me? Will it kill you to take out the garbage for once? Would it kill you to wear a necktie at dinner? Would it kill you to be nice to your brother? And so on. So the writer invented a situation in which the question becomes a real one and the answer is that it does kill the mother to make her son a sandwich. And that ironic fact sets in motion a whole series of jokes built around the ironies to be found in situations taken to their extreme. The son has to administer mouth-to-mouth resuscitation on his mother and worries about her throwing up in his mouth. The mother is on the floor with her bathrobe open when the paramedics arrive. The father is concerned about the boy's hands on the mother's naked body. The father and son don't know how to talk to one another. It's a very funny story that begins with a joke.

T: That's almost the same way I approached the story this time, myself. Though I think I like your piece better. That gives me two good reasons—the other being the pressure of time—not to read my own piece of writing (which I already shared in a small group), but to see what the readings we have heard (and those we haven't) may show us about what is worth saying about a work of literature.

Extending the Workshop from Practice to Theory (10–30 minutes)

ON RIGHT READINGS AND MULTIPLE READINGS

Having heard the range of readings we have just heard for the David Ordan story, many students (and even more of their parents) might be inclined to ask which one among them (or beyond them) is correct, as if the function of literary study were to acquire correct or academically approved interpretations of works of literature, and the function of teachers were to teach those approved readings. There is certainly good reason for students and their parents to think of literary study that way, given much of the history of literary instruction over the past few generations and before. Without presenting a history of literary instruction in America (see, however, Myers 1996), let me point out that for generations in this country, literary study meant reading canonical works of literature and learning what was supposed to be said about them, that is, what the community of literary scholars was presumed to regard as the right way to read them. If there is any doubt about the continuing prevalence of such a view of literary study, one need only look at the stacks of paperback booklets and study guides available in bookstores and supermarkets promising to teach students (especially those who have never actually read the literary works themselves) what teachers and scholars are supposed to regard as the correct interpretations and critical statements to make about those works. And surely the difficulty of many canonical works of literature and the fact that almost all of them originate in earlier centuries and may appear to have been written in a language hardly our own (the English of Shakespeare or Milton, for example) may suggest that literature—at least that brand of it usually taught in schools—can only be read by experts, upon whom ordinary readers must depend for their literary knowledge.

Since I have done it elsewhere (see Chapter 1 of this volume), I won't use this occasion to demonstrate how such a view of literary study is a recipe for illiteracy or pseudoliteracy. Let's note, however, that it surely encourages readers to believe that they have no capacity or authority to produce anything that could be respected in an academic setting as an interesting or useful interpretation or criticism of a text. And this helps to explain why so many students feel utterly empty when called upon to talk or write about a work of literature.

The series of activities we have just completed in reading and writing about a literary work is designed to help students acquire a very different sense of themselves as participants in a literary and academic community, and it would ideally be completed by helping them to recognize the value of what they have produced. Notice that each of the readings we heard represented a different perspective on the story, based on what each reader happened to observe about the story, helped perhaps by the attention drawn to certain lines (during our pointing) by other readers. Sometimes it is clearly based on their own experience with some issue or theme raised by the story.

FROM PERSONAL TO TRANSPERSONAL READINGS

Yet as individual and even personal as these different readings may appear, each one of them can also be said to be transpersonal insofar as the relevant experience that gave rise to a particular reading for an individual also identifies that reader as a member of a group of readers in similar cultural roles—for example, as fathers of teenage boys, or mothers of sons, or women in relationships with uncommunicative men. The particular cultural dimension of each reader's response to the story can often be tapped by asking students to follow up their first written responses with a brief reflection on how what they wrote in their response reveals something about who they are as "situated readers," that is, as readers who occupy particular social roles in a particular cultural moment and setting (along with their roles in their own more personal and specific relational dramas). Such a reflection would invite Sue to speak of her feminist sympathies and perhaps of the cultural as well as personal circumstances that fostered her feminism. Jason might talk about the inclination he acquired, when he was a graduate student in English, to look for language play and irony in works of literature. Maureen might say something about her Catholic school education and her interest in the problem of guilt as a moral and psychological issue. Such reflection can help students see how often we read from a perspective shaped partly by who we are as individuals, but also by the cultural roles we occupy and share with large groups of people who are likely to share our perspective.[2]

But even without engaging in such a reflective exercise, students can be encouraged to recognize how the readings they have constructed, based on where their interests or experience led them to focus in identifying the most significant or problematic line in the story, may be said to be more than a merely private response of interest only to themselves. Each reading can, in fact, be seen as a publicly available and potentially illuminating and persuasive reading for other readers insofar as evidence is marshaled in its support. And in the case of the readings we witnessed here—readings produced by English teachers who are all sophisticated readers and writers—every one was presented with the kind of evidence that would require reasonable readers with different perspectives to acknowledge it as a legitimate or possible reading, even if it was not one they would subscribe to.

In any case, whether little or much evidence is presented in support of a particular reading at this point, the quick drafts produced through this exercise can be seen for all students as potential starts, notes as it were, or first drafts for more fully elaborated essays that approach the text from the perspective they have identified here. This exercise shows them that they do have a perspective worth exploring in an essay on a literary text, and that the essay that such a perspective will yield will probably be useful as an interpretation or reflection on a literary work and one that can make a genuine contribution to the discourse of their classroom community about the text under discussion.

Let's now make a list on the board of the various readings we have heard, thereby dignifying each of them with a label that will identify each as a kind of theoretical perspective that persons of like interest may also be inclined to adopt and that all readers can benefit from attending to.

1. The Freudian reading (Mark's), which sees the story as an Oedipal drama
2. The feminist reading (Sue's), which criticizes the story for representing the exploitation and abuse of women, yet not recognizing its own complicity in and ideological sympathy with the system of injustice it inadvertently reveals

3. The language analysis perspective (Jason's), through which the story is seen as an elaborately constructed joke based on language play

4. The psychological and ethical perspective (Maureen's), focused on the guilt that accompanies the loss of a loved one

5. The family dynamics perspective (Eileen's), focused on the roles of members of the family—on the mother, for example, as the mediator between father and son in the family and on gendered roles more broadly

6. The male-parental phenomenological perspective (Roger's), focused on the lived experience of fathers of teenage boys as it is reflected in the relationships represented in the story. Roger's reading might also be classified as another one that looks primarily at issues of family dynamics, and again at the triangle of mother-father-son, though it speaks particularly from the father's point of view

It is, of course, not necessary to give academic-sounding names to every perspective a reader might take on a literary work, but it is useful for us to show our students (through exercises or workshops such as the one I have been conducting here) that they are capable of producing readings of texts that represent perspectives that are likely to be of interest and value to other readers. And to do that, it helps to name the perspective in a way that demonstrates its transpersonal nature or its character as something more than a merely personal and individual response of no possible value to other readers whose primary interest is in the literary work and the issues it raises and not the personal life or feelings of other readers (even though these may be interesting too). So let's now take another moment to hear from some others in the room who have not read their writing for all of us to hear, but who might be willing to just name their perspective or tell us what angle they took in talking about the story. I'll add these to our list on the board as you tell them to me.

S3: I wrote about the mother as the center of the family. I suppose you could put it with Eileen's, but it was more positive in a way, and more about how everything depends on Mom, and maybe we don't appreciate our moms until it's too late.

T: That sounds like another one from the family dynamics perspective. But maybe it's a different perspective—the mother's perspective, perhaps, speaking for all mothers. Something like that?

S3: Yes, something like that.

S14: I wrote about the other side of the story, about the father as a marginal figure in the family. That may be the American way in families, and it's what we see in a typical situation comedy too.

T: So you are reading the story as a cultural document showing the role of fathers in the American family. And that perspective would invite you to talk about other representations of American families and of the role of fathers, as in situation comedies, and maybe other actual families or accounts of family life. It's also another one about family dynamics, isn't it? But with a fascinating twist. Any others? Monica?

MONICA: I wrote about the way young people are so self-absorbed, they can't see anything except their own needs and the way they might look in other people's eyes. That's what I think this story is about. Even when his mother is dying on the kitchen floor, he's worried about the embarrassment of having an ambulance come to his house and what will the neighbors say and so on.

T: So you'd do something like a character study of the narrator and examine him from the prospective of adolescent psychology as you know about it in other contexts (and maybe from some additional reading?). You already know a good deal from twenty years of teaching adolescents.

MONICA: Yes, and raising four of my own.

T: Okay, let me stop collecting now and put on the board all the perspectives on this story that we've heard so far (and I assume we could collect more), all of which have already been used for very early drafts of papers on this story and any of which might make for a productive line of inquiry for a more fully developed paper about the story. Each of these, in other words, can be seen as a potentially productive way of reading this story and every one of these originated in the reader's own take on the story—that is, in what happened to strike you as significant or problematic or interesting in the story.

1. Oedipal triangle
2. Non-Freudian examination of father-son conflicts
3. Feminist critique
4. Ethical/psychological analysis of guilt
5. Family dynamics/family triangle study/roles of family members
6. Verbal joke analysis
7. Maternal role analysis
8. Paternal role analysis
9. Study of adolescent psychology/egocentricity

What I would ask you to notice about these nine different topics or ways to see and talk about the same text is that each of them is at once a reflection of some individual person's own response and yet an application of some transpersonal theory or generalization about gender roles, adolescence, the psychology of guilt, sexual politics, the culture of the family, and so on. And each of those ways of reading serves as what Deborah Appleman (2000) calls a "lens"—each one like a different colored lens or a lens of different power on a camera—through which to look at a work of literature. You will notice different features of the landscape every time you change your lens, but it will still be the same landscape. No one way of looking necessarily challenges the validity of any other way.

It is obvious to researchers in every field—but insufficiently recognized about literary inquiry—that every way of looking is also a way of not looking. When we pay attention to the microbes in a drop of water under a microscope, we are not paying attention to the experience of fishing in the stream where the water comes from, though it's the same water and our microscopic examination may tell us a good deal about why it's such a good stream for fishing. Similarly, any critical, theoretical, or interpretive perspective we employ in looking at a text implies that we will be noticing some features of the text, but ignoring others. And that fact makes a good argument for the value of multiple and different perspectives in a community of readers. When others offer us their perspectives, we need not think of them as competing interpretations, but as additional perspectives that enrich the totality of our own perception.

Metaprocessing for Teachers: Reflections on Practice

What I now want to add for teachers who would take their students through the sequence of activities I have just demonstrated (or use any part of that sequence, since most of the activities included can be used independently or as parts of other exercises) is a brief recapitulation of the process we have gone through and an explanation or rationale for why we did what we did or what purposes it serves. If we don't understand the rationale or theory informing a practice, we can easily subvert its purposes or blunt them with the minor revisions we inevitably make as we adapt new practices to our own classrooms. So let's begin at the beginning.

We started with a silent reading, which seems to me a useful way to start, before you ask people to read a text aloud. But I must tell you that I was once doing the first part of this workshop (using a very different text) in partnership with a colleague who teaches in the primary grades, and she wanted to start the workshop with jump-in reading. I told her she had it backward. Her response was that in her classroom, if she were to start with the silent reading, half of her students wouldn't be able to read the text. She needed the oral reading to show many of her students how to read and pronounce many of the words. So, in spite of my theoretical preference for reading silently first, we need to acknowledge the wisdom of her practice and the possibility that in some classrooms, even at the secondary level, where there may be a great many English language learners or struggling readers, some teachers may want to start with the jump-in reading.

Rereading as a Reading Strategy

Wherever you start, I want to point out the virtue of a second reading and regular practice in class of rereading texts. I want to assert, in fact, that rereading is the most powerful strategy available to all readers for helping themselves read more profitably, especially when they are reading difficult texts.)How many of you, for example, noticed or understood features of this story through the jump-in reading that slipped your notice or understanding on the first silent reading? Yet you are expert readers who were reading a fairly easy text. So imagine the power of rereading for weaker readers with this same text or more difficult texts.

In my classes, I usually try to get students to do at least two readings, whenever possible, and I usually start with a silent reading in preparation for a jump-in reading. But aside from serving as a second reading, there are other virtues to a jump-in reading for many middle school and high school classes, where teachers typically want students to practice reading out loud. Allowing students to jump in when they choose to relieves them of the worry that the prospect of oral reading creates for many students and frees them to pay attention to the text being read, rather than reading ahead to practice what they figure they'll be called upon to read. It also allows weaker readers to hear difficult and unfamiliar words pronounced, so that they will feel more confident about jumping in later, even though the same difficult words might appear. The fact is that wherever I have demonstrated jump-in reading, teachers have taken it up and have reported to me later that they continue to use it, that their students enjoy it, and that many students will jump in who had been very reluctant to participate in any oral reading in the past.

The Point of Pointing

Let's now think about the value and point of pointing, the next practice we employed. First of all, it constitutes a kind of third reading. It at least highlights selected passages from the text in a way that makes them more visible to all readers in the room.

Second,(by allowing students to hear many lines called out repeatedly by many different readers, you may be able to help some reluctant readers—especially those who would not take the risk of calling out any line—begin to gain valuable confidence in themselves as readers.)One of the differences between strong and weak readers is that strong readers trust that their responses to texts are worth paying attention to and talking about with other readers. It's the exact parallel to a difference between strong and weak writers. Strong writers think that what they think is worth writing down and reporting. Weak writers also have thoughts, but assume they aren't worth anything, so they don't explore them. They think that all they can do in writing is tell what their teacher told them or whatever it is they are supposed to say. They see writing as what Scardamalia and Bereiter (1982) call a "knowledge-telling routine," performed exclusively for their teachers, and not in any way a creative or self-directed act of contributing to anybody's knowledge.

Similarly, weak readers assume that their responses to texts are meaningless and not worth reporting. They would never presume to point to a line that they found interesting or important, because they would claim that they don't know what is supposed to make a line interesting or important. Yet, when these same weak readers hear students known to be strong readers calling out lines that they themselves might also have been struck by, they will start to recognize that they are not so unlike the strong readers as they may have imagined and that their responses may also be worthy of attention.

(The repetitions of lines or of clusters of lines also starts to locate what Elbow might call a "center of gravity" for a reading or interpretation of a text.)For example, in this exercise, the frequent repetition of the lines about "my hands," "her body," "my lips," and "her mouth," and about the open bathrobe suggested that many of us were identifying a theme of something like Oedipal sexuality in this story, a theme that some of the participants mentioned explicitly or implicitly in their brief responses and that we might also want to explore more fully in discussion. In the meantime, the process of pointing honors every individual response and requires no explanation for why any reader decided to call out any line.

This brings me to what I think is the most powerful reason to use pointing as an instructional strategy in classrooms and also the reason why we liked doing it in this workshop and why teachers report that they and their students love to do it:(it acknolwedges and honors each reader's own aesthetic experience in reading this particular text) But before I explain the pedagogical significant of such an acknowledgment, I want to indulge in a longish digression to point out that many teachers in my Writing Project (including me) used pointing for at least a couple of years in their classrooms and we even demonstrated it in workshops for other teachers before we could provide any rationale for it or justify it theoretically. We did it, we liked it, our students liked it, and we thought it was a good practice. But it was a couple of years before we had reflected sufficiently on our practice to offer what I am now offering as a theory for the practice, a theory I developed largely in collaboration with my Writing Project colleagues and through conversations with teachers at workshops where I demonstrated it and then admitted that I couldn't say much to explain its value. The point to this digression is not to tell about the origins of the rationale I am providing, but to demonstrate how, in teaching, practice often precedes theory, and how teachers must be willing to develop and trust practices that they feel work well for their students, even when they can't articulate a rationale for that practice. It is also to say, however, that we still have a professional responsibility to reflect on all our practices and to explore possible ways of explaining and justifying them in collaboration with our colleagues and our students, even as we continue to use and refine those practices in our classrooms.

EFFERENT AND AESTHETIC READING AND THE PROBLEM OF ASSESSMENT

To return to what I think is the best rationale and most powerful explanation of our own pleasure in pointing, I want to cite Louise Rosenblatt's (1968/1938, 1978) now classic distinction between what she calls *efferent* and *aesthetic* reading. To briefly summarize Rosenblatt's formulation, we can say that there are two poles representing the purposes of most readers in reading. At one extreme there is the purely informational pole, where a reader reads for what Rosenblatt calls efferent purposes (from the Latin *effere*, to carry away), which is to say, to take something away from the text (usually information).

If you were reading a biology or chemistry text, for example, and someone were to ask you why you were reading it, you would probably tell them you were reading it because you were going to take a test on the information in a particular chapter or had some similar need for some piece of information contained in the text. If someone offered to give you all the same information in some form easier to digest, you'd probably be happy about the shortcut. You don't really want to read the book. You want what you can get out of it: the information. Or imagine that you want to call someone on the phone and you don't have the number. So you go to the telephone book to look up the number. But your friend says to you, Never mind, you don't have to look up the number. I have it here in my address book. I'll give it to you. Would you ever say, Don't tell it to me; I want to read it for myself? Of course not. You don't want to read. You want a phone number.

Now imagine that you come home from this workshop tonight and your significant other is sitting in the living room reading the evening paper and seems very engrossed in reading it. You might ask, What are you reading? and he might respond with something like, I'm reading about what happened in Los Angeles yesterday. And then you might ask what happened in Los Angeles, and he'd probably tell you. Then, imagine that he puts down his paper and asks you, Did you read anything interesting today? And you respond, Yes, in a workshop I attended I read a very very short story by David Ordan. And imagine that he then asks you to tell him about it. What would you tell him? Oh, it's about a woman who drops dead while she is fixing her son a sandwich? Or, It's about an Oedipal triangle? Could you summarize the story and give a satisfactory account of it? I think not. My assumption is that you wouldn't tell him about the story at all. You'd give it to him to read. Because unlike the news story in the newspaper, you don't read literature for the information it contains. So getting the information can't substitute for the reading experience. The information can't give you what you read a poem or story or novel for. You read literature in order to read it, to have the experience one has in reading (or in hearing the work read to you). That's what Rosenblatt means by aesthetic reading. No one wants you to tell him or her what a poem is about. Most people would prefer to read it themselves, wouldn't they?

Well, no. At least not one group of people we know very well: students! Many of them would be happy with the information rather than the story or poem, because they assume that the information is what they will need for the test. And usually they are right. One of the ironies Rosenblatt points to about the teaching of literature is that we teach students literature because we want them to have a literary experience, but then we test them on it as if they were to have read it for information (1968/ 1938, 285). Not that one acquires no information in reading literature. You can't read *Moby-Dick* without learning a good deal about whaling in the nineteenth century. But one's experience of the novel can't be measured or evaluated by one's knowledge of whaling. Moreover, a system of testing that consistently tests literary or aesthetic reading as if it were efferent reading is going to push students to read for efferent rather than aesthetic purposes when they read literature.

That explains the quite characteristic question I remember being asked by high school students when I was teaching in high school—a question that drove me wild with frustration at what seemed to me its perversity. I would ask my students to read a short story or poem that I thought they would love, and some student, after reading it, would raise his hand and ask, What are we supposed to get out of this? *Get out of it?* It was like asking me what you are supposed to get out of dancing or singing or playing a game of chess. It was a frustrating question for me because I assumed that my assignment was providing students with an opportunity to have a certain kind of experience. But my student, raised as he was in school to be prepared for a test with informational questions, knew that what counted was the information asked for on the test. So he asked—reasonably for him and unreasonably for me—what he was supposed to get out of it. If I would tell him, then he would know and be able to perform well on the test. And why would I want to withhold such information, anyway, if my job was to teach students what they needed to learn?

Part of the problem, of course, is that we don't know how to test students on their literary experience, or we didn't know until recently. In the last decade, however, we have developed a testing expertise (Dudley 1997; Claggett 1999; Blau 2001), now being employed by a number of leading educational agencies, for measuring the proficiency of students in reading literature that addresses the kind of literary experience they have had and evaluates them on the degree to which they demonstrate their capacity to function as engaged, active readers who know how to have a literary experience. Typical questions on such a test might ask students (much as I did in this workshop) to identify what they think is the most important line in a poem and explain why they selected it or to name what they regard as the most important event to the meaning of a story and explain why. Another question might ask students to write a three-line summary of a story for an annotated bibliography and then discuss some of the important features of the story that their summary could not capture.

Our limited repertoire of questions to tap into a student's experience of a literary work may also be a reflection of our limited repertoire of teaching practices that foster literary reading as an aesthetic rather than an efferent process. And this brings us back to the practice of pointing, which seems to me both to foster and to celebrate the reader's aesthetic experience of a literary work. It asks readers to re-create high points of their experience, not by talking about them, but by reliving those moments in the text in their own voices, by simply calling out lines or phrases or short passages that touched them, interested them, struck them for any reason.

And it doesn't ask them to explain, interpret, or justify their choices. We find the experience of pointing an affirming and valuable one, I believe, because we find it so respectful of the text we have read and of our own experience of it. It also happens to provide an excellent transition to and preparation for the more challenging and productive discourse task (also one tapping a reader's experience of a text rather than information acquired from a text) of selecting a significant or problematic line from a text and explaining its importance or exploring the problems it raises.

Writing About a Line

And this brings me to the rationale for the writing assignment that followed our pointing, writing about a line from a text. It is, first of all, a reliable fallback assignment for teachers who assign paper topics and then find that some of their students don't like any of the assigned topics. It is equally valuable for teachers who encounter students who claim not to be able to find their own topics for a literary paper. Such students can be told that if they can't find a compelling topic among the choices provided or on their own, they should simply pick any line in one of the eligible texts that they think is important to the meaning of that literary work and use that line as the topic of their paper. Begin with the line and explain its significance to the work as a whole or reflect on its connection to the moral, psychological, and aesthetic problems raised in and by the work. A variation of this assignment that I frequently use in the study of major canonical texts as an assigned paper topic and as homework in preparation for class discussions is to ask students to identify a line or a passage that they don't understand and write about that, inquiring into how and why these lines are so problematic and possibly (but not necessarily) exploring some plausible solutions. Though some students will feel mystified the first time they are asked to write about what they don't understand in a literary work, all students will eventually realize the power of such an assignment and many will find it the avenue to their most satisfying and productive writing.

This method of developing a discussion of the significant issues of a larger text as an extended commentary on or inquiry into a single line (or short passage) of text has a long and honorable history in the homiletic tradition, the tradition of sermon giving, where a preacher typically builds a sermon as an extended commentary on a single line of scripture. It also has a respectable precedent in the modern critical tradition in the essays and lectures of R. P. Blackmur, one of the leading literary critics of the postwar years (and the son of a minister).

The best justification for the assignment, however, is what it yields in insight and illumination for the students in a class where the assignment is used. A sizeable body of research on the teaching of literature (Marshall 1989; Hynds 1991; Zancanella 1991) shows us that one of the great worries for teachers of English is the anxiety of the right reading, their desire to make certain that their students come away from the study of assigned literary works with the right ideas about those works, which usually means the teacher's ideas or else the normative interpretations and the set of standard critical observations that is so often taken to be the demonstrable outcome of literary study. Teachers typically reread texts and consult their notes and critical editions and scholarly introductions in order to gather together the ideas they regard as the essential or approved body of knowledge about each work studied. Then in class they lead a "discussion" or recitation session designed to bring students to their planned set of insights about the work, a procedure that may actually be experienced by students as a form of intellectual manipulation or else as a naked assertion of the primacy of a teacher's intellectual authority (Hynds 1991).

In contrast, if teachers were to ask their students to engage in a sort of extended commentary on what they have identified as an important (or interesting or problematic) line as I did in this workshop, then put students in small groups to share their commentaries and problems, and then hear some of those commentaries published for the benefit of the entire class, most of the points that a conscientious teacher might want to advance in a lecture or recitation session would get covered by one or more student papers, and many new ideas and insights developed by the students themselves would emerge as well. In the meantime, the crucial point that a teacher would not want to skip in her teaching can also be covered by the piece that the teacher herself writes and shares with her students. The teacher's perspective presented in this manner commands respect not because it is the only one that counts, but because it is a legitimate contribution made by a highly respected member of the class to a discourse in which all members have also been active contributors.

Notice too that in the course of the workshop, as I demonstrated it, students were asked to share their writing in small groups of three before being asked to volunteer themselves or their neighbors to read some pieces to the whole class, thereby publishing them (making them public) for a wider audience. This sequence seems to me important as a way of ensuring that all students function as contributors to the discourse of the literature classroom (in at least small groups) and that the class will also function as a version of the larger academic community with a shared discourse, which includes shared critical texts as well as shared literary works. The small-group work also provides an excellent scaffold or rehearsal for the more risky arena of the whole classroom for students who need both the practice and the encouragement that a rehearsal can give them before they are willing to read their writing aloud to the entire class.

Readings as Theoretical Perspectives

The most difficult step in this workshop conceptually and in practice for many teachers may be the step of treating each student's reading as a kind of theoretical perspective rather than an individual response. It is also a step that many teachers may, quite properly, decide to omit, particularly with less sophisticated students. The sequence of activities I demonstrated leads to a satisfactory end for most students and their teachers without it. Still, some further explanation or possibly a defense of that last segment of the workshop seems called for here.

I think it is fair to say that the responses we witnessed and are likely to get from the exercise are pushed in the direction of something more than the merely individual and personal by the focus of my still clumsy prompt on a particular line in the story and on what was interesting, important, or puzzling about the line as it relates to the meaning of the story, rather than on how the line happened to interest the student in some way unrelated to what the story itself means. Of course, what the story means to any student, as response theorists will readily and correctly point out, will also be influenced by the student's own particular and personal perspective. Yet the personal dimension of the response is mediated in this assignment by the focus on the story's meaning, which requires a discourse that draws evidence from the story and not merely personal or associational observations by the writer. More importantly, I am suggesting through the exercise that we reframe the idea of a personal perspective by acknowledging how much what we are inclined to call personal response—while it seems personal insofar as it derives from our own personal history—is also transpersonal insofar as our history is one whose features are to a very large extent shared by extensive communities of people who occupy similar cultural roles or identities to any position we might identify and assume as an interpreter (cf. Scholes 1985, 23).

Thus, when readers read the David Ordan story from the presumably personal perspective of a mother, or the father of a teenage boy, or an unappreciated wife, those readings may be said to be transpersonal in that they identify cultural roles shared by entire communities of people whose frame of reference and understanding of human experience may be said, by virtue of their experience, to be every bit as authoritative as a Marxist, feminist, or Freudian perspective, and probably more authentic and better informed (in fact, we did get readings that were influenced by Freudian and feminist discourse). And given the contemporary cultural phenomenon of support groups and self-help books for persons who belong to almost any collectivity imaginable or who have suffered with or from almost any nameable loss, malady, or form of victimization, almost any role identifiable for an interpreter can be said to represent a discourse as well, with its own terminology, its own seminal texts, and its own way of describing experience.

It remains the case, of course, that most of the identifiable roles we occupy don't give us the kind of systematically elaborated theoretical frame for analyzing texts that one can obtain from a thorough grounding in the language, concepts, and doctrine of such influential philosophical and ideological traditions as Marxism, feminism, psychoanalytic theory, or more obscure and fashionable contemporary systems of thought. But the reality is that relatively few of the undergraduate essays I have seen by students who are writing from the perspective of one particular critical theory or another represent anything more than a secondhand and superficial understanding of the philosophical position they are pretending to occupy. Nor have I ever read from students taking less exalted perspectives on texts the sort of arrant interpretive nonsense I have seen perpetrated by students in the name of the more sophisticated critical theories that they have naïvely misapplied. I also think that an instructional program may be operating on dubious ethical grounds if it regularly demands that students adopt interpretive and critical perspectives (which inevitably model the perspectives they might take on the texts of their lives) based on theories that the students are in no position intellectually to evaluate or critique, particularly when those theories derive from ideological projects that they may neither understand nor subscribe to.

I hope that these observations about the misuses and difficulties of using critical theory in the classroom will not be read as opposition on my part to most contemporary theory or to exposing students to some of the insights and modes of analysis that the most widely practiced modern critical theories have made available to us. What I want to argue, however, is that the generalizations, practical wisdom, and perspectives on texts that students acquire from their experiences in various roles and relationships can also qualify as valid lenses with which to interrogate texts and events, and deserve to be treated with at least the same respect we grant to the more academic theories and critical lenses that might also be employed by students who have learned to use them. In fact, I would propose that the workshop I have just conducted can serve as a useful introduction to how the academically prestigious critical theories also operate as alternative perspectives on texts and how they too can enable us to observe and interpret features of texts that we might otherwise have missed.

Notes

1. The problem of what to write about a literary text doesn't resolve itself easily for more advanced students or their teachers, either. It has been documented as a serious problem for graduate students in English in master's- and doctoral-level literature courses (Sullivan 1994).

2. It's possible, of course, to get a reading based on cultural sympathy or understanding rather than membership. For instance, a man could produce a feminist reading.

7

Writing Assignments in Literature Classes
The Problem

I call it a problem because it is so widely experienced as a problem by thoughtful teachers, even when they may think they have solved it for one class or some paper assignments. In this chapter I'm going to think through the ways in which writing assignments pose problems (quite aside from the substantive problems the assignments address) for teachers of literature and their students, and then (mostly in the following chapter) offer guidelines for some writing assignments that are designed to help students achieve worthwhile goals as students of literature while giving them opportunities to also become stronger and more confident writers of academic papers. That I offer such advice doesn't mean that writing assignments are no longer a problem for me. Many of the most interesting problems we face as teachers never go away. Our experience over the years simply gives us more skill and insight in dealing with them and makes us more comfortable about our competence as teachers who continue to struggle with the constitutive or defining problems of our professional practice.

Why We Believe in Writing

Most English teachers will probably agree with the Deweyan notion that the only knowledge you truly possess is knowledge you have somehow made. Insofar as we believe that, we will also be inclined to think that nothing a student learns in our literature classes can be more reliably counted on as genuine knowledge than the knowledge acquired through the student's own writing. Most of us would believe this to be the case whether or not we had read Dewey or had thought about learning theory. We understand the value of writing as a way of learning literature because we have had the experience in our own academic lives of coming to know the texts we have written about differently and better than other texts we have studied.

Robert Scholes, in *Semiotics and Interpretation* (1982), claims that the act of writing about our reading is virtually constitutive for our field and for all humanistic study, where the fundamental and defining act is that of producing interpretive texts. Reading and the interpretation of texts are, of course, where humanistic studies begin, he says, "but the process of interpretation is not complete until the student [including the scholar and critic] has produced an interpretive text of his or her own" (4). The reasons for this ineluctable fact of life about literary knowledge, he asserts, may be found in the insights that psychoanalysis offers to us about the difference between what we know secondhand and what we know in a way that makes it available for our use. Both Freud and Lacan, he points out, emphasize the importance of a patient's putting the insights and understandings arrived at during analysis into the patient's own words, if those insights are to have any therapeutic effect.

Such observations, of course, are merely another version of what almost all teachers know and report from their own experience as teachers: that we never really come to know a text until we have taught it. That is, we learn the text when we have to construct our own reading of it and when we articulate that reading coherently and clearly for others. This is also exactly what we do when we write. To ask our students to write, therefore, confers on them many of the same opportunities for learning that are afforded to teachers through teaching. In fact, when we ask our students to write about their reading, we are taking a significant step toward the reversal of roles for students and teachers that is the paradoxical requirement to provide students with genuine opportunities for learning (see my introduction to this volume).

In composing our knowledge, whether as teachers or as writers, we come into possession of what we know in a way that makes it truly ours and not some piece of borrowed intellectual baggage we carry but don't own for ourselves. The difference between what we teach (in our role as teachers or as writers) and what someone else teaches us is often the difference between what we know for ourselves and what we know as hearsay. We believe in student writing as an important element in literary instruction, then, because we want our students to have what counts as firsthand knowledge of literary works, and we believe that the most reliable way to make that happen in the context of an academic course is to have them write papers about their reading. It comes as no surprise to us that there is also powerful research evidence that students who write extensively about their reading (compared with those who don't write or write only in response to short-answer questions) not only remember better what they have read, but through their writing come to think about their reading with greater personal involvement and depth of understanding (Nystrand 1991).

Writing as a Problem

So why is writing a problem? It's a problem because students don't always cooperate by having the kind of intellectual experience we anticipate for them. We want them to write so that they can have the experience of constructing knowledge for themselves, but we get papers that seem to be warmed-over versions of somebody else's cooking. These are papers that largely restate and sometimes misstate what we ourselves said in class or seem so derivative of critical sources or worse (Mr. Cliff, for example) that it's not clear that the student did much independent thinking at all. Some papers that are independently written seem written by a formula, offering a thesis that represents some obvious, hardly disputable fact about a text and then backing it up with three paragraphs of evidence or examples, plus a conclusion that restates the obvious thesis in different words. Another version of this paper is the paper that is built on some conventional topos like compare and contrast and proceeds to compare characters or texts for no apparent intellectual purpose whatever, except to produce a compare-and-contrast essay. In these cases we've gotten the papers we appeared to have assigned, but the students' experience was not one of constructing knowledge. What got constructed was a paper made of prefabricated parts, so that neither the writer nor the reader could learn anything from it.

More commonly, perhaps, we get papers that are so vague and imprecise in their language, so incoherent or illogical in their arguments, or so misguided in their thinking that we feel misplaced in our teaching assignment, or suspect that the students were misplaced in our class or that we need to lower our expectations of what our students can and should be asked to do. And I haven't mentioned the plagiarism cases that make a mockery of all our pedagogical efforts and poison the relationship between teachers and their students. Rampant plagiarism has driven some teachers to become nearly full-time academic detectives and has driven others to give up on assigning papers altogether.

Of course, nothing we do in our teaching can guarantee that students will engage in good faith or with their most focused attention, or in a spirit of genuine intellectual inquiry with the work we assign them. Our best pedagogical efforts can always be defeated by students who refuse to do our assignments or are determined to complete an assignment merely as an act of obedience and not as a task in which they invest themselves as learners (see Sperling and Freedman 1987). For students who see academic work as something like factory work, a job to be finished in order to collect a paycheck (credit and a passing grade) with as little personal or intellectual investment as possible, nothing of intellectual value can be gained from any paper we assign, except possibly the recognition, when they see what some more committed students have produced, that there is another way to engage in academic work that can be more intellectually rewarding and personally satisfying.

But the problem of disengaged students can also be one fostered by writing assignments into which students are unable to read themselves. Student alienation from the intellectual work that papers ought to be calling for can be exacerbated by the way we frame our assignments as well as by the way we respond to the writing we receive. It is pedagogically wise, I believe (even if sometimes unrealistically generous to our students), for us to assume that we generally get the papers we deserve. If we are getting derivative, disengaged, perfunctory, or ignorantly pompous papers—papers written in what Ken Macrorie (1970) calls "Engfish"—from our students, we should ask ourselves what we are doing to deserve such papers.

I recently saw a secondary school paper assignment that required students to write an essay in which they demonstrated how their knowledge of a set of literary terms contributed to their understanding of a literary work. And the teacher wondered why the student writing seemed perfunctory and formulaic! For most students there was probably no way to fulfill the assignment except by trying to figure out what the teacher wanted to hear and then say that—a recipe for alienation. Sometimes students are asked to write papers in support of their teacher's (often secondhand) interpretation or analysis of a text: a five-paragraph essay showing how Hamlet was indecisive, an essay on irony in "Young Goodman Brown," or a postmodern analysis of some pop culture text, employing terms and concepts already demonstrated by the teacher in lectures on that same text or a parallel text. Such assignments may represent typical academic papers and may even have their place in a course of study designed to teach and test an authoritative reading of a text or a body of literary terms and concepts. But we need to acknowledge that such papers function largely as essay tests on what students have already learned and are quite limited as opportunities for students to experience genuine authorship or the benefits that accrue from writing a literary paper worthy of one's time and engagement as a writer. They are certainly not likely to be valued by any reader except the teacher in his role as examiner (Britton et al. 1975).

What About Literature Logs or Journals?

Journals or logs frequently provide a solution to the problem of student alienation from their writing. The genre of the log or journal is generally seen as one calling for writing in what Britton and his colleagues (1975) identify as the *expressive mode*, where the writer addresses herself as her only auditor and writes largely to make sense of what she is reading for herself and to record responses to what is read or to discussions in class. Some teachers also see the log, as I do, as a workshop or laboratory, where experiments in analysis and criticism are conducted and prospective papers are incubated. In this sense I also see the log as a kind of reservoir for storing ideas that may later be drawn on in class discussion or subsequently developed into more formal essays. For teachers like Audre Allison, a high school teacher in Long Island whose work was closely observed by a teacher-ethnographer, Nancy Wilson (1989), the principal use of a log is to encourage students to record the questions, confusion, and difficulties they experience in reading texts, so that these problems can be shared with other students and addressed in class discussions, becoming powerful occasions for advancing student understanding of a text.

Logs do offer more solutions than problems to the problem of writing in literature classes, though a number of students (including some very good students) will always claim that they find their logs a waste of time and an interference with their reading rather than an aid to it. With logs one can find that the perfunctory, careless work—the use of the log as an intellectual trash bin rather than reservoir—sometimes comes from one's best students rather than the worst. And that can be disheartening to a teacher, especially in a class where (as it often happens) many students will claim for the first week or two of work with logs that they are mostly a waste of time.

My own practice, whenever I am almost persuaded to make my journal or log assignment optional in order to accommodate the good students who refuse to do more than perfunctory writing in it, is to write a few log entries myself along with my students. Whenever I do that—whenever I take ten minutes to write a log entry about what I have been reading as I finish a work or a sitting as a reader (which is what I ask my students to do)—I discover that the writing of the entry allows me to think more deeply about what I have read, that it generates important questions about the text and my reading of it and often takes me some distance toward important answers. It does, in other words, what we know writing is supposed to do for reading: it clarifies, advances, and problematizes both what has been read and how one responded to it.

The experience of doing the journal work along with my students (even if for only a few days) is always salutary for me and for my students, with whom I share my journal entries. It always leads me to reconfirm my own commitment to the journal or log assignment and usually persuades reluctant students to invest more of their own intellectual energy in their journal work. I usually get similar results (and need them several times during the course of an academic term) when I ask students to share self-selected journal entries in small groups and then report to the entire class on what sort of entries they heard before we hear a few read aloud to the whole class. (For my next class I plan to have all students post sample entries on an electronic bulletin board.) The virtue of such sharing is that students begin to recognize from the practice of others that there is no fixed form or content requirement for a journal entry, that there are options they might try that they had never thought about, that there is value in writing about and sharing confusion, and that some of their colleagues are having important intellectual experiences by practicing a form of writing that is quite painless, except insofar as genuine thinking is always difficult. But they also see how rewarding such thinking can be and how they too are capable of it.

In the next chapter I'll share the journal or log assignment that I use in my introduction to literature class with college freshmen and sophomores. (I always identify my assignment on handouts as a log and then find myself referring to it as a journal. But I prefer to call it a log to distinguish it from a personal diary and to attempt to dignify it as a literary enterprise.) Right now, I want to mention the best pedagogical use I have heard about for the employment of journals or logs in an advanced literature class in college. It is one I have recently adapted for use in one of my own advanced literature courses with quite satisfying results. But I want to describe it here as it is employed by the teacher from whom I learned it, my colleague Steven Allaback, professor of English at the University of California, Santa Barbara.

Steve teaches upper-division courses (i.e., courses for college juniors and seniors) in American literature and modern fiction and typically teaches novels. In these courses his principal writing assignment is a journal. He asks all his students to keep up with their reading so they can participate actively in class discussions and to make extensive journal entries on what they read at the time they read it. He then collects his students' journal entries once a week and reads them at home, selecting a representative set of entries for reading aloud in the following class hour. Then he devotes an entire class hour each week (out of three class meetings per week) to reading to his class from the journals of the students in the class, commenting as he reads and inviting responsive comments from all members of the class. During his other class hours he conducts a normal class with lecture and discussion. But one day each week is reserved for hearing the voices of the students (through his reading aloud) in his class through their writing. And he selects what he reads for its value in illuminating the literature, in raising critical issues, in advancing or opposing a line of interpretation he or some other member of the class might have offered, in demonstrating a method of response or criticism, or in exemplifying what can be done in a journal entry. Students take pride in having their work read out loud and naturally tend to write up to that possibility and even to compete in order to have their entries selected. They also see very early in the term a standard being set for journal entries and generally try to meet or exceed that standard.

In this use of journals, a genre traditionally identified with an audience of one-self is transformed into one for an audience of one's teacher and colleagues, much like a formal paper. But the fact is that the tradition of journals (think of Thoreau's journals, for example) has always been one that kept in mind a later auditor—one's heirs, one's reading public, or one's older self returning to a scene of earlier experience. And all of us who assign journals know that what gets written as private discourse will (or should) also be written with the consciousness that another reader (namely the teacher) will eventually read it. Since Steve (himself a widely published short story writer as well as the author of scholarly books on American literature and the modern novel) favors writing that has a conversational feel and that avoids pompous and pedantic language, his selection of journal entries for reading aloud encourages students to keep their writing conversational rather than stiffly academic and to preserve the pose of writing for themselves while also writing for an audience largely of their peers.

What About Formal Academic Papers?

Steve's approach to writing about literature in his classes works perfectly with his students and courses, and some adaptation of it would surely work in many classes in college and in secondary schools. But those of us who teach more introductory literature courses (including virtually all English teachers in secondary school) may feel that we have to give a higher priority to teaching more formal academic writing in our literature classes. So while nothing prevents us from assigning students logs or journals, the reality of our classroom context is such that we have to reserve an equally prominent place in our syllabus for a serious effort at teaching and having students work on the formal academic literary paper.

Unfortunately, another reality of classroom life is that such academic assignments often seem self-defeating. Literature teachers in secondary schools and in college English courses typically report that many of their students can engage in intelligent, literate, and even eloquent discourse in journal writing and freewriting exercises, where they give every appearance of understanding and responding insightfully to the texts under study, but not when it comes time for them to write formal academic papers (Hammond 1991). Then these same students appear to have nothing interesting to say and whatever they manage to say sounds as if it were written by a language machine with a hyperactive thesaurus. And this can be the case no matter how well-framed and potentially engaging an assignment might be, because that may be the kind of writing our students think they are obliged to produce.

It's possible, in fact, that previous instruction has disabled some students by convincing them, as some conscientious teachers have been known to do, never to use the first person in formal writing and to avoid any of the flavor of their own idiomatic speech. The result of this largely misguided (but not entirely baseless) advice is that students with native or nativelike mastery of English—students who are capable of intelligent, fluent, and felicitous discourse in their own nearly standard idiom (an idiom easily fashioned into Standard Written English with only a little editing)—produce sentences so wrenched to avoid a natural "I" and so couched in overblown and pretentious diction as to obscure their meaning from the writer as well as the reader.

Equally sad and self-defeating is the fact that such attention to making a particular kind of impression on readers almost always perverts a student's sense of what purposes an academic paper might serve, since it would seem clear that its purpose is to demonstrate one's intellectual credentials by sounding as much as possible like a cartoon version of a professor. Don't imagine that you can make any intellectual contribution to your teacher's thinking or to the conversation of your classroom. Just say what seems to be a safe thing to say or what everybody already knows to be true, and show that you can sound professorial doing it. And remember that you'll never sound intelligent if you sound anything like yourself (and never use "you," which is even worse than using "I").

That reasoning is not a parody of what students think. It captures quite accurately what intelligent and otherwise literate students have told me over the years when I have worked with them to uncover the source of sentences and paragraphs that no native speaker of English would ever produce under anything like normal discourse conditions. For such students, an assignment to write a formal academic paper is an assignment to make themselves stupid. They fall over themselves trying to make what they think of as their own pedestrian thoughts or commonplace ideas (which may, in fact, be quite powerful and interesting ideas) sound smarter than they believe they actually are. Such language use is perverse in the sense that it violates most of the tacit rules or conversational maxims (Grice 1975) that have been found to govern conversations in most ordinary human transactions where people are exchanging information—maxims like try to be as clear as possible, avoid obscurity in expression, avoid excessive wordiness, say what you mean, say what needs to be said, don't try to confuse your auditor, say what you think to be true, do not say that for which you lack adequate evidence, and so on. More simply stated, what students do—and think they are required to do—in their overdressed and underconceptualized formal papers represents in most contexts and communities a dishonest and socially inappropriate use of language.

It is not always easy to persuade students to give up their indecorous pose of premature middle-aged authority in their writing, though they are generally relieved to know that they are free to use the first person, even if they think that my permission is idiosyncratic. The evidence on the use of "I" is quite compelling, however. Our own studies a dozen years ago in California (McClelland, Blau, and Nicholson 1990) revealed that about 20 percent of all high school teachers teaching college prep English courses proscribed the use of the first person in the belief that it was also prohibited by college instructors, while virtually no freshman English instructors at seven campuses of the University of California at that time prohibited the use of the first person in papers written for their classes. My recent conversations with teachers around the country have led me to suspect that in university English departments, the prohibition against the first person remains largely regarded as a misguided high school fetish, but that it has increased its hold in high schools in California and in other states where the standards movement has instigated a (generally healthy) focus on academic writing and college preparatory work in English for all students.

This is not to say that there are no college classes where it would be inappropriate to use the first person in writing assignments. It is generally unacceptable in lab reports in the hard sciences and apparently in a number of other forms of science writing, including papers written in some of the branches of the social sciences (experimental psychology, for example). But it is difficult to read a collection of scholarly or professional articles in any branch of the humanities or in many of the social sciences and in such professions as the law (including legal opinions written by state and federal judges) without noticing the judicious use of the first person, when it is called for and when alternative structures would be infelicitous.

As an empirical test of my claim that first-person discourse routinely appears in the most prestigious and most authoritative academic writing in the humanities and in related fields, I conducted a simple experiment with a collection of documents that represents what has to be the most influential and academically respected body of writing in the contemporary world of literary and humanistic studies, *The Norton Anthology of Theory and Criticism* (2001), edited by Vincent Leitch and a team of prominent American literary theorists. Scrupulously careful not to prejudice my experiment by selecting any passages or section of the volume beforehand, I opened *The Norton Anthology of Theory and Criticism* randomly twenty times and read the page I opened to. I then discounted my initial attempt because I had opened to a page of introductory notes, which necessarily spoke in the corporate voice of a team of editors and could not be classified as the kind of discourse I was examining. Of the nineteen times I opened to a text articulating theory or criticism, I found the author on that page speaking in the first-person singular thirteen times. Only six of the nineteen random pages I examined did not employ a first-person-singular usage on that page. But of the nineteen selections examined, only one avoided the use of "I" throughout the pages of the selection printed in the anthology—and that one, quite ironically, was by one of the leading theoreticians of a personal response to literature, Wolfgang Iser. That is to say, eighteen of the nineteen selections randomly picked from among the most prestigious pieces of academic writing in the field of literary theory were found to employ first-person-singular discourse within the excerpted essay or chapter examined, and sentences employing "I" representing the voice of the author (excluding quotations from other authors within the text) actually appeared on 68 percent of the total number of randomly selected pages.

If such writers and such pieces of writing (see endnote for a list of authors and works examined) do not eschew the first-person singular, by what authority do any teachers of English counsel their students to avoid the first-person singular in essays on literature because it is a practice unacceptable in the academic community? Recently a junior high school teacher, willing to defend her practice of forbidding the use of "I," told me quite forcefully that she was not seeking to exclude the first person, but trying to prevent her students from indulging in what she saw as a rhetorically disempowering habit of prefacing every idea with the phrase "I think." I wasn't sharp enough at that moment to suggest that she would then more logically forbid the use of the word *think* rather than the word *I*, or, most logically, forbid the whole offending phrase rather than any innocent word at all.

But I don't mean to blame secondary school teachers or the misguided prohibition of the first person for most of the troubled prose produced by college students in literature classes. Many students who are willing to believe that they don't have to disappear linguistically as agents in their academic writing are reluctant for their own reasons to relinquish their conviction that academic writing requires a kind of pedantic posturing. And their reluctance may seem supported by what appears to be empirical evidence. Certainly most of the authoritative academic discourse they hear and read appears to them (and is) far more sophisticated in language and conception than anything they feel capable of producing themselves (see Fleischer 1992). And it is surely the case that most of us who teach writing in the context of any academic discipline want our students to become conversant with the technical terms and jargon that allow us to make subtle distinctions and articulate ideas with some exactitude in our field. It is also the case that the discourse communities into which undergraduate courses and advanced high school courses initiate students are defined in part by a shared specialized language.

Looking back at the previous few pages in this chapter, I can identify several terms that would not be familiar (at least as they are used here) to most undergraduates or to most adults outside the academic community and perhaps outside the community of specialists in language and literature. These include, among others, *genre*, *problematize*, *discourse*, *auditor*, *infelicitous*, *derivative*, and one that my editor will probably question—*topos*. But the use of such terms and the relative sophistication of my vocabulary (compared with that of an average college freshman, for example) is not evidence that in my writing I am trying to sound like someone other than the person I am in my ordinary conversations with colleagues and friends. In fact, most scholars would regard it as a compliment to be told by colleagues that their academic writing had the flavor and sound of their spoken discourse. I know (having read transcripts of my talk) that I don't speak exactly as I write, but I hope and trust that my writing is something like the flower of the way I talk on similar topics and to similar auditors, with the dirt that is the growth medium invisible and the thorns, unsightly stems, and extra leaves thoughtfully pruned.

If my writing includes phrases and terms that identify me with the academic community to which I belong, that's because I am a member of such a community and my working vocabulary naturally includes the specialized lexicon of my professional life. In other words, when I compose in my writing, I do not adopt a special language in order to sound academic. I am an academic. I simply write in the language I ordinarily use in my professional life (with some editing to reflect conventions of writing that differ slightly from conventions of written speech) to talk about and even to think about similar topics. If I were consciously trying to sound like somebody who is not I, I couldn't think about the topic of my discourse very well, because I would be giving too much attention to the way I sounded. Moreover, to try to sound academic is a formula for sounding foolish. It's very much like the impersonation of the cool American swingers produced by the wild and crazy immigrant brothers (played by Dan Aykroyd and Steve Martin) in the classic shows of *Saturday Night Live*.

The language that academics use, like the language everybody else uses, reflects their experience and is acquired gradually through their participation in an academic community. And it will come to all students in the same way as they too participate in a particular academic community, which will almost inevitably mean that they will learn, in part, by imitating in their own speech and writing the speech of their teachers and respected peers. They will, at least, if they feel able to identify themselves as members or potential members of the community into which they are becoming initiated.

There is a subtle but important difference here that we ought to observe between imitation or what we can also call *appropriation* on the one hand and *impersonation* on the other. The difference closely resembles the difference T. S. Eliot pointed to when he quipped that minor writers borrow and major writers steal. When students who identify themselves as members of a classroom community adopt some of the verbal mannerisms of their teachers and colleagues to articulate concepts and use ideas that are becoming their own, they are engaged in the same kind of process that defines the learning of language and thought by children in their interactions with parents and older siblings (Bruner 1978). We can also say that they are operating in what Vygotsky (1978) called the zone of proximal development, the zone where genuine learning takes place as learners use the assistance of others to achieve what they are just about capable of achieving on their own, but can't quite achieve without such assistance. Learning that takes place in such a manner (as described by Lee and Smagorinsky [2000, 2] in their summary of Vygotskian principles) often involves mentoring by more knowledgeable colleagues or teachers. What is learned in such a social context, moreover, constitutes jointly constructed knowledge produced through the interactions of each learner and the other participants. The language and concepts learned and taken up by a student through such an *interpsychological* process are said to be *appropriated* (i.e., stolen, not borrowed) by the student, which is to say, taken up in genuine use and employed as if they were the learner's own.

The difference between such a use of appropriated terms and concepts and the borrowed language adopted by a student who is doing what I have called an impersonation of an academic is the difference between experiencing an engaged and authentic relationship to one's discourse and experiencing an alienated and inauthentic relationship to one's discourse. Students who feel alienated from their discourse tend to experience the act of writing much as Cathy Fleischer's (1992) former student did when, speaking of academic writing in the university, she complained: "Even when I'm writing, I don't feel like I'm writing," with the emphasis, I assume, on the second "I," saying, in other words, that in academic writing, it is not I who writes (183). We can't help wondering if the absence of the "I" that she reports is a linguistic as well as a psychological fact.

To try to get a college freshman or sophomore in an introductory literature course to sound like a graduate student in English may seem like a good idea to a graduate student instructor who likes being a model for his students, but it makes little psycholinguistic, pedagogical, or rhetorical sense. What does make sense is to encourage all students to participate as actively and as much as possible in the discourse of a discipline (mainly through writing and talking as well as through reading and listening) so they can build the kind of authentic knowledge that they can possess as their own rather than as borrowed from someone else. In the course of such active learning, students will also acquire and begin to use the language of the discipline, sometimes, perhaps, stumbling in its use as may be necessary for any novice, but always in the interest of extending the boundaries of their own thought and language rather than trying to do an impersonation of some speaker more intellectually sophisticated than themselves.

My own cautionary rule for students, designed to counteract their self-defeating ambition to adopt an alienating and falsely elevated discourse, is to "try to sound as dumb as you are." It's a maxim that can work well for students because it functions as a therapeutic double bind. That is, if you try to sound as dumb as you are, you won't really have to try at all. You will simply trust your own voice and not give any attention to trying to sound any particular way. Your attention will then be free to focus on your ideas and getting them straight and clear and not on how they sound. And if that's where you put your focus, you'll surely produce prose that is a good deal smarter than it would be if you were trying to sound smart. By trying to sound as dumb as you are, in other words, you allow yourself (without trying) to also sound as smart as you are. And that is as well as any of us can do.

Let us now turn to some model assignments that may encourage students to be as smart as they are and to grow smarter, not through the self-betrayal of trying (like Adam and Faust) to be someone they have not yet become, but through the slow and sometimes difficult development of authentic knowledge that is fostered (in the Vygotskian zone of proximal development) through discourse with teachers and peers as members of a learning community and through the instructive process of writing itself.

Note

The authors and excerpts I randomly examined in *The Norton Anthology of Theory and Criticism* for first-person usage were (in chronological order) the following:

Giovanni Boccaccio, from *Genealogy of the Gentile Gods*

Giacopo Mazzoni, from *On the Defense of the Comedy of Dante*

Samuel Johnson, from "Preface to Shakespeare"

Mary Wollstonecraft, from *A Vindication of the Rights of Woman*

Percy Shelley, from "A Defense of Poetry"

Sigmund Freud, from the "Uncanny"

Boris Eichenbaum, from "The Theory of the 'Formal Method'"

Martin Heidegger, from "Language"

Cleanth Brooks, from *The Well Wrought Urn*

Northrop Frye, from "The Archetypes of Literature"

Louis Althusser, from *On Ideology*

Hans Robert Jauss, from "Literary History as a Challenge to Literary Theory"

Wolfgang Iser, from "Interaction Between Text and Reader" from *The Act of Reading*

Adrienne Rich, from "Compulsory Heterosexuality and Lesbian Experience"

Stuart Hall, from "Cultural Studies and Its Theoretical Legacies"

Edward Said, from *Orientalism*

Stanley Fish, from "Interpreting the *Variorium*"

Jane Tompkins, from "Me and My Shadow"

Gloria Anzaldua, from *Borderlands*

Homi Bhabha, from "The Commitment to Theory"

Judith Butler, from *Gender Trouble*

8

Writing Assignments in Literature Classes
Models for Solutions-in-Progress

In this chapter I want to present some writing assignments that are designed to help students in literature classes become producers as well as consumers of literary knowledge and active participants in a version of an academic community—in this case, the community of the classroom, including the students and the teacher who constitute it in any particular academic term and those students who will arrive in subsequent academic terms or years. With each of these assignments I'll also describe the preparatory or corollary teaching that I have found useful to do in support of the assignment, and I'll comment on problems I have encountered and sometimes solved in implementing each assignment in my own classes.

The Reading Log

Here is how I describe this assignment in my syllabus:

> Every student will be required to maintain a reading log to record impressions of, responses to, and reflections on assigned and self-selected literary works as they are being read and studied and at the conclusion of each reading. These logs should be useful to you in several ways. First, they will help you to notice what you notice as you read—the first step toward becoming an independent and powerful reader. Recording what you notice in your log will also help you discover the value of your own

impressions, observations, questions, and other responses as starting points for illuminating discussions of literary works. Your log will also provide you with a place to do some low-stakes writing, experimenting with critical approaches and new strategies of analysis introduced to you in this course. Finally, the responses, reflections, and experiments recorded in your log will serve as a reservoir of ideas and first-draft writing you can draw upon for the public and more formal papers you will be asked to submit during the quarter. Although your log is largely a private document, written primarily for your own use, you will be asked occasionally to share some entries with classmates and to allow your instructor to audit your logging work. Your log entries will thereby document your reading for the course.

Your log will be of most use to you as a resource and as a record of your reading if you carefully date each entry and make it clear what text or segment of text you are writing about. So that you might periodically turn in sections of your log, it is wise to use a loose-leaf binder for your log.

To introduce students to the work of keeping a reading log, I read them a range of what I regard as exemplary log entries collected in previous classes and I ask them to read a short (fairly easy) poem and write a log entry for it in class and then share their entries in small groups. I also share with them an entry I made on the same poem some years ago. The idea of this introductory work to reading logs is to give students a sense of the almost unlimited range of possibilities for writing in their logs and to foster in them a sense of their ownership of the writing they do in their logs. Yet, at the same time, I am trying to help them experience how their log entries are also potential contributions to the discourse of our classroom as we read, interpret, and reflect on a variety of literary works, and especially as we identify questions and problems that trouble us in our reading of the assigned texts.

The real difficulty and the advantage that the log presents for many students are the discipline it requires to use it regularly when reading and the necessity it imposes for actually keeping up with the reading assigned in the course. These are also a difficulty and an advantage for the teacher. The advantage is that the log can become a substitute for quizzes or other forms of monitoring student work in the course. And it is a better monitor than quizzes because we get the opportunity through the log to see how our students are responding to what they are reading and what sorts of problems they are encountering and so on. We get much more information and more reliable information about their reading, in other words, than we are likely to get from any short quiz. The problem for us is that we only get the information if we read or otherwise check the log. Many students need to know that we will be checking up on them regularly in order to keep them on track with their reading and log work.

The logs become almost pointless and little more than a bureaucratic hurdle when a student who has been doing the reading but not writing in his log tries near the end of the term to fill up a log to satisfy the requirement. So it is very much in our students' interest and in ours if we collect the logs often (even if we merely spot-check a few of them) or find some other way to monitor students' use of their logs at fairly frequent intervals. And this becomes even more important with younger and academically less committed students.

My own very imperfect method with my university students (mostly college sophomores who are extremely responsible) has usually been to ask students to show me their logs in office visits (and sometimes as I make rounds during class time) throughout the academic term and to collect their logs for a formal review at midterm and at the end of the term in a ten-week academic quarter. My end-of-term review of their logs takes place in the context of my review of their portfolios, when I ask them to also review their own log or journal work for the entire term and reflect in a written introduction to the log (which I quite inconsistently call a "journal") on how their journal writing may have changed in the course of the quarter, how their journal may reveal changes in their reading practices, what they think of various kinds of journal entries, which entries they now find most or least interesting, and so on.

The midterm check on student journals has always been an enormous problem for me (as it will be for almost any teacher, already burdened by too much student work to read in an overcommitted schedule), and it became more problematic during the years when my travel schedule took me out of town by airplane three out of every four weekends during the academic year and I didn't want to pack thirty reading logs to review on the plane. So (inspired by a practice the eminent author and teacher-educator Dan Kirby employs to keep track of student progress in a writing workshop), I began to ask my students to do the midterm review of their journals for me and to report the results to me in a short report that I called the midterm reading log audit. Here are the instructions I gave to my students for such an audit for a fall-quarter introduction to literature course, where all our reading for the first five weeks of the course was in poetry.

Reading Log Audit

As a way of reporting your work-in-progress on your reading logs, please conduct the reading log audit described here and submit an audit report by Wednesday, October 25. Your audit report will include two major sections: your own descriptive, analytic, and reflective account of what you find in your reading log (about two to three pages in length) and three sample entries from your log. In composing and putting together your report, make sure you address the kinds of questions listed under each heading below:

1. Description: A Brief Tour. The idea of the description is to show your reader what he would see if he were to read your log. That means your description should include information answering such questions as the following: How many entries have you written? What is their average length? How many are

long or short or in between? How many poems have you written about? What does your log look like?

2. Analysis. In this section of your report you should discuss the content of your log entries, answering such questions as the following: What do you usually talk about in your log entries? What elements of poems do you tend to comment on, or what is it that you tend to talk about in your commentaries on the poems? How have your log entries changed (if they have) over the past few weeks? What changes do you notice in length, topics, language, and so on? What might account for differences in the content, length, or quality of your entries? What else do you notice about your log entries? Refer to specific entries as examples. Feel free to quote from your entries as needed.

3. Reflection. Think about what your log entries amount to. Do you find any worthwhile writing in your log? What value do you place on this log or on some of its entries? Have you found any reason for keeping a reading log other than because the instructor assigned it? If you were the teacher of this course, would you ask your students to keep a reading log? Why or why not? What do the sample entries you have included show your reader about your log?

4. Sample Log Entries. Choose three log entries that you feel are representative of the content of your reading log. These need not be the "best" entries, but rather those that you feel offer the most accurate picture of the kind of writing your journal contains. Please photocopy these entries for submission as part of your audit report, showing the date when each was originally written. If the entries that you would like to submit as most representative are not legible, please type them out or otherwise rewrite them legibly before including them in your report.

I have been pleased with what my students have done in their audits over the past couple of years and I am convinced that I'm getting fairly accurate information on what their journals contain. (My understanding with my students has been that I would also look over their logs informally at various points during the quarter, so there was an unspoken presumption that I would know whether their audits were honest.) More importantly, I believe that their midterm reflections on their logs as documents of their recent intellectual history and as evidence about the character and focus of their thinking have encouraged them to take the activity of writing in their logs more seriously as an intellectual event. It's my impression, in fact (though it may be an illusion), that the midterm audit has led many students who were initially reluctant journal writers to take their journal work more seriously in the second half of the term and to write more thoughtful and useful entries. Some students actually mention such a change in their end-of-term reflections on their journals, though I doubt that any analysis of the data could isolate causes for detectable improvements in journal work. One would hope that the journal entries of all students would become more sophisticated in the second half of the academic term as a function of their growth as readers.

Finally, I should note that I like the audit assignment for the way it gives students practice in and provides them with a model and a kind of scaffold for them in the production of literary discourse, taking them in their audit of their own log entries from reading or describing texts, to interpretation or the analysis of texts, to criticism or the evaluation of texts. But unlike most writing students are asked to produce about their reading, in this case the texts under analysis are those they have themselves written and have presented in the audit report as the focal objects for their literary discourse.

The Reading Process Research Report

This assignment asks students to engage in a systematic study of their own reading process as they read a challenging poem. It is usually the first major paper I require in my introduction to literature courses. I confess, however, that I have never come up with an entirely satisfactory solution to the problem of when to collect it.

I'd prefer to collect this paper from my students in the first week of the course, but because it takes about a week before my class roster is stable, I've never been able to set the paper deadline before the end of the second week. On the other hand, if I spend more time doing more preparatory work with students, as I have in some years, I can help my students conduct their study more effectively. With this paper, it even makes sense to have students conduct a pilot study to experiment with research methods. That would mean not collecting the paper before the end of week three. Yet I want the results of their study to be influenced as little as possible by what they are concurrently learning in my class about how to read literary works, partly so their process study can represent a benchmark for them of where they were at the beginning of the course and allow them (and me) to observe changes. But even if the paper is due at the end of the second week of the course, it has already probably been "contaminated" by my instruction in the first week. So the timing of this paper remains a problem for me, but a minor one, given what I believe the paper achieves whenever it is written.

Here is how I frame the assignment in my syllabus:

Reading Process Research Report

This paper will be an informal research report on your own mental processes as you attempt to read and make sense of an assigned short poem. The idea will be for you to conduct a study of yourself as a reader of a difficult text. Your paper will be an account of what you do as a reader from the first time you look at a poem until you complete your reading of it and have acquired some satisfactory sense of its meaning. Your report must also include a reflection on what your self-study reveals about you as a reader or about the particular demands of the work you are reading or about the reading process in general. A good research tool for you to use might be that of the think-aloud protocol, a transcript or portions of a transcript of a tape recording of you thinking out loud as you engage in the process of reading and rereading and trying to figure out a poem. In class we'll examine some ways of engaging in this sort of study. The poem to be used for this study will be announced in class. Additional guidelines for this paper will follow.

To lend importance to the study and the report, I used to call this a "formal" paper rather than the "informal research report" I call it now. But I have found that the unprecedented nature of the assignment panics many students who assume that they don't have any idea of how to go about conducting such a study and discourages them from experimenting and speculating freely about their findings, especially if they think they have to meet the constraints of some predetermined academic form. So I now emphasize the experimental nature of the study they are undertaking and invite them to do it in the spirit of play—which is to say, with all the seriousness of attention that children devote to their best moments in play, and with the same freedom to improvise and experiment that children feel because nothing is really at stake.

To dignify the entire study they are undertaking, I point out that literary theorists and specialists in reading at least since the time of I. A. Richards' *Practical Criticism* (1929) have puzzled over how readers come to make or to mistake meanings from texts. The progress of the mind in moving from a state in which a reader reads a poem but doesn't understand it, to a point at which he understands it—especially the moment in which there is a sudden sense of illumination—has long been a tantalizing mystery to literary criticism as well as to psychology and remains an insufficiently explored area of research to which our own experiments, including those we will be conducting through this research assignment, can now make a contribution.

To prepare students for their study of their own reading process, I conduct an exercise in class where I assign a poem that offers some challenge and then ask students to work in pairs and take turns playing experimental subject and researcher in a reading think-aloud experiment (see Wilhelm 2001). First, one student in each pair will read the poem aloud and say aloud everything she is thinking as she tries to make sense of the poem or as she experiences the poem. Some of what she will say are the words and lines of the poem itself. Some will be the thinking she is doing directed toward making sense of the poem (questions, translations or paraphrases, observations about the poem's language, images or memories that come to mind, and so on). Some of it will be about the strategies or process she is engaged in: what researchers who conduct protocol analyses call metaprocessing—for example, "First, I'm just going to try to get a general feel for the meaning," or "I usually like to read it twice." While the first student of the pair is doing this work out loud, her partner is listening and observing carefully and taking notes on what he hears and observes: does she point to lines with her finger, does she fidget, what questions does she ask, what does she do and say when she is stuck, and so on.

Then the partners switch roles and do the same thing again with the same poem, an easier task in some ways for the person who now has the role of reader, but no easier for the observer/note taker. (To avoid disputes about which partner should take which role first, I ask students to assign themselves a letter, A or B, as soon as they form the pairs but before they know what they will be doing, and then I tell them which letter takes which role first.) After the second round of the experiment, the students take turns telling each other what they observed and then discuss their find-ings. I urge them to try their hand at classifying the various acts of mind or reading strategies they observed or can infer from what a reader said aloud. Did readers visu-alize what they were reading, for example? Did they connect what they were reading to other poems they had read? Did they ask questions? And so on. The findings from various pairs are reported to the class and further discussed as data suggesting some tentative hypotheses about the reading process or what some people do in the pro-cess. The idea, of course, is to begin to develop a model and a language for examin-ing and describing one's own reading process and reflecting on findings from that examination.[1]

When I formally make the paper assignment and hand out the poem to be used, I warn students to start tracking their thinking process from the first moment they lay eyes on the poem and urge them to feel free to experiment with various methods for conducting their study (most use note taking instead of a tape recording of a think-aloud). I mention as well that whatever they do or want to do in working on the poem is of interest in this experiment and that if they want to call a friend for help with the poem or discuss it with their roommate, that would be fine and needs to be in-cluded as part of their data and in their report. I then read aloud and comment on sample papers from students from previous years (working on different poems), not-ing some great variations in the forms chosen for the report. These include a paper written in the form of a lab report and another taking the form of a familiar essay. Finally, I give out the following guidelines (based on past experience) for writing a successful paper.

Reading Process Research Report: Some Features of Successful Papers

- *They capture the reading process as a process.* They are based on a carefully con-structed record of what the reader actually did and thought.
- *They show the progress of a mind.* They show (they don't merely tell about) how the writer was thinking in the course of reading the poem, but they se-lectively show. They don't present more raw data than an auditor can make use of. Additional data can go in an appendix.
- *They interpret the poem and explain how the interpretation emerged and changed.* They show the substance of the meaning that the reader constructed in the

course of the reading. They explain the meaning that emerges from the process and how it changes and what is and isn't clear.

- *They refer specifically to the text.* They refer to specific words and lines in the
  poem, so the auditor can see how the reader moved from the lines in the poem
  to the interpretive statements offered about those lines.
- *They capture this particular experience.* They are based on the reader's experience with this poem and not with poems in general, and they distinguish carefully between what happened with this poem and what usually happens or is
  supposed to happen.
- *They include some analysis and/or reflection.* They provide some analysis of the
  process shown or reflect on the process to draw conclusions about what usually happens or might happen.

Here I want to emphasize what I repeatedly emphasize for my students: the importance of making sure the report includes the substantive thinking that is going on in
the process as well as the naming of the mental actions that are taking place. It is
not enough to say: "Then I put the poem into my own words." We need to see the
words that the poem was put into. We need to see at every moment, insofar as possible, precisely what meaning the reader is making of the poem in the very words (or
images) that the reader is using in his or her thinking. It's the careful record of the
content of such thinking that reveals how meaning comes into being and gets reshaped
in the reading of a poem.

During the week or two that students are working on their papers, I invite them
to report in class on how they are collecting their data and what problems they are
finding. These reports by some students on their research-in-progress help others
anticipate and solve problems they are having or might have, and encourage all students to begin work sometime before the usual last minute. I push my class, in other
words, to function like a research community of genuinely interested participants,
where methods and problems are shared and discussed in the interest of advancing
methodology as well as substantive knowledge.

Over the past couple of years I have sometimes added a twist to the reading process research study that seems to me to enrich the research experience of students
from the point when they would ordinarily submit their papers for evaluation. When
students bring their papers to class expecting to submit them to me, I have them read
them to each other in small groups and discuss the experience of the experiment as
well as the poem itself. Then, instead of asking my students to turn their papers in, I
invite them to postpone submission until the following class meeting, so they can add
an additional section to their currently completed paper describing the impact of the
group discussion and of the readings of others on their own reading. In other words,
I invite them to extend their paper on their reading process and their conception of
what that process includes to include the classroom work on the poem that takes place
when students share their papers and their readings with their classmates. Most students take up the opportunity to revisit the poem and revise their papers with the

benefit of their colleagues' readings and responses. And the results seem to me useful and reflective of authentic practice in my classroom, since virtually all papers written for my courses and surely all readings of difficult poems in my classes are discussed in groups before the readings or the papers are treated as submissible drafts.

Pedagogical Aims

The reading process paper serves a number of pedagogical aims, aside from that of getting students to write about their interpretations of texts, but it is also an excellent introduction to such writing. The focus on process frees students to engage in their interpretive writing with what they generally experience as a refreshing honesty. Moreover, for many students it is their first experience in writing a literary paper where they were not working to approximate an existing correct interpretation that they presumed their papers would be measured against. Here, the interest they have in their teacher's interpretation and in the interpretations of peers is likely to be an expression of genuine intellectual interest derived from a common intellectual project and not a self-protective or self-serving interest. The reading process research paper puts a premium not on coming up with the right reading, but on students noticing, recording, and sharing the workings of their own minds as they make their way through a difficult text. Thus, it shifts the intellectual focus of the classroom from an interest in right answers to an interest in problems and in strategies for solving them.

Two important additional instructional aims are achieved with this shift. First, it moves the classroom toward becoming a laboratory for investigating thinking processes and problem-solving strategies, thereby privileging and enhancing metacognitive skills and helping students become more conscious readers, better able to monitor and control what and how they are thinking as they read. Such skills are crucial to the development of the kind of disciplined or strategic literacy that sustains students in the reading of difficult texts and that is essential to an advanced literary competence (see Olson 2003; Schoenbach et al. 1999; Wilhelm, Baker, and Dube 2001; and Chapter 2 of this volume). Additionally, in sharing their reading processes in class, students learn about strategies they may never have tried and get to share tips on how they might refine or otherwise revise strategies they already employ in the reading of literature, thereby expanding and enriching their own strategic repertoire as readers.

Finally, the reading process paper shifts the focus of learning in the literature classroom away from what students can come to know as novices or recipients of the learning of others and toward what they can achieve as persons who are capable of producing knowledge and making a contribution to the collective expertise of their classroom community, which is surely what they do in conducting and sharing what amounts to original research on their own reading processes. That shift is important not simply to foster the development of a classroom that functions as a learning community but to help students take an important step in defining their own roles as active and valuable members of that community.

The Formal Literary Paper: The Interpretation Project

This assignment represents my attempt to re-create in a writing assignment for students the intellectual tasks and benefits that are entailed in the production of an academic or professional paper by a member of an academic or professional community. Those benefits need to be rehearsed briefly as a rationale for requiring formal papers in literature classes in the first place.

I have already made the case for writing in the literature class—a case that rests, first, on the value of writing as a way of constructing and thereby acquiring and taking first-hand possession of one's knowledge. It may not be fair to say, as Scholes (1982) and others might say, that we know a literary work only to the extent that we articulate what we know in speech or in writing, but the advantages that writing offers for refining, clarifying, and making our knowledge more coherent for ourselves as well as for our auditors still make a compelling case for requiring a good deal of writing in connection with literary study and making sure that at least some of the writing is directed to an audience beyond the self. Where, then, in the academic community or elsewhere in the universe of discourse can we look to find the models for such writing?

The Need for Models

Every act of writing (and possibly every utterance) is shaped and understood by the constraints and traditions of the genre in which it participates. No one entering a field of discourse can know how or what to write without some tacit or explicit knowledge of the discourse types available for imitation. One cannot tell a story without having in one's head a story grammar—the knowledge needed to present characters, develop a plot, create conflicts, and so on. Even children of preschool age know enough about the conventions of a story to recognize that when they hear "once upon a time," they are going to hear a story, and that when they want to tell a story they can begin with the same phrase.

A law student learning how to write a brief must first know what a brief looks like. A medical student writing up a report on a patient will typically look at available files to see several model reports in order to know what is expected in that particular hospital or clinic setting for the form and content of a report. A student asked to write a paper in a literature course similarly needs to know what such a paper looks like. But it appears from the classrooms I have visited that very few teachers actually show students any models for use at any grade or level of schooling before graduate school.

Teachers who are asked about what they imagine as the real-world models for the literary papers they assign in high school or in lower-division college English courses will usually acknowledge that they have hardly thought about the question or else point to a model for a five-paragraph essay—such as will never appear in the real world—in some textbook. College teachers will more often respond by identifying scholarly articles in professional journals, or the tradition of the literary essay in nonacademic publications like *Harper's* and *Atlantic Monthly*, or the highly professional, elegant, but consciously nonacademic essays that appear in such journals as the *Yale Review*, the *Kenyon Review*, or the *New York Review of Books*.

But very few teachers outside of graduate programs ever ask their high school or college literature students to read literary articles in the journals where presumed exemplars might appear or show students any examples at all of what might be identified as a model in the real world. And with good reason. For if students were to read any of the presumed models for what they are being asked to write, they would find the gap between what they had thought they were doing and what is being presented as their model so wide as to be unbridgeable, either condemning them to failure in their writing or rendering the model irrelevant.

They would at least feel incapable of inhabiting the role (the ethos) of the speaker in a professional article about literature—a role that would require them to represent themselves as conversant with the body of contemporary and traditional critical discourse on the work and author being discussed, knowledgeable about the cultural and literary context for the work, and in possession of sufficient expertise to speak for and to an entire field of study. Such knowledge and expertise may be desiderated for graduate students who are preparing for academic careers, but can hardly be expected of students early in their undergraduate education or before.

The most honest or the most realistic answer about where to find models for student literary essays may be that they are implicit in the heads of teachers, based on their experience in writing such papers as students and reading them as teachers. And this suggests that if there is a model for the student literary paper, it is the genre of the student literary paper itself and not any essay or article form that can be found outside of school.

The cultural power of the school to create and sustain genres of discourse is explicitly recognized in a good deal of recent work written for teachers directed to helping them raise test scores and improve the writing performance of middle school and high school students. The most helpful and demonstrably successful programs I have seen of this kind tend to treat the literary essay, not surprisingly, as a version of the traditional school-sponsored thesis-argument or thesis-proof essay, in which the writer advances a thesis and then produces warrants and arguments to prove it (see Olson 2003, Chapter 8). Similarly, college textbooks in composition and literature typically present the literary essay as a subspecies of the argumentative essay, in which one advances an interpretive or analytic claim as a thesis and then gives evidence to support it (see, for example, Griffith 1998, 175; Axelrod and Cooper 2001). My own conversations with college prep and college literature teachers around the country suggest, moreover, that even where the scholarly article in journals for literary studies is cited as the real-world model for student essays, the thesis-proof essay remains the prevailing form for college prep (especially AP) classes and undergraduate literary essays, and that mastery of that form is widely seen as a key to success in college literature courses and, apparently, in graduate courses as well (Sullivan 1994, 43).

While I have serious concerns about the intellectual limitations of the thesis-argument essay, I am not inclined to argue with the wisdom of the teaching tradition that has led to its dominance in literature instruction. In fact, I argued earlier (Chapter 1) that the teaching of literature necessarily entails teaching students to interpret literary texts, and that the thinking that informs interpretation is fundamentally a form of evidentiary reasoning of the kind that would be practiced in a thesis-argument essay. My principal concern with the tradition of such an essay form in literature classes is that its unquestioned dominance in schools and colleges and the virtual absence of living models of such essays in the real-world reading experience of students (even if such essays are dominant—and I think they are not—in the published writing of the academic world[2]) have rendered it an ossified and ritually practiced form unlikely to be perceived by students (or their teachers) as having much authentic social or intellectual purpose, even if it will produce a respectable score on an Advanced Placement test or on similar assessments of competence in writing about literature. (For an excellent account of the limitations of the thesis-driven essay, see Chapter 7 of Bruce Pirie's *Reshaping High School English*, 1997.)

The assignment I am presenting here for a formal paper represents an attempt to recover the social and intellectual benefits of professional academic papers for essays written by students within the context of an introductory literature course. It takes as its model the professional academic paper in the sense that it is based on a conception of the classroom as a version or microcosm of the academic community constituted by a specialized field of study with its own professional journals and conferences. It then asks that students become active contributors to knowledge within the academic community of their classroom by producing papers that function much in the same way that papers function within any academic community—to refine the discourse of the community by advancing knowledge, clarifying concepts, challenging theories, and uncovering problems within the discursive space constituted by the topics, problems, texts, and methods of inquiry that define an academic field.

It might be argued that all classrooms are academic communities (whether teachers and students in them realize it or not) in which all writing serves the cultural purposes honored or allowed within that community. The question then becomes one of how such a community may be organized, what counts in the community as learning and knowledge, who or what is regarded as a source of knowledge, and what sorts of opportunities for learning and for communicating knowledge are made available to whom, for what purposes, under what conditions, and so on (Green and Dixon 1993; Yeager, Floriani, and Green 1998). The question is, To what extent will a classroom community function as a healthy learning community for all its members and imitate the most productive and intellectually vital academic communities and not the most repressive or stagnant ones? Even professional academic communities (particularly those operating under totalitarian regimes) have been known to operate in ways that have suppressed knowledge, limited opportunities for learning, and invested the power to determine what counted as knowledge in unworthy and arbitrary authorities.

The paper assignment I am presenting here is one designed to nurture and to reflect an ideal, healthy, and democratic academic community that provides rich opportunities for learning for all its members. And since ideals are usually defined more by what is sought than what is achieved, I will acknowledge at the outset that this paper assignment and the classes where I have employed it have never quite achieved all that I have hoped for them. But I have seen results that are highly satisfactory and that give me sufficient confidence in the assignment to offer it to colleagues not as a recipe, but as an unfinished blueprint for an instructional strategy that I plan to continue revising and refining and that I trust will be improved upon by teachers who appropriate these plans for the classroom cultures they are coconstructing with their students.

Here is the assignment as I have most recently presented it on a handout to my students.

The Interpretation Project: Poems and Stories

For this project you are to take on an interpretively difficult or problematic poem or short story (or passage therein) and write a brief paper presenting the interpretive problem and exploring possible solutions. Ideally, in the course of working on this paper, you will resolve the problem in a way that is satisfying for you and convincing to your reader. However, it is possible—even likely—that your work on the problem will advance your understanding of the problem and clarify its dimensions for your reader, but that your paper will still not reach any conclusion that might be called a solution or resolution for the problem you have examined.

This project and the study it entails will be completed in two stages, with each stage yielding a paper or a draft of a paper. The two stages of the project are described below.

Stage 1

The first stage of the project requires you to write an interpretive paper as described above on one of the texts listed below (all in our anthologies). Your choice of a text will be complicated, however, by the need to join a group of four to six students all of whom are required to agree on the one poem or story from the list that all the members of your small group will write about (or form your group with class members who come to class already interested in the same text you want to write about from the list below). However you form your group with members who will be writing about the same literary work, your job will be to write your paper and bring it with you to class on the specified date (see below) with copies for every member of your group (and one for your instructor). At that point you and the members of your group will read and respond to each other's papers and discuss the story or poem at length within your group during the class period.

In completing the paper for stage 1 you will not be expected to engage in any library research or use web-based resources (though there is no prohibition against them), but it would be wise to read the biographical sketch of your author either preceding the story or (for poets) at the back of our anthology. If you are writing about a poem, you may also want to read some additional poems by the same poet in our anthology. Stage 1 paper due Monday, November 4.

Read all eight of the eligible texts for this assignment ASAP, so that by Monday, October 28, you'll be able to join a group and select the text you'll be writing about. The eligible texts are the following:

John Donne, "The Flea"
Andrew Marvell, "To His Coy Mistress"
Robinson Jeffers, "Carmel Point"
Langston Hughes, "Theme for English B"
Gabriel Garcia Marquez, "A Very Old Man with Enormous Wings"
Ernest Hemingway, "Hills Like White Elephants"
Kurt Vonnegut Jr., "Harrison Bergeron"

Stage 2

This stage asks you to revise your paper in any way that you think will strengthen it, but with the one additional requirement that you now draw upon one or more of the papers written by your colleagues to support, clarify, or stand in contrast to your own ideas about the text. In other words, you are obliged to acknowledge in your paper the existence of a body of writing by your colleagues about the same literary work you are explicating and to incorporate the ideas of your colleagues (at least one of them and preferably more) into your paper, either to illuminate or support some point you wish to make or to show a contrasting or alternative point of view. You may quote from your colleague's paper or paraphrase or summarize what he or she has written, acknowledging your sources by using parenthetical abbreviated citations within your text and a list of references at the end. (Conventions and forms for citation will be discussed in class, well before the due date.) Stage 2 paper due Monday, November 11.

What the assignment attempts to do, in case it is not obvious, is acknowledge the classroom as the academic community to which students belong as students of literature and create in the classroom (through the collection of papers by peers on the same text) the kind of body of criticism or interpretive literature that would be found in the professional journals of any group of literary specialists on any subject likely to be addressed in a conference paper or article submitted for publication. It also draws upon the collective expertise of the classroom community to respond to and inform the emerging drafts of the papers of the members. Yet it avoids the fatal problems of using secondary sources that have led most undergraduate and precollege teachers to discourage rather than require the use of secondary sources by their students for critical or interpretive papers. Those problems include the tendency of many students to be overwhelmed by the authority of their sources and make their essays entirely derivative from what they read and the tendency to misunderstand or misuse—if they understand at all—the technical and deeply contextualized arguments and ideas they read in professional essays. Even in the context of this paper designed to enhance the authority of each student-author, some students may be inclined to relinquish their own most insightful interpretive ideas in favor of a colleague's less plausible but more forcefully presented interpretation. Follow-up work on the paper then provides a good opportunity to help students learn the value of weighing arguments carefully and both trusting and questioning their own ideas.

Of course, the assignment also presents students with the challenges that many teachers want to introduce in high school and in introductory college literature courses of citing sources and integrating quotations and ideas derived from sources into the texts and arguments of their own papers. That many if not most students need direct instruction in how to cite sources and, more importantly, how to incorporate derived ideas and language appropriately and accurately into their own texts will be revealed readily by the papers submitted in response to this assignment, unless those problems are anticipated and addressed in advance.

The follow-up paper to this assignment in my course has been a modified version of it (following three more weeks of reading short fiction) that actually does require students to make some use of secondary sources (at least one) but invites them to use only sources reprinted in their textbook and therefore preselected by the textbook editor for their readability and utility for undergraduate students. This assignment, like the previous one, also invites students to think about their essays rhetorically and structurally as representing a discourse type that is or may be something other than a thesis-proof essay.

Interpretive or Critical Paper on Short Fiction

In this paper you may explore any problem raised for you as a reader of one or more of the assigned stories or raised through class discussion of a story or its author. Or you may write an interpretive or critical paper on a story (or group of stories), offering simply to help a reader read it (or them) more deeply or comprehensively or pleasurably. Or you may want to advance some idea you have about a story or reflect on some idea you find advanced or illustrated by a story or several stories by a single author or different authors.

Whatever issue you address or problem you explore in your paper, please be certain to do some reading about the stories or authors or contexts and make some use of your reading in your essay. You may read any of the supplementary readings in our anthology—readings that were included to illuminate the stories—or you may use other resources that you find in journals or in books (or online) about the author or the story. The idea is simply to make sure that your essay is informed in some way by your engagement in a conversation that goes beyond your discussions with colleagues and your teacher to include perspectives available through the wider and more carefully constructed conversations that are represented by the body of published literature about literature.

Challenging the Hegemony of the Thesis-Argument Essay

While my assignment never mentions a thesis, argument, or proof and would seem to invite students to think about what they are writing as something other than an argument in support of a thesis, I have found that the thesis-argument structure is so fixed for many students as a model for writing that they can't imagine how to think about any topic they might write about through any other frame. I have therefore lately taken to offering students some additional models and definitions for formal essays, making the case that the alternative models I am suggesting appear in our professional literature and include some classic and influential essays and books about literature and particular literary texts. In fact, reviews of literary studies often refer to essays and books not as arguments but as "explorations" or "meditations" on particular topics, texts, or literary problems (also see my endnote).

Thus, I propose to students a discourse typology that offers them three different rhetorical or cognitive modes for structuring a literary essay and one alternative to what they think of as the essay form itself. The first three essay types are the following:

- The conventional thesis-argument or thesis-proof essay
- An exploratory essay—one that does not so much advance an argument as examine and explore avenues for solving an interpretive or critical problem (e.g., an exploration of the problem of point of view and narrative evaluation in Alice Walker's "Everyday Use")
- A meditation (which may be very close to an analysis) on an issue or topic or critical question about a text (e.g., the vexed relationship between the man and woman in Hemingway's "Hills Like White Elephants")

It might be possible to make the case that all of the forms I have listed are really versions of a thesis-argument essay, since both the alternative forms I have identified would probably need some focal issue or question that could be called a thesis as an organizing principle and source of coherence, and either of them could and very well might lead to something like a conclusion. Students would also need to provide support or illustrative examples and quotations to clarify and elaborate any points they might make in their papers. And if they didn't have any points to make, we would hardly find their papers worth reading.

Nor would I find it useful to offer a counterargument to that criticism. The issue is not what we call the discourse types that are allowable for literary essays, but that students understand that a literary essay need not be argumentative or driven by a thesis in the sense that it make a claim and then set out to prove it. I would like students to understand that a literary essay need not be more devoted to demonstrating the validity of a particular point of view than to illuminating and clarifying a sometimes uncertain and multidimensional reality (see Fort 1971; Zeiger 1985; Vinz 2000). While I am not arguing for the abolition of the thesis-argument essay in literature classes, I am arguing that students should be encouraged to sometimes abandon it, if the form of that essay requires them, for example, to argue for one interpretation over another when it might be more critically useful to open up additional possibilities for reading a text than closing down any one of them. I want them to abandon the thesis-argument essay, in other words, insofar as they believe that the form requires them to prove a particular point of view over others when their own understanding of a story or issue might be more richly illuminated by recognizing and affirming the value of multiple perspectives or uncertainty about any stable or single position as a correct one (see Bartolomae 1983, 311).

Finally, I offer students the option to adopt a fourth form, which is not so much an alternative to the thesis-argument essay as one to the essay form itself. That is, it offers an alternative idea about the form of the essay, as the essay is conventionally imagined in English classes:

- A collection of loosely connected notes or comments on a text or topic, each identified by a heading or number, requiring no transitions between them

With this alternative as an optional form for my students to adopt for their papers I am happy to instigate a minor revolution against the long single-topic paper as the only model for literary essays in English classes. Students have told me repeatedly over the years that they often respond to an assignment to write an eight- or ten-page paper with a paper that meets the length requirement, but that would have been better written in four or five pages (though I suspect that what some students think of as padding is actually useful and needed elaboration). It has also been my observation that many students, in discussing possible topics for papers, will eliminate some of the most promising and potentially illuminating topics because they can't see how they can write more than a couple of pages on the topic, rather than the four or five pages that they believe would be the minimum expectation in my courses (where I typically give no length requirements except to observe that papers in the past—some of which I show as models—have tended to be four to six pages in length). I have also noticed that I sometimes receive papers from students where two ideas are discussed and connected by a transition that doesn't work, so that the paper would have been more elegantly and honestly structured as a two-part paper with the two parts identified by numbers.

As a solution to all of these problems, I have found it productive to introduce to students the genre of the *note* or *comment* as a structure that may be too short for a conventional essay, yet adequate for the exploration or explanation of some idea worthy of attention in a smaller rhetorical package. My invitation to students is to recognize that they have the option of making their four- to seven-page paper a gathering of two or more or notes on some topic or text or group of related topics. They could simply call their paper "Notes on Ivan Illych" or "Interpretive Issues in X" and then write a series of notes or comments on the separate topics they wish to explore, not worrying about transitions between them, and certainly not creating false or strained transitions just because they are required by the protocol of the essay form. In this case no transitions are required or expected. The separate parts could be labeled by numbers or given distinct subtitle headings.

In practice I receive very few papers that take the form of a collection of notes or comments, though some students every term make excellent use of the option and produce papers that are among the best in the class. But many students have told me that they were liberated by the option to begin a paper on a topic they were interested in but would otherwise have dropped because it wouldn't yield more than a couple of pages of writing. Yet, having begun a paper as a note or comment—which is to say, without having to worry about going beyond one or two pages—they found that the one little topic they were working on as a short comment became, much to their surprise, a complete and highly satisfying five- or six-page paper. With the option of writing a series of short notes, students find no need to engage in the intellectually fraudulent practice of padding their papers; they find, instead, that their papers grow to a length dictated legitimately by the demands of their topic and the limits of their knowledge. They write either one unpadded long paper or a composite paper of equal length consisting of two or more short notes or comments.

Grading Papers and the Portfolio Assignment

I have no wish to enter into any debate on the best policy for grading papers, because I am so often ready to change my mind about how to do it. So I will share my policy here as one that serves my present purposes and fits the kind of writing assignments I make. I have not put a grade on an individual paper since 1967 or possibly 1968. And I have not had a complaint about that in at least twenty-five years. My reasons are fairly simple and fairly compelling for me, though every year for the past several years I have reconsidered my policy at the end of each term and thought that maybe next term I'll use grades. It might be easier.

The principal reason I give no grades to individual papers is that I don't know how I could encourage students, as I do, to take chances, to try experiments, to challenge themselves with new forms and a more honest style, and so on, if I were at the same time to give them a grade for every effort. I would then be asking them to do more than take the risk of trying out a new rhetorical approach or a more honest mode of self-presentation; I'd be asking them to risk consequences for their final grade in the course and possibly for their future as applicants for fellowships or graduate programs, where grades and grade point averages can matter. I also think that student work can be very uneven from paper to paper and sometimes within the same paper, so that grades for papers added up and averaged for a course may not reflect very well what a student has accomplished over time and at various moments in a course of study. Finally, once I stopped giving grades, many years ago, I found that I could talk to students more honestly and informatively about their papers and write more informative comments on their papers, because I didn't have to think about whether my commentary justified or failed to justify the grade I was awarding the paper (also see Elbow 2000, 399–421). A grade for an entire course or for a body of written work is another matter, however. It's been my impression that the prospect of an eventual grade is a help to most students, because it serves as an incentive for them to work hard and productively on all of their papers and throughout an academic course.

I do respond to the papers students submit at the time that they are written, however, and I respond both as an editor and a teacher, but largely to substantive matters. I often enter into conversations with students in my comments and invite them to write back (which they sometimes do). For my later use in awarding end-of-term grades (and for legibility), I try to type my comments on the computer and print them out for students, so I'll have a record of my comments to consult later. At the end of the term I collect the entire body of my students' written work for the course (with my earlier comments attached, I pray) to review for the final grade.

I didn't start calling these collections portfolios until the mid-seventies, when I did so in imitation of my wife's practice as a college art teacher who never graded any individual drawing or painting, but based her grades instead on what her students submitted in their end-of-term portfolios. With the advent of the portfolio movement in composition in the eighties, I began to reconceive the function of portfolios and to look at them as more than an opportunity for me to review student work for a grade. But they remain for me the principal collection of evidence I use to award final grades to my students in most of the courses I teach, for graduate students as well as under-graduates.

I'll present here the portfolio assignment I now give to undergraduate students in my lower-division introduction to literature course, English 10 (though it's hardly different from what I use for more specialized upper-division courses or graduate courses). I think it will be self-evident how the portfolio assignment as it has evolved for me avoids the pedagogical problems posed by grading individual papers, at the same time that it encourages students to take all their work seriously and give their best effort when producing written work on which their final grade will largely depend.

Portfolio Assignment

As a record and final product of your effort in this course, you are required to submit a portfolio representing the quantity and quality of your work in English 10. Your portfolio will represent a collection, a selection, and a reflection. It will constitute a collection of the body of your work, showing the quantity of your work for the quarter; it will allow you to identify a selection of the best work you have produced—the work that can best show the quality of your reading, writing, and thinking for the quarter; and it will afford you the opportunity to reflect on what your work has meant to you, what kind of development in your thinking or reading it represents, and what you think about what you have accomplished.

Content and Format

The Collection

Your collection may include everything you write in connection with this course this quarter. This includes your journal or log, all your papers in all their drafts, all in-class writing, notes, creative pieces written in class or inspired by the reading, letters you may have written to friends telling about your reading, or anything else that can be said to represent the reading, writing, and thinking you engaged in for English 10. Make sure that your collection is easy to handle (bound between covers or placed securely in a well-marked folder) and organized so that a reader will be able to locate sections and particular materials readily. Label sections clearly and provide a table of contents for the whole collection and possibly for whatever subsections you choose to create. Also provide a rough word count as a measure of the quantity of your writing for the quarter.

The Selection

This will represent your best writing and thinking for the quarter and the work that you choose to submit for the most rigorous evaluation. For this section of your portfolio, select carefully from the work in your collection and feel free to revise any writing before you include it in your selection. You may select (and revise) whole essays or parts of essays, pieces of in-class writing, or sections of your journal just as they appeared in your journal or edited and revised. You may want to photocopy pages of your journal and show them as they were written (assuming that they are legible) or type out selected passages from your journal. Your whole selection may consist of copies of what you regard as your best two or three papers. The only constraint is one of length. Please limit your selection to 2,500 words or approximately ten pages.

The Reflection

You are required to include in your portfolio a general introduction to the whole collection and an introduction to the selection of your best work. You may also include introductions to other sections of your portfolio. Your introductions (informal essays or notes) should describe the materials you are including and provide any background information about the submitted work that might aid the reader in appreciating it.

Your own reflections on the range of work included and its characteristics, qualities, development from piece to piece, and so on will be especially valuable. It would also be useful for a reader to find some reflective remarks on your reading journal and on how your journal writing may have changed in the course of the quarter, how your journal may reveal changes in your reading practices, what you think of various kinds of journal entries, which entries you now find most or least interesting, and so on.

Grading

Your final portfolio will receive a single grade, which will count as approximately two-thirds of the final course grade (class participation will count for the rest). A strong portfolio will include a large collection of material, showing evidence of a serious and thoughtful engagement with all or most of the assigned texts, a willingness to take risks with difficult texts, a willingness to read a variety of texts and authors, thoughtful engagement in the assigned writing tasks, participation in a variety of in-class writing exercises, intellectual honesty throughout, and eight to ten pages of especially thoughtful writing (the selection) that addresses particular texts or problems in reading or criticism. A strong portfolio will also be well-organized and include helpful introductions to and reflections on the work submitted.

Space constraints have forced me to delete the samples I had planned to include as an appendix of the reflective essays and notes my students have written for their portfolios. So readers will have to trust my naked assertion that whenever I am tempted to give up on portfolios and give up on my practice of withholding grades until I review all the work included in a student's portfolio, I look at the kind of reflective thinking about their work and about their intellectual growth that the portfolio assignment occasions for students. Then I am much more willing to accept the extra burden that the portfolios require of me, along with the considerable pleasure I derive from the chance to see, as I could never otherwise see (even discounting the self-interest of students in pleasing and impressing me with their claims of accomplishment), just what my students have accomplished in my course.

Notes

1. When I have asked my students to identify the acts of mind or reading strategies that they observe in their partners or themselves, they usually respond with blank stares, expressing their lack of any idea about what they should be looking for or how it might be classified. I was at first surprised by such blankness, until I reflected on the fact as a teacher-educator in English I regularly participate in a discourse that is characterized by a rich lexicon and set of concepts for describing skilled and unskilled reading performances, but that my students have no experience with that discourse or the concepts it employs. What they need, of course,

are examples of what might be identified as a reading strategy and how it might be observed. In their inability to understand what I was asking them to do, we see an example of how concepts are instruments for thinking and how sometimes a simple instructional scaffold of concept building is required before a student can engage in a task that might seem deceptively easy for the teacher who assigns it. The problem is that we don't want the examples we might give to dictate what our students will observe. Yet, the examples are needed to make observation possible.

How often is it the case that we assign tasks to our students without recognizing their need for such instructional scaffolds? Moreover, the more our students differ from us in their cultural experience, the more likely it is that we will mistakenly assume that they are in possession of concepts that we are hardly aware we possess, but that are necessary for the academic tasks we assign.

2. An Excursus on the Thesis-Argument Essay as a Model for Academic Writing
Readers who assume that the thesis-argument essay or thesis-proof essay is alive and well in the real world of literary essays and academic writing (or ever was) might test their assumption by looking through some literary and academic journals to find examples. In an experiment I recently conducted myself, I examined a dozen or more published essays and articles in three locations: a major journal of literary criticism and scholarship, a leading journal on literary and professional issues in the field of English, and a collection of essays in a volume on the teaching of English. Nowhere could I find an example of an essay that bore a sufficiently close resemblance to the models ordinarily posited by teachers and by textbooks that it could serve the students as an example of such writing. The essays I found all could be said to have made arguments (as I do in all of the chapters in this book), but they tended not to be developed in support of what could be identified as a single discernible thesis.

The one that comes closest to stating a thesis, an MLA essay on a Conrad novel (Henricksen 1988), describes itself (in a passage that might be said to constitute a thesis statement) as an essay that "explores the dialogical tendencies in *The Nigger of the "Narcissus,"* particularly in relation to the problem of point of view," while serving "a larger purpose," which is "to suggest how contemporary theories of the subject—understood in their properly political dimension—might encourage a general reorientation of our thinking about point of view and its relation to ideology." So there is an argument here to be made. But is there a thesis? There is in the sense that what is largely an exploratory essay about point of view in a particular novel might also encourage some new theoretical reflections about point of view in general. But that thesis, if it is one, does not organize the structure and thought of this largely exploratory essay in anything like the form that the top-down model of a thesis-argument essay demands. And this is the only essay of the dozen I examined that even had a candidate for a thesis.

Where we will more easily find a discernible thesis in academic writing in English studies, I suspect, is not in essays or whole articles but in long passages within essays or sections of an essay that constitute arguments like this one, where my thesis is that the thesis-argument essay is probably not the dominant form of the professional and published literary or academic essay, even if we can find numerous instances of formal thesis-driven arguments (that might well be used as rhetorical examples for our students) within sections of such essays, where particular points need to be driven home. Thus, like the compare-and-contrast essay or the essay of definition, the thesis-argument essay may be another instance where what is often treated in school as an essay type is actually more often used in real-world writing as a topos or rhetorical method for elaborating or developing a point or idea within a larger discourse in the service of a broader rhetorical purpose. That observation would also make a good argument for teaching students how to develop effective arguments in their writing, at the same time that it encourages us to become more flexible in our thinking about the purpose and shape of the academic literary essay.

9

Honoring Readers and Respecting Texts
Value and Authority in Literary Interpretation

The Double Bind for Teachers of English

For many conscientious and well-informed teachers, the teaching of literature often feels like a double bind or at best a pedagogically uncomfortable balancing act, particularly when they are teaching what they regard as difficult literary works. On the one hand, we want our students to be active readers who are engaged in a process of making sense for themselves of what they are reading. The battle here, or what feels like a battle, perhaps especially with high-achieving students—high school seniors preparing for Advanced Placement tests for example, or college students worried about grades and eventual graduate school applications—is to push students to enter for themselves into the hermeneutic arena and engage in acts of interpretation that will produce meanings that they themselves can trace back to the evidentiary reasoning, textual facts, and ideological engagement that plausible meanings are built on. These are earned interpretations and, for many teachers, the only ones worth acquiring. Unearned interpretations—those taken on trust from teachers or sourcebooks—are merely hearsay, knowledge borrowed rather than owned.

Nevertheless, it is secondhand teacher-dictated interpretations that our students (and their parents) often demand, since what they want is not so much direct and authentic literary knowledge as the certitude that they are in possession of an interpretation that is approved as correct. "Just tell us what it means," they often insist. They do not understand the point of Louise Rosenblatt's admonition that taking somebody else's interpretation as your own is like having someone else eat your dinner for you. Nor do they realize that the danger of such a diet is that it is likely to lead to the atrophy of the literary digestive tract or to a kind of intellectual infantilism, whereby the student experiences himself as incapable of eating and digesting his own literary dinner and thereby becomes permanently dependent on someone else for interpretative nourishment.

On the other hand (the irreconcilable second strand of our pedagogical double bind), it remains the case that virtually all of us who choose to teach literature in our classrooms choose to teach particular texts because we believe that those texts will provide students with important and even transforming literary experiences. The works we select to teach we select precisely because we believe that in them a reader will find intellectually significant or spiritually nourishing meanings—particular meanings that account for their importance in the literary canon or at least in the canon of our own literary experience and the one we are ostensibly helping our students to build for themselves.[1]

Not surprisingly, then, any casual conversation with English teachers about the books they choose to teach will reveal what research has consistently confirmed (Marshall 1989; Hynds 1991; Zancanella 1991): that among the greatest pedagogical anxieties for teachers of literature is the anxiety of the right reading. By this I mean the anxiety that I assume we all sometimes feel about whether our students will come away from their experience of an assigned text with a reasonably accurate understanding of the meaning of the text—with a sense of a meaning that captures at least roughly the values, ideas, wisdom, or insights that a particular work of literature, as we see it, offers to readers and that accounts for the intellectual or aesthetic importance of that work and for our having chosen it in the first place. Students sense this, of course, which is another reason they are so insistent that we tell them what amounts to the correct interpretation of the texts we are teaching them.

The difficulty with being invested in teaching particular meanings for assigned texts, however, is that such an investment sets up the problematic pedagogical dynamic I have already described—a dynamic that is at odds with a conscientious teacher's equal desire to see students construe texts for themselves and become autonomous readers capable of producing their own interpretations of texts (cf. Chapter 1 of Marshall, Smagorinsky, and Smith 1995). In fact, the greater the teacher's investment in a particular interpretation, the greater the danger that variant student readings will be suppressed and that alternative perspectives and intelligent readings against the grain will be discounted or marginalized. The conflict becomes less complicated ethically, but no less problematic pedagogically, under the conditions that most typically and most often obtain in actual literature classes in secondary schools and colleges: when students appear not to be offering alternative readings, but merely failing to apprehend the difficult or subtle meanings that a text offers, or when they attempt to avoid the challenges of an assigned text by declaring it stupid, boring, or a waste of time. A similar problem occurs, of course, whenever any student, no matter how competent or gifted, construes a text in a way that represents what a more knowledgeable and experienced teacher can demonstrate to be a misreading or misinterpretation of a text.

On the Possibility of Misreadings

In speaking of the possibility of a misreading or misinterpretation, I may appear to be ignoring the body of modern theory and contemporary practice that would argue that there is no such thing as a correct or incorrect reading of a text, but merely a range of possible readings (Mellor, O'Neill, and Patterson 1992, 44). Yet, as I have already suggested, and as every classroom teacher knows, many student-produced readings that might be said to challenge a normative or traditional reading do not represent an alternative perspective at all, but a failed or incomplete reading or a reading that misapprehends the text in the way that an observer of a visually obscured object from a distance might render a judgment about its identity, but would, upon closer inspection, regard his initial judgment as mistaken and now irrelevant.

When literary critics and theorists debate the status of alternative readings of texts, they do not entertain alternatives that might be introduced by readers of questionable competence, but limit their attention only to the theoretically possible readings that might be offered by expert readers or readers who by virtue of their education and academic position may be regarded as members of the literary community that determines what counts as a possible competing interpretation (Fish 1980, 345). Only I. A. Richards (in *Practical Criticism*, 1929) among major literary theorists has seriously attended to the ways in which student readers may misread literary works and what these readings suggest about the nature and apprehension of poetic meaning.[2] But even the student readers in Richards' study were much more literate and accomplished than the great body of students who inhabit classrooms in typical American secondary schools and colleges. They were Cambridge undergraduates of the 1920s, most of whom were "reading English with a view to an Honours Degree" (4), a population that Richards himself claims could not be surpassed in their "capacity for reading poetry" by any group of university students in the world (292).

Moreover, the reading task Richards assigned to his students—which asked them to comment freely on poems presented to them—was rendered highly artificial by the fact that the poems were presented with titles and authors' names removed. The absence of such information for the readers, whose readings Richards so influentially analyzed, has invited many recent theorists to regard Richards' experiment as an invalid one and Richards' conclusions about the causes of misreadings largely erroneous (see Graff 1987, 174–77, and my discussion of decontextualized readings in Chapter 2). It is also the case that many of the student commentaries that Richards finds problematic and counts as misreadings would be defended by many modern critical theorists as possible alternative readings, legitimate personal responses, or resistant readings.

For most contemporary literary theorists, all readings are phenomenologically equivalent if not the same. Student readings, however (as even Richards' study demonstrates), often differ not as a consequence of ideological or theoretical or even cultural differences, but as a consequence of inattention, inexperience, or ignorance (among other causes). It is precisely such matters, generally ignored in the discourse of literary theory or criticism,[3] that I want to address through the value-authority distinction that I'll explain shortly.

First, however, given the current critical culture and its inclination to celebrate the democratic equality of all readings, I may need to demonstrate (with examples drawn from my own classes and workshops) the possibility that some readings can be wrong and many may be inadequate. Ironically, even most of my examples represent readings produced by readers who in most contexts would be regarded as highly competent if not expert readers. Yet the instances of misreading that I'll cite all constitute mistaken or inadequate readings rather than theoretically defensible alternative readings. These misreadings do not derive from experiments, like the one conducted by Richards, that imposed artificial constraints that may be said to invite if not encourage misreading. Rather, the misreadings I'll be discussing here are all versions of the kinds of errors that students (and other readers) make out of ignorance, inattention, lack of experience, or in some cases the vagaries of a momentarily mistaken perspective.[4]

The simplest examples to cite are those that derive from a lack on the part of the reader of what reading specialists have long called the "prior knowledge" that any text presupposes in its readers (what E. D. Hirsch [1987] discusses under the rubric of "cultural literacy"), where students don't know what a text is talking about, even in instances where they may know what most of the words mean in other contexts. We don't have to teach Shakespeare, where the language is so dramatically different from our own, to see how such problems can overwhelm a reading and make any interpretation produced obviously limited and inadequate, if not flat wrong.

When I first read Randall Jarrell's classic war poem "The Death of the Ball Turret Gunner," in about 1958, I found it, even on the first reading, a powerfully moving poem with memorable visual images. Not so many years later, it has to be translated even for audiences of English teachers, most of whom don't remember or may not have seen films depicting American bombers in World War II, with their transparent ball turrets protruding from the belly of the plane, where an airman (with his fur-collared flak jacket) would sit in an almost fetal position to operate the machine gun that protected the bomber from fighter planes that attacked from below. Without such a translation, most readers now misread the poem (see Chapter 4) as one that directly describes—without metaphoric reference—some kind of a dead animal being washed out of a container. Not a stupid or an entirely inattentive reading; but in what universe of discourse is such a nonmetaphoric reading not wrong or at least inadequate compared with one based on an accurate understanding of what a ball turret gunner was?

The Death of the Ball Turret Gunner

From my mother's sleep I fell into the State,
And I hunched in its belly till my wet fur froze.
Six miles from earth, loosed from its dream of life,
I woke to black flak and the nightmare fighters.
When I died, they washed me out of the turret with a hose.

—Randall Jarrell (1914–1965)

Or consider what may be seen as a contrasting case, the short lyric of Wordsworth's that I have already examined at some length (in the introduction), "My Heart Leaps Up":

> My heart leaps up when I behold
> A rainbow in the sky:
> So was it when my life began;
> So is it now I am a man;
> So be it when I shall grow old,
> Or let me die!
> The Child is father of the Man;
> And I could wish my days to be
> Bound each to each by natural piety.
>
> *(1807)*

What most English teachers would probably identify as the most important line of the poem is also the one that is most problematic for many student readers: "The Child is father of the Man." This line can be understood easily—lexically and syntactically— by even the least literate students in any high school or college class. It also expresses an idea that is probably more current now than when it was written. Yet, as I demonstrate in the introduction, many students will claim that they can make little or no sense of a line that seems to be stating the opposite of what is literally and universally true, or else they will interpret it as a reference to Jesus as the child who is also the father (the Son and the Father being two persons in one God). Again, this isn't a foolish or entirely implausible reading, but it is one that becomes obviously inadequate once the discussion pays enough attention to the context of the line within the short poem itself and begins to address a range of ideas about how adults are shaped by their own childhood experiences. If the first kind of misreading (of "The Ball Turret Gunner") can be said to represent some insufficiency in the student's prior knowledge, then we can say that the second kind of misreading arises not so much from insufficiencies located in the reader's knowledge or cultural experience as from conceptual difficulties located in the text.

Another source of misreadings located more in the difficulty of the text rather than in any defect in what the reader happens to know is the linguistic difficulty presented, particularly in poetry (and I am using poems exclusively here only because they are short texts and provide readily visible examples), by syntactic complexities or oddities. A familiar example for experienced readers may be the frequent instances in *Paradise Lost* where the Latinate structure and poetic rhythms of the lines sustain for the ear sentences that are longer than the mind can hold. Readers therefore often lose track of the subject or verb of the sentence and need to parse the lines carefully to make sense of them. How much this difficulty is a function of the fact that Milton, already blind by the time he wrote most of *Paradise Lost*, composed only by ear and was unable to read his own text we can only speculate. But the sentences create problems for all readers and invite misreadings or confusions, which are not difficult to clear up for readers who happen to need help. Nor would any confused or mistaken reader (except out of sheer perversity) ever reject the corrected reading in favor of the uncorrected one that never apprehended the syntactically whole sentence contained in the lines in question.

We can find a different version of linguistic difficulty in a highly accessible and widely anthologized poem by William Stafford. Most students, after two or three readings, can make good sense of the poem and even find themselves engaged by its ethical dimensions.

Traveling Through the Dark

Traveling through the dark I found a deer
dead on the edge of the Wilson River Road.
It is usually best to roll them into the canyon:
that road is narrow; to swerve might make more dead.

By glow of the tail-light I stumbled back of the car
and stood by the heap, a doe, a recent killing;
she had stiffened already, almost cold.
I dragged her off; she was large in the belly.

My fingers touching her side brought me the reason—
her side was warm; her fawn lay there waiting,
alive, still, never to be born.
Beside that mountain road I hesitated.

The car aimed ahead its lowered parking lights;
under the hood purred the steady engine.
I stood in the glare of the warm exhaust turning red;
around our group I could hear the wilderness listen.

I thought hard for us all—my only swerving—,
then pushed her over the edge into the river.

There are a couple of places in this fairly transparent poem where readers are likely to falter, at least momentarily. The one I find most interesting occurs with a line that will puzzle about half its readers, though it doesn't significantly impair their understanding or appreciation of the poem. In the meantime, the other half of the poem's readers (not generally distinguishable as stronger readers, but more on target in this instance) will encounter no difficulty in the line whatsoever. I am speaking about the third line in the next-to-last stanza: "I stood in the glare of the warm exhaust turning red." The question, for readers who feel uncomfortable with the line (and I was once among them), is, Why is he turning red? And the interpretative answers they come up with are always plausible, though rarely entirely satisfying: he is red because he is angry at nature; he is red because he is embarrassed by his hesitation; he is red because he is literally hot from the car exhaust and the emotions he is feeling. But these speculations generally vanish once a student who has not had the problem offers the commonsense reading (as my students did for me) that it is not he who is red, but the exhaust that is turning red from the taillights of the car, though the lines might also plausibly suggest that, standing in the exhaust, he too is turning red from the glare of the taillights.

In this case I have sometimes found students who remain disinclined to abandon their former interpretation, wanting to insist that he is red and that when a person turns red it has to have some psychological or symbolic significance and can't be seen as a fact located only in external circumstances. But even these readers will acknowledge that until they heard the physical explanation for the turning red, they had missed something.

A fourth cause of misreadings arises neither from a lack of prior knowledge on the part of the reader, nor from conceptual or linguistic difficulties located in the text, but from the nature of poetic meaning and, in the actual instances I will cite, from the process some readers employ in the course of reading and construing a text. Consider another poem we have examined in an earlier chapter (Chapter 2), Pat Mora's "Sonrisas":

Sonrisas

I live in a doorway
between two rooms, I hear
quiet clicks, cups of black
coffee, *click, click* like facts
    budgets, tenure, curriculum,
from careful women in crisp beige
suits, quick beige smiles
that seldom sneak into their eyes.

I peek
in the other room señoras
in faded dresses stir sweet
milk coffee, laughter whirls
with steam from fresh *tamales*
    sh, sh, mucho ruido,

they scold one another,
press their lips, trap smiles
in their dark, Mexican eyes.

This poem is not very difficult, even for people who speak no Spanish, if they will read it a few times and pay careful attention to the location of the speaker and the topics discussed by the persons described in the poem. But, as we saw in the workshop of Chapter 2, readers who read this poem only once are likely to misread it in a number of ways, the most amusing of which suggests to them that the speaker of the poem is an insect or mouse who lives in a doorway. A variation of that reading is that the speaker is a homeless person. Again, these are not readings that represent abject ignorance. But they are wrong, and they will be seen as wrong once the reader rereads the poem enough to abandon a first impression created by the first line of the poem and realizes that the speaker is speaking metaphorically about living in a doorway between two rooms. In this case I have never encountered any reader who was inclined to retain the initial misreading in the face of the more attentive and thoughtful corrective reading.

These misreadings of "Sonrisas" may have derived from a failure to reread in all the instances where I have encountered them, but they can also be seen as a failure to recognize the metaphoric character of literary language—to do what many inexperienced readers do when they treat a text as a literal statement and nothing more, attending only to what I have referred to elsewhere (see Chapter 5) as the *representational* meaning of a text without attending to what I have called its *evocative* meaning. And this leads me to the last type of misreading I want to describe—something like the reverse of the previous case and of particular interest to us, because I have witnessed this misreading being committed mostly by experienced and fairly sophisticated readers, including (as in the case I'll describe here) some highly distinguished professional readers who are themselves eminent contributors to literary scholarship and criticism.

Some years ago I was invited by a group of university alumni and faculty who raised money for programs in English and the humanities to talk to them about my research and professional development work on the teaching of English. So I decided to conduct one of the workshops I regularly conduct for high school and college teachers. This time, however, a number of my own departmental colleagues were among the participants, including some internationally distinguished literary scholars. The poem I used for this workshop, and that I use in many of my workshops, was "For Julia, in the Deep Water" by John Morris, a poem that appeared in the *New Yorker* about twenty-five years ago (when I first saw it) and that has been reprinted since in a volume of Morris' collected poems (1980, 55). I'll print it here and ask readers to read it two or three times before reading ahead in this discourse.

For Julia, in the Deep Water

The instructor we hire
Because she does not love you
Leads you into the deep water,
The deep end
Where the water is darker—
Her open, encouraging arms
That never get nearer
Are merciless for your sake.

You will dream this water always
Where nothing draws nearer,
Wasting your valuable breath
You will scream for your mother—
Only your mother is drowning
Forever in the thin air
Down at the deep end.
She is doing nothing,
She never did anything harder.
And I am beside her.

I am beside her in this imagination.
We are waiting
Where the water is darker.
You are over your head,
Screaming, you are learning
Your way toward us,
You are learning how
In the helpless water
It is with our skill
We live in what kills us.

I will not re-create or describe the workshop in which I use this poem in any detail, except to say that it entails a series of steps whereby readers read the poem three times, tracking their difficulties in understanding the poem, and then meet in groups of three to discuss those difficulties and how they resolved them or didn't. Then in combined groups of six they work on the most refractory problems remaining for them in the poem. Then we reflect on the entire sequence of activities that has just transpired and discuss the value and impact of the various stages of the process they have just experienced. On this particular occasion, when my colleagues were participants in my workshop, when I came to the point in my presentation where I always ask participants to talk about how their understanding of the poem was enhanced by the rereading process and then by the discussion process, I discovered that some of the most highly accomplished and professional readers in the room, including the authors of influential critical studies of poetry and prose, had missed the metaphoric vehicle of the swimming lesson (they saw that the poem referred to swimming but not the drama of the swimming lesson), until they joined a group that included some alumni and spouses who were far less sophisticated readers and for whom the swimming lesson was plainly visible, though it might have taken them two readings to construe it.

I tell this story in all my workshops with this poem now, partly because it gives comfort to the many sophisticated readers who in every workshop where I use this poem make the same mistake my eminent colleagues did (and that many readers of this chapter have, no doubt, also made). It is a misreading deriving not from any deficiency in a reader's knowledge, skill, or performance, nor from features of the text that make it especially difficult. It arises rather from the reader's extensive experience and skill as a reader of literary texts and the inclination that such experience confers to look for what is most significant about a text in the meanings it evokes rather than in those more directly represented by its language. In other words, sophisticated readers often reach immediately for the larger and deeper meanings suggested or evoked by literary texts, and in the course of doing so, can miss a more readily accessible and instrumental meaning.

Another way of describing the problem is to observe that the poem uses the metaphor of the swimming lesson as a vehicle to carry or evoke a set of larger and more general meanings (the *tenor* is the technical term for meaning evoked by the *vehicle* of a metaphor) about the life of learning or the process of maturing that all human beings experience and about the role of parents and possibly other teachers in that life. In this case many sophisticated readers fail to notice the details of the instrumental metaphor or vehicle as they leap directly to its tenor or to what they apprehend as the more significant evoked meanings. Once the vehicle is pointed out to them, of course, they will immediately see what they had overlooked and regard their failure to notice it as an interesting and illuminating misreading.

Cutting the Knot of the Double Bind

The question remaining for us to address, then, given that misreadings are not only possible but common (even among highly proficient readers), is how we can help our students become autonomous readers of texts, capable of producing their own interpretations, at the same time that we demonstrate respect for accuracy and correctness in interpretation and respect for the important meanings and ideas that make texts worth reading in the first place. Or, to look at the problem as it is more typically experienced by teachers in classroom contexts: How do we encourage our students to trust and employ their own powers as interpreters of texts at the same time that we exercise our responsibility in class discussions of literature to point out how some of the interpretations our students offer are more adequate than others and some may be wrong—not merely different from our own or resistant to the ideology that is inscribed in a text, but wrong or inadequate in the sense that they are flatly contradicted by the evidence of the text, or based on a superficial apprehension, a misapprehension, or a lack of comprehension of the language or meaning of the text?

The answer—or at least an avenue for developing a teaching practice that might offer a solution to the problem—may be found in thinking about literary interpretations and the process of producing them in terms of distinguishing characteristics that we can call their *value* and their *authority*. These two terms alone can clarify our thinking about students' readings in ways that will allow us to deal more productively and honestly with the double bind I have described for most classroom teachers. That is, again, the problem of our wanting students to have enough confidence to produce their own readings of texts yet also wanting, without undermining their confidence, to help them distinguish the degree to which their own readings and those of their colleagues are correct, accurate, well-informed, or thoughtful.

Let me begin to explicate the idea of value in literary reading by telling a story about an event that took place a few years ago in one of my classes in a course called Introduction to Literary Study—a true story about the first time I asked my students to write a research paper based on a detailed self-study of their own reading process. The assignment (described in detail in Chapter 8) was to write a research paper on their process or experience in reading and making sense (producing an interpretation) of a short assigned poem (in this instance, a twelve-line seventeenth-century lyric, Lovelace's "To Lucasta on Going to the Wars"). The idea was for students to keep track of everything they thought and did in the course of trying to understand the poem and then to use their notes on the process to write a paper about how they went about interpreting the poem and what meanings they produced for the poem at different stages in their reading experience.

In reading the student papers about their reading process, I noticed that one of the students described his first reading of the poem as "a complete waste of time." That is, he realized through his second and subsequent readings of the poem that his first reading was completely mistaken and took him in an entirely wrong direction in thinking about the poem. The next day in class I asked all the students how many of them regarded their first reading of the poem as a "complete waste of time." About half of them raised their hands, claiming that they too misunderstood the poem completely on their first reading or else found it so confusing and devoid of any meaning at all that they regarded their first reading, from the perspective of subsequent readings, as a complete waste of time. My response to this classification of their experience was to suggest to my students (largely tongue-in-cheek, but not entirely in jest) that the next time they read a difficult poem they should try to be more efficient and not waste any time. Why couldn't they, I asked, skip their first reading and go directly to their second—or more realistically, do what they did in their second reading, but do it right away; do it in their first reading?

The answer, of course, is that it can't be done. As much as you might want to abbreviate the process, you can't get to your second reading except by way of your first. And if in your first reading you feel completely lost (a familiar feeling to all experienced readers), well then, that's what it takes to get to the second reading, in which you begin to find your bearings. In other words, you sometimes have to lose your way in order to find it.

We see in this story a suggestive paradox of the reading process. The very students who judged their own first readings as most worthless managed through subsequent readings to arrive at thoughtful, well-observed, and fairly comprehensive interpretations of the poem. In fact, it was precisely because they came to understand the poem so well through their persistence in rereading and reinterpreting it that they could look back at their first readings as worthless and declare them a complete waste of time. Conversely, if they had not proceeded beyond their first readings to subsequent and more adequate readings, they might have mistakenly regarded their first readings as finished or the best they could do, even if such readings did not produce what they themselves regarded as adequate interpretations. What the story also dramatizes is the related paradox of the inestimable value of a wrong or apparently worthless reading for those who will engage in the reading process beyond a first reading, particularly when their first reading includes numerous gaps in their understanding and many unaccounted-for elements in a text.

Given the nature of the reading process and the contribution of rereading and reflection to textual understanding, we can say that any reading is *valuable* insofar as it is the product of a student's own engaged and mindful act and leads to subsequent readings and further reflection on a text in a way that might yield a more adequate or even a confirming interpretation. A reading is *not* valuable, however, if it is unengaged and inattentive or merely borrowed from someone else, or if it serves as an impediment to any further interrogation of a text or more considered reflection on textual meaning.

Indeed, one of the reasons that a borrowed interpretation often deserves to be classified with what Milton calls "false" knowledge (*Paradise Lost*, XI, 412–14) is that it becomes an obstruction to learning in the sense that it is what a student holds on to and insists on dogmatically and uncritically as constituting knowledge (even against contradictory evidence), precisely because it was borrowed and therefore not arrived at experientially or through a process of evidentiary reasoning. That is, insofar as the borrowed knowledge has taken the place of what might have accrued for the student through his own intellectual work and experience of a text, the recitational knowledge itself often becomes what the student takes to be a source of intellectual power and efficacy and thereby becomes a possession that the student (or, unfortunately, sometimes a teacher) must protect in order to preserve a sense of his own power and efficacy. Having put his trust in such unearned knowledge (the forbidden fruit in the Garden of Eden) rather than in his own power to acquire it through the experience of his own reading and reasoning processes, such a student becomes a kind of idolater who will revere his knowledge more than his own capacity to learn anything that might challenge it.

On the other hand, a misreading, a mistaken interpretation of a text, or a confused sense of the meaning of the text honestly arrived at (in the sense that the student was actually engaged in some mindful effort) and provisionally held may be regarded as true knowledge and valuable learning and even a necessary kind of knowledge insofar as it represents a way station in a process of textual interpretation that entails reading, rereading, and reflection as well as refinements in understanding through conversation with other readers and possibly through research. Moreover, what such continuing interpretive work will yield at every stage is what we can call an increasingly more authoritative reading. In other words, all genuinely earned readings are equally *valuable*, but some will be more *authoritative* than others. Moreover, it is possible to produce a reading that has great authority but no value, just as it is possible to produce a reading that has great value but no authority.

Imagine a student who on an essay examination or in a class discussion of a short lyric poem offers an interpretation that seems largely accurate and consistent with conventional academic accounts of the poem but which is based entirely on what the student has read about the poem in a crib like Cliffs Notes or on what the student learned from a teacher's lecture in a previous course. Imagine further that the student has actually read the poem once, but only once, and that his reading of it was perfunctory, yielding for the student almost no sense of a meaning, except a sense that by himself he couldn't make any sense of it at all. Assume further that this student's borrowed statements about the poem are hardly distinguishable from those that the most conscientious student readers are likely to arrive at for themselves through a process of rereading, discussion, and reflection under the guidance of a patient and well-informed instructor. What can we say about interpretative or critical statements that are arrived at in either of the ways I have described, that is, by the individual student who took his interpretation secondhand from a sourcebook or lecture or by the students who arrived at the same interpretation through their own active engagement in a process of rereading, discussion, and reflection on the meaning of the text?

We can say that they both have great authority insofar as they represent well-informed, accurate readings that are the product of some reader's attentive, responsible intellectual work, but that they are very different in their value for the students who offer them, according to how they were arrived at by those students. For students who do the intellectual work of reading, rereading, reflecting, and responsibly constructing an interpretation, the interpretations they offer may be said to have both great authority and great value. For the students whose similar interpretations are borrowed from others and do not represent their own reading experience, the interpretations they offer can be said to have authority (depending on the authority of their source) but little or no value. They have no value because they are grounded in no experience or process of reasoning that the student may consult to confirm or test them, and they may even represent false knowledge to the degree to which they become impediments to further learning. In contrast, for students who will do the work of building an interpretation for themselves, even their first confused readings—readings that may later seem to have been a complete waste of time—may be said to have great value as indispensable steps toward more considered readings. But these first readings, as valuable as they are to a process that will lead to more adequate readings, cannot yet be said to have much if any authority.

With this conceptual scheme in mind, it is possible to imagine a classroom in which, without condescension or false enthusiasm, (the teacher honors all student readings as valuable insofar as they represent steps toward more authoritative and comprehensive readings, while at the same time prodding and encouraging students to reread texts, to discuss and reflect on them) and even to read related texts that will build for students the kind of cultural knowledge needed to produce what Peter Rabinowitz and Michael Smith (1998) call an "authorial reading," a reading that is in touch with the public knowledge that might be presupposed for readers contemporary with an author or otherwise presumed by an author.

However, for students to acquire such knowledge—knowledge that may be essential for anything like what I have been calling an authoritative reading—it may appear that they will need instruction of a kind that is problematic in ways I have already described in my account of false knowledge. The danger in having our students read and reread texts that emerge from cultural contexts very different from their own is that we may be tempted to provide lectures designed to bridge cultural differences, so that students will possess the kind of informational knowledge they need for effective engagement in the reading process. I speak of such lectures as temptations, because I think they often entail a suspiciously easy pedagogical compromise leading to what I have referred to earlier as a kind of interpretive welfare system—a system that keeps student readers dependent on teachers and never able to exercise or realize their own interpretive powers.

I do not want to argue here in favor of teaching only contemporary literature; nor do I want to indict all lectures on literary background and contexts or all footnotes that provide historical glosses for unfamiliar terms—not any more than I would argue against the judicious use of the *Oxford English Dictionary* or against all headnotes that might give useful contextualizing information. The essential pedagogical issue is whether the extratextual information provided by a teacher or other sources is *enabling* for students in the sense that it assists them in becoming autonomous readers or whether it is *disabling* in the sense that it overdirects students to a particular interpretation or otherwise renders students overly dependent on their teachers in the production of interpretations, so that students do not recognize or never have the opportunity to discover the efficacy of their own experience and persistence as readers. The decision on how much historical or contextual information it is necessary for a teacher to give to students in order to foster rather than preempt their autonomy as readers is one that each teacher must make based on a knowledge of the students as well as of the texts being taught (cf. Rabinowitz and Smith 1998, 103–11).

I would point out, however, that it is frequently the case that (most of the background information readers need for an authoritative reading of older texts can be acquired through reading those texts themselves or in some instances from reading a number of texts by the same author or by related or contemporary authors.) Half the time when I assume that my students need my expert guidance to prepare them to read an older literary work that I judge to be inaccessible to them I turn out to be wrong. I discover that they are capable of filling in the crucial gaps in their knowledge through discussion with other students and through careful attention to the text they are studying.

Moreover, when I examine the difference between my own well-informed reading of a text that appears to be inaccessible to my students and my students' reading of the same text, I find it often the case that the "specialized" knowledge I appear to possess derives merely from my experience with a few additional texts by the same author or by contemporaneous authors—texts that can often be added to a syllabus with little inconvenience. It is often possible and relatively easy to avoid making students dependent on a teacher's specialized knowledge by enabling those same students to acquire at least the rudiments of that specialized knowledge for themselves, at least insofar as such knowledge is necessary for their well-informed reading of an assigned literary work (for a more complete treatment of this issue see Chapter 4).

Of course, students will still be dependent on their teachers and their teacher's specialized knowledge to guide them to the related texts that might inform their readings of other texts, but that is the dependence that defines all teaching relationships and accounts for the responsibility of a teacher to prepare a syllabus or conduct an examination. It is not unlike the dependence, or more accurately, the interdependence, that enables learning to take place in what Vygotsky (1978) calls the zone of proximal development, where learners perform with the assistance of their teachers at more advanced levels of skill or competence than they could exhibit on their own and through which they acquire those more advanced competencies for themselves. It is, in short, an interdependence that fosters the acquisition of true rather than false knowledge, thereby leading students to greater independence as readers and giving value as well as authority to their literary learning.

Notes

1. We are all, as Terry Eagleton (1983) wistfully observes, unreconstructed Leavisites, whether we realize it or not, the heirs and continuing exponents of the faith that F. R. Leavis (and Matthew Arnold before him) held in a literary education as a source of psychological and moral wisdom and a humanizing bulwark against the crass materialism, ethical obtuseness, and intellectual crudity of contemporary commercial and political discourse (30–34).

2. Northrop Frye is the only theorist I know of who explains why he would locate the problems of student misreading outside the purview of literary theory. In his proposal (an earlier version of the second essay in his classic *Anatomy of Criticism*) to revivify medieval literary theory for modern criticism ("Levels of Meaning in Literature," *Kenyon Review*, Spring 1950), he begins by removing the literal level of reading, where most student misreadings originate, from the province of literary criticism, claiming that it represents a level of reading that is prior to literary study. Literal reading, he says, "occupies the same place in criticism that observation, the direct exposure of the mind to nature, has in the scientific method" (248), as if both reading at the literal level and scientific observation were nonproblematic and could be bypassed in a disciplinary theory. That assumption would not be acceptable in any modern discussion of the

scientific method and deserves to be challenged in any modern discussion of the discipline of literature.

3. Among major literary theorists, Louise Rosenblatt (1968/1938) is the only one who has seriously examined the implications of theory for classroom instruction and for real readers—including struggling readers—who inhabit real classrooms (which may explain the degree to which she was for so long neglected by mainstream literary theorists). She even deals with the general causes and cures for unsound reading practices among the least literate students (280–290), though she doesn't attempt to develop any systematic analysis of how readers can misapprehend a text.

   One study subsequent to Richards' that extensively examines readings produced by different readers at various levels of skill and experience is that of Harold Vine and Mark Faust in *Situating Readers: Students Making Meaning of Literature* (1993). But their interest is entirely in response and in how students construct meaning, not in misreadings. However, they do acknowledge and reflect on the fact that one-third of the readers in the youngest group of readers whose responses they examined "were unable to sense the general situation" (93) represented in the poem presented to them.

4. *In Practical Criticism* (1929) Richards himself finds ten causes of misreading in the student commentaries he examines. These causes include such problems as failing to construe meaning correctly, failing to apprehend rhythm and meter, improper visualization, "mnemonic irrelevancies" (irrelevant emotional associations or personal connections), doctrinal adhesions (ideological resistance), stock responses, and technical and critical presuppositions. Many of these difficulties would be treated by modern theorists and teachers as representing viable alternative readings rather than errors. Almost all the misreadings I will discuss would be classified by Richards in the category of difficulties arising from a failure to construe a poem correctly, which he acknowledges to be the most common difficulty to appear in his collection of commentaries and which he recognizes as a difficulty to which no reader, not even the "most reputable scholar," is entirely immune (12). Also see Purves and Beach (1972) for an account of student difficulties in responding to literature and a review of research replicating Richards' study.

10

What Do Students Need to Learn?
The Dimensions of Literary Competence

Any curriculum we construct in literature, any set of lessons, any practices we employ in our teaching or teach to our students as readers is necessarily based on some model of what it means to read and what it is that skilled or competent readers do or think about when they engage in the process of reading and talking about or writing about their reading. The workshops, stories, and principles for practice that have constituted the chapters of this book all lead to and derive from an implicit theory about what constitutes competence in the discipline of literature as a field for academic study and a practice for readers of literature in and beyond academic settings. In this chapter I want to make that implicit theory explicit and elaborate a theory of literary competence that can serve as a conceptual and generative framework for continuing to think about our work as teachers of literature and the work of our students as learners.

Let me begin by postulating three crucial domains of knowledge or ways of knowing that also constitute three different forms of literacy. Together these three define the literary competence or disciplined literacy that I propose as the aim and proper end of literary study for all students, but especially for high school students preparing for college and for students enrolled in introductory college-level literature courses.[1]

1. Textual literacy, or *procedural knowledge*
2. Intertextual literacy, or *informational knowledge*
3. Performative literacy, or *enabling knowledge*

Taken together, these three domains of knowledge may be said to map the instructional territory of the literature class and the goals and most efficacious strategies for literary instruction. Two of the three domains will be familiar to most readers from other contexts (as well as from two of the workshops I have presented in this volume). The last represents a less well-explored region of our pedagogical thinking, though virtually every chapter of this book either suggests its dimensions or exemplifies instructional strategies developed in their service.

Textual Literacy, Critical Thinking, and Reading the World

When I speak of textual literacy, I have in mind the kind of *procedural knowledge* and experience in evidentiary reasoning (described in Chapter 2) that accounts for a reader's knowing how to construe the plain sense of a text, apprehend its evoked meaning, and evaluate or challenge its significance—activities that Robert Scholes (1985) labels under the three headings of *reading, interpretation,* and *criticism.* We teach such procedural knowledge to our students through direct instruction in literary language and analysis, through workshops of the kind I have demonstrated in this book, by our example in the way we talk about literature, and most often through the questions we ask of students as readers: What happens here? What is the character's motive? What evidence do you have for that claim? How would such behavior be treated in our community? What do you think of the doctor's treatment of the mother?

We may use Scholes' theoretical formulation and terminology to describe the activity of accomplished readers in their encounters with literary and other texts and also as a conceptual framework for thinking about how we want to focus our instruction or classify various teaching strategies. Moving beyond Scholes' frame of reference, we also find (as I demonstrate in Chapter 2) that if we reframe these textual activities in terms of the kinds of cognitive demands they make, we will recognize their nearly universal utility as critical thinking skills applicable in all academic fields and disciplines. Thus, our textual literacy directs us in the study of literature to ask some form of the following questions: What does it say? What does it mean? and What does it matter? But, if we are reading a cultural event, a crime scene, a body of survey data, or a scientific experiment instead of a literary text, we might represent the same cognitive sequence by asking three analogous questions: What are the facts? What inferences may be drawn from them? and Of what value are these findings? or How may we apply them? In other words, while reading, interpretation, and criticism define the overt focus of instruction in the academic discipline of literature, they also analogously describe the sort of critical thinking that is required for responsible intellectual participation in most civic, economic, and moral transactions and in virtually every academic discipline and learned profession.

The idea that textual literacy defines or is analogous to critical thinking in every intellectual enterprise and human endeavor might also suggest to us a related idea that was a commonplace of medieval and Renaissance thought and one that has lately been revived by the postmodern inclination to textualize all experience (see, for example, Freire and Macedo 1987; Scholes 2001, 76–103): the idea that the world is a difficult text and we are reading it all the time. Nor is this merely a metaphoric and theoretically interesting extension of our conception of reading. Rather, it explains the centrality of literary study and the role of the teacher of literature in the larger enterprise of education for all students. For if the world is a difficult text, with every event, conversation, and experience demanding careful reading, yielding multiple and competing interpretations, and subject to various sorts of criticism, then English teachers, who are the principal teachers of reading as a disciplined process, are teaching students to read not only the literary texts that are in and beyond the prescribed curriculum but all the texts of their lives as public and private persons. Disciplined instruction in literature, in other words, can powerfully influence our students' capacity to negotiate, interpret, and evaluate all the events of their lives, from the most ordinary to the most momentous.

In making such claims about the value of literary study I do not mean to assert that the literature class is the only site for learning to engage thoughtfully in one's transactions with the world, that students do not learn to be critical thinkers at home, or that only literate people can live intellectually responsible and reflective lives. But I don't think that the kind of analytical, interpretive thoughtfulness that characterizes literary discussion arises naturally in children. My middle child, who is now the parent of school-age children and is herself an accomplished and perceptive writer of fiction and a teacher of writing, is an extraordinarily thoughtful and insightful adult. But she used to be a fourteen-year-old. I remember a day when she came home from school at about age fourteen and told me of some offense committed against her by a boy in her class whom she had previously liked. I asked her why she thought the boy had acted in such an uncharacteristic and brutish manner. Her response was to look up at me, with an expression that did not disguise her feelings of disappointment and contempt, and say, "Who are you, Mr. Professor? I'm not going to tell you anything anymore!" And with that she left the room.

I do not read this incident as evidence merely of some male brutishness on my part, though I acknowledge that most mothers and a savvier father than I was at the time might have first responded to a daughter's story of hurt feelings with expressions of sympathy and support rather than with a question asking for psychological analysis. But most readers of this discourse, even parents more emotionally literate than I was at that moment, would have later asked a question much like the one I asked too soon. That's what we do with our children. We regularly ask them questions about how they interpret the facts that upset them, what evidence they have for the claims they make, how they read their own reactions to events, what motives they read behind actions or words they report to us. Like Emerson (1836), we tend to see a spiritual or psychological fact behind every physical fact, and we raise our children to do the same. Our children learn interpretive analysis, evidentiary reasoning, and critical thinking at the dinner table before they learn it at school. But they also learn it in literature classes at school.

And many children can learn it only in school, because they have not had the good fortune to grow up in homes where children have much opportunity for extended conversations with thoughtful adults. The studies documenting the differences between the home language experience of the least privileged and least successful children in school and that of the most privileged can be disheartening to even the most optimistic teachers of youngsters who seem ill-prepared for the linguistic and cognitive demands of school (Traub 2000). But if an important function of education is (as I think it is) to overcome disabling social class differences and provide all children with an opportunity to enter the common culture represented by the practice of critical thinking and the intellectual liberation conferred by literacy, then the teacher of literature and the literature class are among the best instruments available for addressing the social injustice that much else in schooling appears to perpetuate rather than correct (see, for example, Oakes 1986; Kozol 1991).

Intertextual or Cultural Literacy

Let me now turn from procedural knowledge or *knowing how* to what I am proposing as the second major dimension of literary competence—*informational knowledge* or *knowing about* (also see Chapter 4), the dimension that I have labeled *intertextual literacy*, appropriating (or misappropriating) a term from contemporary theory as an alternative to E. D. Hirsch's term *cultural literacy*, largely to avoid association with the political and educational controversies that Hirsch's widely influential book (1987) and concept have occasioned. Hirsch, however, did not discover nor does he claim to have discovered the constraint on reading that he named cultural literacy. Reading specialists had been speaking of the same idea for a number of years as *prior knowledge*. All of these terms are roughly equivalent and serviceable for referring to the knowledge of other texts (including knowledge of literary genres and of such texts as social and economic practices, history, religious controversies, and so on) that is presupposed by most written texts and without which otherwise simple texts can become unintelligible.

What the issue of cultural or intertextual literacy is usually about for most student readers is a distinction between two kinds of understanding that language philosophers, following Frege (1892), refer to with the related but contrasting terms *sense* and *reference*. One may very well understand the sense of a locution—a word, phrase, or sentence, for example—without knowing what it refers to. Thus, every speaker of English is able to understand the sense signified by the phrase "Joseph's coat of many colors," but only those who are familiar with the biblical story will understand what that coat refers to. To not know the referential meanings of the words and phrases of a text is to read a very different text from the identical text read by a more intertextually literate reader. That difference can appear to discredit completely some readings of some texts—even or especially in the eyes of naive readers, once the references are made clear.

But the knowledge differential between sophisticated readers and unsophisticated readers of many texts (as I have demonstrated in my workshop on intertextual literacy in Chapter 4 and as Hirsch also suggests) is often trivial; and, even when it is substantial and significant, it can often be traversed fairly easily with some minimal amount of preparatory reading in related texts, so that students can acquire through their own reading rather than from their teacher's the kind of background knowledge that is presupposed for particular canonical texts they are typically assigned in their English classes. In the meantime, teachers need to be particularly sensitive (again, see Chapter 4) to the often trivial and accidental nature of the prior knowledge that they themselves depend upon as readers. They need to recognize and unpack such knowledge or otherwise make it available to their students, so that in their teaching they do not exaggerate for themselves or for their students their own virtuosity as interpreters of texts and, by comparison, the insufficiency of student readers.

Teachers of literature at advanced levels of instruction must also be alert to the tendency of students to use ignorance of contextual knowledge as an excuse for not doing the interpretive work that texts demand of all readers. In my upper-division Milton class, for example, students often complain at the beginning of the term that they can't understand *Paradise Lost* because they don't know enough about seventeenth-century religious belief in England and therefore can't understand the theological issues that are so central to the action of the poem. Yet almost any account they might read of conventional religious belief in England in the seventeenth century is likely to encourage a misreading of Milton's quite extraordinary theology (see Hill 1978 for an account of Milton's unconventionally radical thought), which can be better learned directly from *Paradise Lost*, where it is available to any attentive reader, than from any crib giving conventional and misleading background information.

It remains the case, however, that some specialized cultural knowledge is often highly advantageous and frequently necessary for a reading that would make sense of a text in terms that are respectful of its provenance, its cultural perspective, and the contextual meaning of its language—a reading that approaches what Peter Rabinowitz and Michael Smith (1998) would call an authorial reading. In my assumption that such a reading is both achievable and desirable, I am not presuming to join the contemporary critical debate among theorists about whether a historically determined meaning or a presently relevant meaning should be privileged in the enterprise of literary interpretation (see Bahti 1985; Hirsch 1985). I am speaking rather from a pedagogical perspective about why students find it difficult in reading historically distant texts to apprehend any coherent or reasonably accurate meaning at all. I am speaking, in other words, mostly about the same kind of prior knowledge a reader needs to make sense of any text, including contemporary texts that presuppose a reader's familiarity with the key terms and concepts informing the text.

As readers of texts composed in the distant past and in diverse cultural contexts, our own position is much like that of ethnographic researchers, who attempt to read the cultures they study from the perspective of insiders or participants as well as from their own perspective as observers. Ethnographers learn how to read as insiders by immersing themselves as deeply as possible in the lifeworld of the cultures they study while seeking interpretive assistance by interrogating or conducting formal ethnographic interviews with insiders or native informants. Literary texts offer us the opportunity to immerse ourselves in alternative cultures. The equivalent of an ethnographic interview for readers who wish to enter the world in which older literary texts were composed may be the testimony of other texts by the same author, the testimony of similar texts by other writers of the same period, and possibly earlier texts in the same genre.

Of course there are severe limitations in how far teachers can go within the scope of a class or academic term to help their students read ancient texts with anything like native comprehension. Yet any argument that student readers should be encouraged to read texts merely from their own parochial and culturally limited perspective will reveal its own limitations as students demonstrate how confused and alienated they are in their encounters with texts whose worlds they are unable to enter imaginatively. Moreover, to encourage readings that shirk the responsibility of attempting to understand historical and cultural contexts is ethically equivalent to telling our conversational partners or anyone with whom we have entered a dialogue that we aren't interested in making any effort to understand their point of view, if we don't already happen to share it. This does not mean that readers should be obliged to embrace rather than resist the culture and ideology of the texts they read. It only means they are obliged to understand as well as possible what it is that they might claim to be resisting.

Performative Literacy

I now come to the dimension of literary competence that I regard as foundational to the cognitive processes that most teachers identify with literate behavior, but that literary instruction and the culture of school (see McCaslin 1990 and endnote 3) may seem more intent on nullifying rather than nourishing. I am talking here about a competence that is not unlike what Hymes (1972) referred to in sociolinguistic accounts of language use as "competence for performance" and that I am now inclined to call performative literacy, though I have referred to it in the past (Blau 1990) as personal literacy. This is the competency that I identify with *enabling knowledge*, and that accounts, as I'll explain shortly, for the quality of a reader's performance in exercising textual literacy in transactions with challenging literary texts and in acquiring the intertextual literacy that supports such transactions.

As a way of approaching what I mean by performative literacy I want to begin by describing its opposite, the kind of pseudoliteracy or counterliteracy that many conventional practices in the teaching of literature—including well-intentioned practices that all of us sometimes engage in—seem designed to foster. And the best way for me to describe that kind of literacy would be with the classroom stories I have already told in Chapter 1 of this book. Instead of retelling those stories in all their

(I hope) interesting and amusing detail in this chapter, let me merely evoke a memory of them by summarizing them here very briefly so that they may be available to us as examples of what I mean when I speak of instruction that fosters the opposite of performative literacy.

The first story I told was of the ninth- or tenth-grade English class where the teacher was teaching *Julius Caesar* and responded correctively and with a lecture on Shakespeare's classic stature when a confused student complained about the play being stupid because it didn't make sense that Brutus, who loved Caesar so much, would be involved in a plot to kill him. From this story I derived the principle that confusion often represents an advanced state of understanding and yields the best opportunity we have in classrooms to help students advance in their knowledge.

My second story also recounted events I witnessed in the teaching of a Shakespearean play. This time it was *Macbeth* in a class of twelfth graders. In this instance an excellent teacher did an excellent job of teaching an entire scene, but never talked about the lines that gave him and me the most trouble. He felt unsure of what to make of those lines, so he avoided them. Yet upon later inspection, they turned out to be the most interesting and informative lines in the scene. From this story I derived the somewhat tongue-in-cheek principle that the texts most worth reading and teaching are those we don't understand, because those are precisely the texts that have the most to teach us. I also observed how misleading it is for students when their teachers avoid teaching the parts of texts that are most puzzling to the teachers themselves, thereby falsely suggesting that these are the easiest parts of the text (because they require no instruction), while also denying students the opportunity to learn what a strong reader can do in an encounter with a challenging text.

My third story told of a typical literature class in college where students were assigned difficult poems to read and then, finding that they couldn't understand the poems, came to the next class to have the professor tell them what the poems mean, rendering the teacher the only reader of the poems and the students merely the witnesses and recorders of the instructor's reading. I went on to confess that I have myself sometimes taught in this manner, feeling required to do so by my commitments to my syllabus, my sense of responsibility about covering texts and authors that my students ought to know before they enter more advanced courses, and the severe time limitations of a ten-week academic quarter. But I acknowledged that such instruction encourages students in two mistaken beliefs. First, it encourages them to believe that they are incapable, without more advanced and specialized training, of reading the difficult texts I have "taught" them. Second, it encourages in them the equally mistaken belief (especially counterproductive for those who will become teachers) that they have acquired something that can be called worthwhile literary knowledge by possessing notes on my readings.

My fourth story followed an experiment with a passage from Thoreau where I demonstrated how skilled adult readers engage in the task of reading difficult texts through rereading and the allocation of concentrated attention. My story told of the contrasting response of high school students to the same difficult text and how they immediately retreated from the difficult task of reading it because they interpreted its difficulty as a sign of their own insufficiency as readers. From this story I derived the proposition that a significant difference between highly accomplished readers and poor readers is that accomplished readers have a greater tolerance for failure.

What I am calling pseudoliteracy or counterliteracy, then, is the kind of literacy that students acquire when they depend on authoritative sources for their readings of difficult texts or when they have been convinced by their instructional experience not that they are capable of making sense of texts that at first seem unintelligible, but that any encounter they have with such a text is evidence that they are insufficient readers, either by virtue of their lack of specialized expertise (their widely advertised cultural illiteracy) or perhaps their insufficient reading level ("This text must be at a twelfth-grade reading level and I'm a tenth grader,") or worse, "I've been tested, so I know that I can't read anything above the seventh-grade level," (whatever that might mean).

If such ways of thinking on the part of students (which surely reflect beliefs held by some teachers and many parents about students) may be said to constitute disabling knowledge or what Milton would call false knowledge (see Chapter 9), what I am calling performative literacy represents its opposite and what we may therefore characterize as a corrective or enabling kind of knowledge.

The Dimensions of Performative Literacy

Performative literacy, then, refers to that kind of knowledge that enables students to perform as autonomous, engaged readers of difficult literary texts at any level of education. These are readers who, in encounters with difficult texts, demonstrate a particular set of attributes or dispositions that may seem more like character traits than academic or literary skills. Yet this set of attributes or habits of mind can be said to constitute the foundation for a related set of literary actions or an intellectual discipline that expert adult readers characteristically exhibit and readily recognize as the discipline and behaviors of the most accomplished student readers (cf. Rosenblatt 1968/1938, 285).[2]

I have identified seven traits as constitutive of performative literacy and associated with actions and dispositions that I have found to be marks of competent readers or marks that distinguish more competent readers from less competent. I proposed these traits initially as hypotheses derived largely from intuition, observation, and analysis of my own reading processes and that of colleagues compared to those of a wide range of student readers (Blau 1990). Many of the traits I identified were later confirmed by reading process data collected in connection with California's 1993 and 1994 statewide reading assessment for students in grades four, eight, and ten (Blau 1994a, 2001; Claggett 1999). They are also consistent with more recent research on proficient student readers as compared to struggling readers (Wilhelm 1997; Schoenbach et al. 1999; Beers 2002; Olson 2003), though there is relatively little obvious overlap between the focus of that research on strategies and the kind of ethical and character traits that I have emphasized. The seven traits are listed below, followed by an explanation and rationale for each.

1. Capacity for sustained, focused attention
2. Willingness to suspend closure
3. Willingness to take risks
4. Tolerance for failure
5. Tolerance for ambiguity, paradox, and uncertainty
6. Intellectual generosity and fallibilism
7. Metacognitive awareness

1. *A capacity for sustained, focused attention.* This attribute may seem so obviously required for the reading of difficult texts that it hardly needs to be mentioned. Yet student failure to give close, sustained attention to texts accounts for much of the illiterate behavior that some educators have been inclined to attribute to more complicated and refractory problems. Surely it is the case, for example, that when students come to class claiming not to have understood an assigned text, few of them have actually given the time and attention to the work of understanding that text that any of us who are expert readers would expect to invest in a similarly unfamiliar work. However, when simple lack of appropriate effort is treated—as it often is—as a symptom of cultural illiteracy or insufficient mastery of some subskill of reading, students are likely to be offered forms of instructional assistance that support inattention and confirm the students' own mistaken notion that they lack some specialized body of knowledge or reading skills that distinguish them from their teachers.

2. *Willingness to suspend closure*—to entertain problems rather than avoid them. Again, the difference between many student readers and the most accomplished readers seems to reside in the operation of the will rather than in the wit. It's not that expert readers immediately apprehend meaning in a text and do so with a sharper vision than less skilled readers, but that they are more willing to endure and even to embrace the disorientation of not seeing clearly, of being temporarily lost. The most productive readers will even sacrifice whatever comfort they may find in a coherent and apparently complete reading to notice discontinuities or possible contradictions in their understanding of a text. Instead of ignoring or rushing in to plug up such gaps with weak evidence or rationalizations, they will probe them, opening up the possibility that their own formerly comfortable reading will collapse or require reconstruction. It is ironic that the same problems that a student reader may avoid acknowledging because they threaten his sense of sufficiency as a reader will be embraced by a literary critic or scholar as an occasion for research and publication—that is, for opening up possibilities for a new and more insightful analysis of a text.

3. *Willingness to take risks*—to offer interpretive hypotheses, to respond honestly, to challenge texts, to challenge normative readings. This characteristic is closely related to a willingness to entertain problems, and both of them are functions of what we might more globally identify as intellectual courage. First, we want to note that any time a reader offers an independent interpretation of a text in a classroom or community of other readers, she takes a risk and assumes a responsibility. The responsibility is to make the case (Rex 1997) in support of her interpretation through a process of evidentiary reasoning. The risk she takes is that her case won't hold, that the interpretive hypothesis presented won't stand up to interrogation by other readers or even to the reasoning process necessary to demonstrate its plausibility.

Intellectual courage may also be required when readers feel called upon by their own experience and knowledge to offer readings that might appear to be unacceptable or socially stigmatized in particular communities of readers. Such readings and such courage may be particularly appropriate, however, in the most traditional English classrooms where literature is sometimes offered up by teachers in what they may see as their obligatory role as the high priests of the canonical culture—a role that many parents and school boards continue to think appropriate for teachers (see Blau 2001)—and where all texts taught seem to demand reverence as the only acceptable response, a reverence that often requires the deadening of perceptiveness and critical inquisitiveness rather than their quickening.

I saw such a deadened response in my own reading experience, when it wasn't until I first taught Sidney's *Arcadia* to undergraduate students (having read it in graduate school some years earlier) that I first experienced any moral shock over Sidney's treatment of the lower classes in a scene in which he makes a joke out of the maiming and dismemberment of a clownish group of farmers and artisans who dare to rebel against the rule of their aristocratic "betters." I had not skipped the scene in my earlier reading and, in fact, remembered it vividly. Yet I remember having had no sense of Sidney as the spokesman for any values that I wasn't prepared to embrace and even celebrate in my general enthusiasm at the time for Renaissance British culture. Nor was my reverence for Sidney's text one imposed on me by my teachers, since I did all of my reading of Sidney independently.

If we want our students to be engaged readers, likely to notice what they notice in the course of their reading and to record it for later reflection, we will probably value their literary irreverence as much as their sense of literary awe. Students need at least enough lack of reverence—or, more positively, a sufficient sense of the value of their responses and their right to talk back to texts—to be willing to recognize when a text speaks against them as well as for them, when it represents an ideology that they might prefer to resist rather than admire.

It may require even more courage to articulate a response that challenges a reading (which is to say an interpretation and possibly an evaluation) of a text for which a teacher and class have colluded in constructing a normative and apparently authoritative meaning. I suspect that most teachers have had the experience of first rejecting out of hand and then later recognizing the indispensable insight made available by the interpretation of the student who took the risk of offering what Derrida calls an "exorbitant" reading (in Scholes 1989, 77–79). Such readings are often valuable not for the sake of their exorbitance or what Thoreau might call their extravagance (literally, going beyond the boundary), but for the contribution that extravagance can make to a normative reading by pointing to an unrecognized yet plausible interpretive possibility or showing a dimension of meaning ignored by most readers. Actors in rehearsal are often prodded by the most creative directors to experiment with the principle of the exorbitant reading as a way of testing the interpretive boundaries of a scene, either to discover new dramatic possibilities or to locate more securely its dramatic center.

4. *Tolerance for failure*—a willingness to reread and reread again. This attribute is probably related to intellectual courage and is surely related to a capacity for sustained attention, but it refers more specifically to a reader's possession of a kind of faith in the process of reading and faith in oneself as a reader that allows a reader to read a text a second time after feeling bewildered or blank in a first reading, and then to reread again when the second reading is hardly more satisfying than the first. How much rereading and frustration can a competent reader tolerate? More than an incompetent reader can. In fact, as I have demonstrated elsewhere (Blau 1981 and Chapter 1), one of the principal differences between expert readers and those who appear less skilled is that the more accomplished have a greater capacity for failure. They are at least willing to experience failure more often, framing their failure not so much as failure but as a part of the difficulty that comes with the territory of reading difficult texts. That is, they construe their failure as a temporary function of the difficulty of the task they are engaged in rather than as a symptom of their own insufficiency.[3]

5. *Tolerance for ambiguity, paradox, and uncertainty.* Closely related to an ability to suspend closure, this tolerance is less a matter of patience and faith in one's capacity to solve problems than one of accepting the limitations and developmental nature of our understanding and the paradoxical, ambiguous, and provisional condition of most human knowledge at any moment. The least competent readers tend to confuse intellectual sufficiency with certainty and completed knowledge, and are inclined to equate uncertainty with ignorance, and ambiguity or paradox with confusion. Readers who read texts looking for secure and certain answers to their questions may also read the world with a similar passion for certainty and with a similar intolerance for the moral complexity and ambiguity that resist simplistic formulations.

A conviction of certainty is one of the most certain signs of ignorance and may be the best operational definition of stupidity. It is surely an indication of false knowledge, the knowledge that originates in pride and eventuates in an incapacity to learn. Those who insist on fixed and certain knowledge as a condition of happiness in this world, warns the poet and exemplary pastor, George Herbert (in his poem "The Flower"), not only squander the modicum of happiness that may be available in this world, but eventually "sacrifice their paradise with their pride."

6. *Intellectual generosity and fallibilism*—willingness to change one's mind, to appreciate alternative visions, and to engage in methodological believing as well as doubting (Elbow 1986). This characteristic refers to a constellation of related traits that allow readers to learn from and be influenced by texts and discourse about texts. The strongest readers will generally argue persuasively for their own readings of texts and be able to demonstrate the deficiencies of arguments for alternative readings. But they also show a capacity to experiment with—to try on and, as it were, to believe—alternative perspectives and to recognize the possibilities of alternative or multiple constructions of meaning. In this process they also show themselves to be fallibilists, persons capable of changing their minds, capable of learning from their encounters with other readings to look in a new way and therefore to adopt a perspective that is more comprehensive than their own former vision. Similarly, such readers can learn from text, in the sense that they will sufficiently enter the world of a text emotionally and intellectually so as to be changed by their experience in their sympathies, in their knowledge of a represented world, and in the ways they apprehend or construct themselves.

7. *Metacognitive awareness*—a capacity to monitor and direct one's own reading process. A number of experiments I have conducted in the various chapters of this book as well as teacher observations and a growing body of more formal reading research (see summaries of research in Schoenbach et al. 1999 and Olson 2003) demonstrate that a major difference between strong and weak readers has to do with the way that strong readers monitor the progress of their understanding as they move through a text, self-correcting as necessary and recognizing when they need to reread or refocus their attention or take some other step to assist themselves in understanding what they are reading. Readers who are used to monitoring their reading are less likely to feel defeated by difficult texts, because they are aware of the difference between understanding and not understanding and recognize their own resources for focusing or redirecting their attention in precisely the ways I have been describing under the other dimensions of performative literacy (see Vygotsky 1962, 8).[4]

Fostering Performative Literacy in Classrooms

Most of the characteristics of readers that I have identified with performative literacy can be developed in students once literature is taught in a way that recognizes that reading, like writing, is a process of text construction—a process through which meaning is made in the head of the reader (and later reconstructed and made more visible, perhaps, through writing) through the reader's encounter or transactions with words on a page and in the course of conversations with other readers. To recognize that reading (including interpretation and criticism) is a process of meaning making or text construction is to recognize that it is a process very much like writing, involving the same false starts, the same vision and re-vision, drafting and redrafting, as well as the same perils, opportunities (including opportunities for collaboration and consultation), and recursiveness of writing.[5]

To see reading as such a process of composition will not only link the teaching of reading with the teaching of writing but also foster in students the kind of respect and capacity for tentativeness, for confusion, for sustained attention, for failure, for metacognitive awareness, and so on that I have identified with the enabling knowledge that constitutes performative literacy. This is particularly so if what we foreground and honor in the course of instruction is the efficacy of the reading process rather than any predetermined product or content knowledge that we feel obliged to transmit. To put the case more succinctly, instruction directed toward fostering performative literacy must focus on the processes of reading and rereading, placing an *equal or greater emphasis* on what student readers learn about their own capacity as readers in their transactions with difficult texts as on any established body of knowledge about those texts.

A number of instructional approaches meet this criterion, including the following:

- Assignments that make reading processes visible. These might include double-entry journals in which students record lines and responses and reflections on them from each reading and rereading of a text; or reading logs that ask students to keep track of their questions and other responses with each reading and rereading; or reading process self-studies as described in Chapter 8 (also see Wilson 1989; Schoenbach et al. 1999).
- Assignments that invite students to examine variant readings and that honor multiple responses, for example, through Elbow's (1986) strategy for methodological believing and doubting (where pairs of students with opposing interpretive or critical views in turns give each other three reasons to believe their opponent's point of view, then three reasons to doubt it). Or assignments that invite students in groups to compare their different responses to a text and to try to account for the differences by dealing with such questions as what those differences tell about different readers, about different cultural experiences, about ideological differences between readers and readings, and about the reading process (see Chapters 3, 5, and 6 for specific exercises).
- Writing assignments that invite students to examine the history of their own changing reading of a text or to explore the multiple possibilities for constructing meaning for a given text, rather than presenting an argument for a single authoritative reading (see Chapters 2, 3, 5, 6, 7, and 8).
- Writing assignments addressed to significant unresolved problems rather than problems with known answers.

- Any approach that honors problems and questions, foregrounding in stages what the reader *doesn't* understand (see, for example, Newkirk 1984; Schoenbach et al. 1999; and Chapters 2, 3, 5, and 6 in this book).
- Pants-down reading—a term coined by my colleagues in the South Coast Writing Project and Literature Institute for Teachers for the experience of working with students on a poem or short story that the teacher has never read before and with which he is likely to experience difficulties in understanding that will enable him to collaborate authentically with students in the construction of meaning and to exemplify the traits and actions that constitute performative literacy.

Finally, just as the teaching of writing as a process has been found to require or to thrive most successfully in a culture of instruction that supports collaboration, tentativeness, risk taking, collegiality, and opportunities to publish written work for an identifiable community of readers, so will classrooms fostering performative literacy need to be communities of practice in which the traits that I have identified as performative literacy will be culturally valued and honored in daily conversational practices as well as in theory. And this calls for the wholesale transformation of the conventional culture of instruction in the English classroom in precisely the ways I have described in the earlier chapters of this book.

Notes

1. Some of my readers will recognize in what I am now calling disciplined literacy the same concept and constellation of ideas that I used to refer to in my teaching and in presentations and conference papers (e.g., Blau 1990) as "humane literacy."

2. Some of the most important dimensions of literary competence that I enumerate under the heading of "performative literacy" were anticipated (as was much of what I have struggled to learn and share about the teaching of literature) by Louise Rosenblatt sixty-five years ago!

3. The culture of school, at least in elementary and middle grades, apparently conspires to discourage three of the first four traits that characterize performative literacy as I have defined it. Mary McCaslin (1990) summarizes a body of research and provides her own case studies of sixth graders to demonstrate the degree to which students equate speed with ability and regard effort as inversely related to ability. Moreover, since ability grants status in the classroom and school, students who demonstrate a capacity for sustained attention, a willingness to suspend closure, or a tolerance for failure also risk a serious loss of social status.

4. In this sense metacognitive awareness might be said to be the foundation for all the other dimensions of performative literacy that I have named. Furthermore, in identifying the construct of literary competence or skill with metacognitive awareness and with the self-regulation that is entailed in concentrating attention, tolerating failure, enduring a lack of closure, and exercising all the other traits or virtues that define performative literacy, I am not so much proposing a view of competence that substitutes virtue or will in place of skill, but linking skill inextricably with will, much in the spirit of Vygotsky's call (1962) for education studies that integrate the operations of thought with "the needs and interests, the inclinations and impulses of the thinker" (8). On this issue also see McCaslin 1990.

5. In proposing a process-oriented pedagogy for the literature class at the same time that the field of composition studies has begun to speak of a postprocess pedagogy (Kent 1999), my book might be identified as another exhibit to show how far literature instruction continues to lag behind composition instruction. My notion of the reading process, however, and the models I present for teaching it do not suffer from the inflexibility, artificiality, and social decontextualization that have been so troubling to critics of a simplistic writing process pedagogy. The process model I have described imposes no fixed set of procedures or method upon students beyond those associated with reflective thought, including evidentiary reasoning, consciousness of the state of one's understanding, and provisionality or fallibilism (which would entail drafting and revision). Thinking may be a process and may be described in terms of various subprocesses (observing, analyzing, hypothesizing, and so on), but it is not a process that can be reduced to a method. Thinking, as Dewey observed, is the method. The process model I have proposed also acknowledges the situatedness of the reader as an interpreter and critic and calls for an instructional culture that is emphatically social, where interpretation and criticism arise from processes of conversation and negotiation in the context of a community and culture, and where members learn and coconstruct the rules of discourse through their active participation.

Works Cited

Adams, Hazard. 1991. "The Difficulty of Difficulty." In *The Idea of Difficulty in Literature*, ed. Alan Purves, 23–50. Albany: State University of New York Press.

Alter, Robert. 1989. *The Pleasures of Reading in an Ideological Age*. New York: Simon and Schuster.

Applebee, Arthur. 1993. *Literature in the Secondary School: Studies of Curriculum and Instruction in the United States* (National Council of Teachers of English Research Report #25). Urbana, IL: National Council of Teachers of English.

Appleman, Deborah. 2000. *Critical Encounters in High School English: Teaching Literary Theory to Adolescents*. New York: Teachers College Press.

Appleman, Deborah, Susan Hynds, and James Marshall. 1998. "Things Fall Apart: Reader Response, Multiculturalism, and the Limits of Belief." Presentation at the Third International Conference: Global Conversations on Language and Literacy (Aug. 3–6). Bordeaux, France.

Axelrod, Rise, and Charles Cooper. 2001. *The St. Martin's Guide to Writing*. New York: Bedford/ St. Martin's.

Bahti, Timothy. 1985. "Historical Realities" and "Short Reply to E. D. Hirsch, Jr." In *Criticism in the University*, ed. Gerald Graff and Reginald Gibbons, 224–28, 231–32. Evanston, IL: Northwestern University Press.

Barthes, Roland. 1975. *The Pleasure of the Text*. Trans. R. Miller. New York: Hill and Wang.

Bartolomae, David. 1983. "Writing Assignments: Where Writing Begins." In *Forum: Essays on Theory and Practice in the Teaching of Writing*, ed. Patricia Stock, 300–312. Portsmouth, NH: Boynton/Cook.

Beach, Richard, and James Marshall. 1991. *Teaching Literature in the Secondary School*. New York: Harcourt Brace Jovanovich.

Beers, Kylene. 2000. "From Hall Talk to Classroom Talk to Book Talk: Helping Struggling Readers Connect to Reading." In *Middle Mosaic: A Celebration of Reading, Writing, and Reflective Practice at the Middle Level*, ed. Elizabeth Close and Katherine Ramsey. Urbana, IL: National Council of Teachers of English.

———. 2002. *When Kids Can't Read—What Teachers Can Do: A Guidebook for Teachers, Grades 6–12*. Portsmouth, NH: Heinemann.

Berthoff, Ann. 1981. *The Making of Meaning: Metaphors, Models, and Maxims for Writing Teachers*. Portsmouth, NH: Boynton/Cook.

Blau, Sheridan. 1981. "Literacy as a Form of Courage." *Journal of Reading* 25 (Nov.): 101–105.

———. 1983. "Invisible Writing: Investigating Cognitive Processes in Composition." *College Composition and Communication* 34 (Oct.): 297–312.

———. 1990. "Humane Literacy: Literary Competence and the Ways of Knowing." Paper presented to the Conference of the International Federation of Teachers of English. Auckland, New Zealand. Redacted with a response by Carol Bencich and a reply by Sheridan Blau in *Global Voices: Culture and Identity in the Teaching of English*, ed. Joseph Milner and Carol Pope. Urbana, IL: National Council of Teachers of English, 1994, 174–82.

———. 1993. "Constructing Knowledge in a Professional Community: The Writing Project as a Model for Classrooms." *The Quarterly* 15 (1): 16–19.

———. 1994a. *The California Learning Assessment System Language Arts Test: A Guide for the Perplexed*. Sacramento: California State Department of Education.

———. 1994b. "Transactions Between Theory and Practice in the Teaching of Literature." In *Literature Instruction: Practice and Policy*, ed. James Flood and Judith Langer, 19–52. New York: Scholastic.

———. 1999. "The Only New Thing Under the Sun: 25 Years of the National Writing Project." *The Quarterly* 21 (3): 2–7, 32.

———. 2001. "Politics and the English Language Arts." In *The Fate of Progressive Language Policies and Practices*, ed. Curt Dudley-Marling and Carol Edelsky, 183–208. Urbana, IL: National Council of Teachers of English.

Bloome, David, and Ann Egan-Robertson. 1993. "The Social Construction of Intertextuality in Classroom Reading and Writing Lessons." *Reading Research Quarterly* 28 (4): 304–33.

Booth, Wayne. 1988. *The Company We Keep: An Ethics of Fiction*. Berkeley: University of California Press.

Britton, James, Tony Burgess, Nancy Martin, Alex McCleod, and Harold Rosen. 1975. *The Development of Writing Abilities in Children, 11–18*. London: Macmillan Education.

Bruner, Jerome S. 1978. "Learning the Mother Tongue." *Human Nature* September: 43–49.

Carey-Webb, Allen. 2001. *Literature and Lives: A Response-Based Cultural Studies Approach to Teaching English*. Urbana, IL: National Council of Teachers of English.

Ciardi, John. 1959. *How Does a Poem Mean*. Boston: Houghton Mifflin.

Claggett, Fran. 1999. "Integrating Reading and Writing in Large-Scale Assessment." In *Evaluating Writing: The Role of Teachers' Knowledge About Text, Learning, and Culture*, ed. Charles Cooper and Lee Odell. Urbana, IL: National Council of Teachers of English.

Cunningham, J. V. 1966. "Lyric Style in the 1590s." In *The Problem of Style*, ed. J. V. Cunningham, 159–173. New York: Fawcett Publications.

Cunningham, Valentine. 2002. *Reading After Theory*. Oxford: Basil Blackwell.

Dewey, John. 1910. *How We Think*. Buffalo, NY: Prometheus Books, 1991.

———. 1938. *Experience and Education*. New York: Collier, 1963.

Dixon, Carol, Carolyn Frank, and Judith Green. 1999. "Classrooms as Cultures: Understanding the Constructed Nature of Life in Classrooms." *Primary Voices* 7 (3): 4–8.

Dudley, Martha. 1997. "The Rise and Fall of a Statewide Assessment System." *English Journal* 86 (1): 15–20.

Durst, Russel. 1999. *Collision Course: Conflict, Negotiation, and Learning in College Composition*. Urbana, IL: National Council of Teachers of English.

Eagleton, Terry. 1983. *Literary Theory: An Introduction*. Minneapolis: University of Minnesota Press.

Elbow, Peter. 1973. *Writing Without Teachers*. New York: Oxford University Press.

———. 1986. "Methodological Doubting and Believing: Contraries in Inquiry." In Peter Elbow, *Embracing Contraries: Explorations in Learning and Teaching*, 253–300. New York: Oxford University Press.

———. 1995. "Breathing Life into the Text." In *When Writing Teachers Teach Literature*, ed. Art Young and Toby Fulwiler, 191–93. Portsmouth, NH: Boynton/Cook.

———. 2000. *Everyone Can Write: Essays Toward a Hopeful Theory of Writing and Teaching Writing*. New York: Oxford University Press.

Elbow, Peter, and Pat Belanoff. 1989. *Sharing and Responding*. New York: McGraw-Hill.

Emerson, Ralph Waldo. [1836] 1957. "Nature." In *Selections from Ralph Waldo Emerson*, ed. Stephen E. Whicher, 31. Boston: Houghton Mifflin.

Fish, Stanley. 1980. "What Makes an Interpretation Acceptable." In *Is There a Text in This Class? The Authority of Interpretative Communities*, 338–355. Cambridge, MA: Harvard University Press.

Fleischer, Cathy. 1992. "Forming an Interactive Literacy in the Writing Classroom." In *Cultural Studies in the English Classroom*, ed. James Berlin and Michael Vivion, 182–99. Portsmouth, NH: Boynton/Cook.

Floriani, Anna. 1994. "Negotiating What Counts: Roles and Relationships, Texts and Contexts, Content and Meaning. " *Linguistics and Education* 5: 241–74 .

Fort, Keith. 1971. "Form, Authority, and the Critical Essay." *College English* 32 (6): 629–39.

Freire, Paulo, and Donaldo Macedo, eds. 1987. *Literacy: Reading the Word and the World*. Boston: Bergin and Garvey.

Frege, Gottlob. 1892. "On Sense and Reference." Trans. Max Black in *Translations from the Philosophical Writings of Gottlob Frege*, ed. Peter Geach and Max Black. Oxford: Basil Blackwell, 1952.

Frye, Northrop. 1950. "Levels of Meaning in Literature." *Kenyon Review* (Spring): 247–62.

———. 1957. *Anatomy of Criticism: Four Essays*. Princeton: Princeton University Press.

Gilbert, Pam. 1987. "Post Reader-Response: The Deconstructive Critique." In *Readers, Texts, Teachers*, ed. B. Corcoran and R. Emrys, 234–50. Portsmouth, NH: Boynton/Cook.

Graff, Gerald. 1985. "The University and the Prevention of Culture." In *Criticism in the University*, ed. Gerald Graff and Reginald Gibbons, 62–82. Evanston, IL: Northwestern University Press.

———. 1987. *Professing Literature: An Institutional History*. Chicago: University of Chicago Press.

———. 1992. *Beyond the Culture Wars: How Teaching the Conflicts Can Revitalize Higher Education*. New York: W. W. Norton.

———. 2001 (originally 1986). "Taking Cover in Coverage." In *The Norton Anthology of Theory and Criticism*, ed. Vincent Leitch et al. 2059–67. New York: W. W. Norton. Reprinted from *Profession 86* of the Modern Language Association.

Gray, James. 2000. *Teachers at the Center: A Memoir of the Early Years of the National Writing Project.* Berkeley, CA: National Writing Project.

Green, Judith, and Carol Dixon. 1993. "Talking Knowledge into Being: Discursive and Social Practices in Classrooms." *Linguistics and Education* 5: 231–39.

Grice, H. P. 1975. "Logic and Conversation." In *Syntax and Semantics, 3: Speech Acts*, ed. P. Cole and J. L. Mogan, 41–58. New York: Academic Press.

Griffith, Kelley. 1998. *Writing Essays About Literature: A Guide and Style Sheet.* 2d ed. Fort Worth, TX: Harcourt Brace.

Gunn, Giles. 2001. *Beyond Solidarity.* Chicago: University of Chicago Press.

Hammond, Lynn. 1991. "Using Focused Freewriting to Promote Critical Thinking." In *Nothing Begins with N: New Investigations of Freewriting*, ed. Pat Belanoff, Peter Elbow, and Sheryl Fontaine, 71–92. Carbondale, IL: Southern Illinois University Press.

Harris, Joseph. 1997. *A Teaching Subject: Composition Since 1966.* Upper Saddle River, NJ: Prentice Hall.

Henricksen, Bruce. 1988. "The Construction of the Narrator in The Nigger of the "Narcissus." *PMLA*, 103 (December): 783–95.

Hill, Christopher. 1978. *Milton and the English Revolution.* New York: Viking Press.

Hirsch, E. D. 1967. *Validity in Interpretation.* New Haven: Yale University Press.

———. 1977. *The Philosophy of Composition.* Chicago: University of Chicago Press.

———. 1985. "Back to History" and "Short Response to Timothy Bahti." In *Criticism in the University*, ed. Gerald Graff and Reginald Gibbons, 189–97, 229–30. Evanston, IL: Northwestern University Press.

———. 1987. *Cultural Literacy: What Every American Needs to Know.* Boston: Houghton Mifflin.

Hymes, D. H. 1972. "Speech and Language: On the Origins and Foundations of Inequality Among Speakers." In *Directions in Sociolinguistics: The Ethnography of Communication*, ed. J. J. Gumperz and D. H. Hymes. New York: Holt, Rinehart.

Hynds, Susan. 1991. "Questions of Difficulty in Literary Reading." In *The Idea of Difficulty in Literature*, ed. Alan Purves, 117–39. Albany: State University of New York Press.

Hynds, Susan, and Deborah Appleman. 1997. "Walking Our Talk: Between Response and Responsibility in the Literature Classroom." *English Education* 29 (December): 272–94.

Iser, Wolfgang. 1974. *The Implied Reader: Patterns of Communication in Prose Fiction from Bunyan to Beckett.* Baltimore: Johns Hopkins University Press.

Jennings, Louise. 1998. "Reading the World of the Classroom Through Ethnographic Eyes." *The California Reader* 31 (4).

Kennedy, X. J., and Dana Gioia. 2000. *Literature: An Introduction to Fiction, Poetry, and Drama.* (2d compact ed.) New York: Longman.

Kent, Thomas, ed. 1999. *Post-Process Theory: Beyond the Writing Process Paradigm.* Carbondale, IL: Southern Illinois University Press.

Kirby, Dan, and Carol Kuykendall. 1991. *Mind Matters: Teaching for Thinking.* Portsmouth, NH: Heinemann.

Kozol, Jonathan. 1991. *Savage Inequalities.* New York: HarperCollins.

Kutz, Eleanor, Suzy Groden, and Vivian Zamel. 1993. *The Discovery of Competence: Teaching and Learning with Diverse Student Writers*. Portsmouth, NH: Boynton/Cook.

Langer, Judith. 1990. "Understanding Literature." *Language Arts* 67 (Dec.): 812–16.

Lave, Jean, and Etienne Wenger. 1991. *Situated Learning: Legitimate Peripheral Participation*. Cambridge: Cambridge University Press.

Lee, Carol, and Peter Smagorinsky. 2000. "Introduction: Constructing Meaning Through Collaborative Inquiry." In *Vygotskian Perspectives on Literary Research: Constructing Meaning Through Collaborative Inquiry*, ed. Carol Lee and Peter Smagorinsky, 1–15. Cambridge: Cambridge University Press.

Leitch, Vincent, gen. ed. 2001. *The Norton Anthology of Theory and Criticism*. New York: W. W. Norton.

Lieberman, Ann, and Diane Wood. 2002. "The National Writing Project." *Educational Leadership* (March): 40–43.

———. 2003. *Inside the Writing Project: Network Learning and Classroom Teaching, A New Synthesis*. New York: Teachers College Press.

Lish, Gordon. 1986. "Skippers, Snappers and Blasters." In *Sudden Fiction: American Short-Short Stories*, ed. Robert Shapard and James Thomas, 255. Salt Lake City: Peregrine Smith.

Luke, Alan. 1988. "The Political Economy of Reading Instruction." In *Towards a Critical Sociology of Reading Pedagogy: Papers of the XII World Congress on Reading*, ed. Carolyn Baker and Alan Luke, 3–25. Amsterdam: John Benjamins.

Macrorie, Ken. 1970. *Telling Writing*. New York: Hayden.

Marshall, James. 1989. *Patterns of Discourse in Classroom Discussions of Literature* (Report No. 2.9). Albany, NY: The Center for the Learning and Teaching of Literature.

Marshall, James, Peter Smagorinsky, and Michael Smith. 1995. *The Language of Interpretation: Patterns of Discourse in Discussions of Literature*. Urbana, IL: National Council of Teachers of English.

McCaslin, Mary. 1990. "Motivated Literacy." In *Literacy Theory and Research: Analyses from Multiple Paradigms* (Thirty-ninth Yearbook of the National Reading Conference), ed. Jerry Zutell and Sandra McCormick, 35–50. Chicago, IL: National Reading Conference.

McClelland, Kathleen, Sheridan Blau, and Stan Nicholson. 1990. "College Preparatory Versus College Reality." Santa Barbara: Office of Instructional Development, University of California, Santa Barbara.

McCormick, Kathleen, Gary Waller, and Linda Flower. 1987. *Reading Texts: Reading, Responding, Writing*. Lexington, MA: D. C. Heath.

Mellor, Bronwyn, Marnie O'Neill, and Annette Patterson. 1992. "Re-reading Literature Teaching." In *Reconstructing Literature Teaching: New Essays on the Teaching of Literature*, ed. Jack Thompson, 40–55. Norwood, Australia: Australia Association for the Teaching of English. Reissued for North America in Portland, ME, by Calendar Islands Publishers, 1998.

Mellor, Bronwyn, and Annette Patterson. 2001. *Investigating Texts: Analyzing Fiction and Nonfiction in High School*. NCTE Chalkface Series. Urbana, IL: National Council of Teachers of English.

Mellor, Bronwyn, Annette Patterson, and Marnie O'Neill. 2000a. *Reading Fiction: Applying Literary Theory to Short Stories*. NCTE Chalkface Series. Urbana, IL: National Council of Teachers of English.

———. 2000b. *Reading Stories: Activities and Texts for Critical Reading.* NCTE Chalkface Series. Urbana, IL: National Council of Teachers of English.

Mitchell, W. J. T. 1985. "Introduction: Pragmatic Theory." In *Against Theory: Literary Studies and the New Pragmatism*, ed. W. J. T. Mitchell, 1–10. Chicago: University of Chicago Press.

Moffett, James. 1968. *Teaching the Universe of Discourse.* Boston: Houghton Mifflin.

———. 1981. "Integrity in the Teaching of Writing." In James Moffett, *Coming on Center: English Education in Evolution*, 81–93. Portsmouth, NH: Boynton/Cook.

Moon, Brian. 1990. *Studying Literature: Theory and Practice for Senior Students.* Scarborough, Australia: Chalkface Press.

Morris, John. 1980. *The Glass Houses.* New York: Atheneum.

Myers, Miles. 1996. *Changing Our Minds: Negotiating English and Literacy.* Urbana, IL: National Council of Teachers of English.

Neves, Sylvia. 2001. *Presentations Matter: An Ethnographic Study of the Life and Practices of a Writing Project's Professional Development Community.* Ph.D. dissertation, University of California, Santa Barbara.

Newkirk, Thomas. 1984. "Looking for Trouble: A Way to Unmask Our Readings." *College English* 46 (Dec.): 756–66.

Nystrand, Martin. 1991. "Making It Hard: Curriculum and Instruction as Factors in the Difficulty of Literature." In *The Idea of Difficulty in Literature*, ed. Alan Purves, 141–56. Albany: State University of New York Press.

———. 1997. *Opening Dialogues: Understanding the Dynamics of Language and Learning in the English Classroom.* With A. Gamoran, R. Kachur, and C. Prendergast. New York: Teachers College Press.

Nystrand, Martin, and Adam Gamaron. 1991. "Instructional Discourse, Student Engagement and Literature Achievement." *Research in the Teaching of English* 25: 261–90.

Oakes, Jeannie. 1986. *Keeping Track: How Schools Structure Inequality.* New Haven: Yale University Press.

O'Connor, Flannery. 1979. *The Habit of Being.* Letters ed. Sally Fitzgerald. New York: Farrar, Straus, Giroux.

Olson, Carol Booth. 2003. *The Reading/Writing Connection: Strategies for Teaching and Learning.* New York: Allyn and Bacon.

Ordan, David. 1986. "Any Minute Mom Should Come Blasting Through the Door." In *Sudden Fiction: American Short-Short Stories*, ed. Robert Shapard and James Thomas, 196–197. Salt Lake City: Peregrine Smith.

Patterson, Annette. 1992. "Individualism in English: From Personal Growth to Discursive Construction." *English Education* 24 (3): 131–46.

———. 1993. "Personal Response in English Teaching." In *Child and Citizen: Genealogies of Schooling and Subjectivity*, ed. Denise Meredyth and Deborah Tyler. Australia: Griffith University Institute for Cultural Policy Studies.

Pirie, Bruce. 1997. *Reshaping High School English.* Urbana, IL: National Council of Teachers of English.

Polanyi, Livia. 1979. "So What's the Point." *Semiotica* 25 (3/4): 207–41.

————. 1985. *Telling the American Story: A Structural and Cultural Analysis of Conversational Storytelling*. Norwood, NJ: Ablex.

Polanyi, Michael. 1966. *The Tacit Dimension*. Garden City, NY: Doubleday.

Pradl, Gordon. 1996. *Literature for Democracy: Reading as a Social Act*. Portsmouth, NH: Boynton/Cook.

Preminger, Alex, T. V. F. Brogan, et al. 1993. *The New Princeton Encyclopedia of Poetry and Poetics*. Princeton: Princeton University Press.

Probst, Robert. 1988. *Response and Analysis: Teaching Literature in Junior and Senior High School*. Portsmouth, NH: Heinemann.

Purves, Alan. 1993. "Toward a Reevaluation of Reader Response and School Literature." *Language Arts* 70 (Sept.): 348–61.

Purves, Alan, and Richard Beach. 1972. *Literature and the Reader: Research in Response to Literature, Reading Interests, and the Teaching of Literature*. Urbana, IL: National Council of Teachers of English.

Rabinowitz, Peter, and Michael Smith. 1998. *Authorizing Readers: Resistance and Respect in the Teaching of Literature*. New York and Urbana, IL: Teachers College Press and National Council of Teachers of English.

Resh, Celeste. 1987. "Experimenting with Response to Literature." *Language Arts Journal of Michigan* 3 (Spring): 14–21.

Rex, Lesley. 1997. *Making a Case: A Study of the Classroom Construction of Academic Literacy*. Unpublished doctoral dissertation, University of California, Santa Barbara.

Rex, Lesley, and D. McEachen. 1999. "If Anything Is Odd, Inappropriate, Confusing, or Boring, It's Probably Important: The Emergence of Inclusive Acaademic Literacy Through English Classroom Discussion Practices." *Research in the Teaching of English* 34: 65–131.

Richards, I. A. 1929. *Practical Criticism*. New York: Harcourt Brace.

Rose, Mike. 1984. *Writer's Block: The Cognitive Dimension*. Carbondale, IL: Southern Illinois University Press.

Rosenblatt, Louise. 1968 (originally 1938). *Literature as Exploration*. Rev. ed. New York: Noble and Noble.

————. 1978. *The Reader, the Text, the Poem: The Transactional Theory of the Literary Work*. Carbondale, IL: Southern Illinois University Press.

Santa Barbara Classroom Discourse Group. 1993. *Talking Knowledge into Being: Discursive and Social Practices in Classrooms*. Special issue of *Linguistics and Education* 5 (3 and 4). Norwood, NJ: Ablex.

Scardamalia, Marlene, and Carl Bereiter. 1982. "Assimilative Processes in Composition Planning." *Educational Psychologist* 17: 165–71.

Schaefer, Jane. 1995. *Teaching the Multiparagraph Essay: A Sequential Nine-Week Unit*. San Diego: Jane Schaefer Publications.

Schoenbach, Ruth, Cynthia Greenleaf, Christine Cziko, and Lori Hurwitz. 1999. *Reading for Understanding: A Guide to Improving Reading in Middle and High School Classrooms*. San Francisco: Jossey-Bass.

Scholes, Robert. 1982. *Semiotics and Interpretation*. New Haven: Yale University Press.

———. 1985. *Textual Power: Literary Theory and the Teaching of English*. New Haven: Yale University Press.

———. 1987. "Textuality: Power and Pleasure." *English Education* 19 (May): 69–82.

———. 1989. *Protocols of Reading*. New Haven: Yale University Press.

———. 1999. "Mission Impossible." *English Journal* 88 (July): 28–35.

———. 2001. *The Crafty Reader*. New Haven: Yale University Press.

Scholes, Robert, Nancy Comley, and Greg Ulmer. 2002. *Text Book: Writing Through Literature*. 3d ed. Boston: Bedford/St. Martin's.

Shapard, Robert, and James Thomas, eds. 1986. *Sudden Fiction: American Short-Short Stories*. Salt Lake City: Peregrine Smith.

Shaughnessy, Mina. 1977. *Errors and Expectations: A Guide for the Teacher of Basic Writing*. New York: Oxford University Press.

Shklovsky, Viktor. 1917. "Art as Technique." In *Contemporary Literary Criticism: Literary and Cultural Studies*. 3d ed., ed. Robert Con Davis and Ronald Schleifer, 260–72. New York: Longman, 1994.

Smith, Michael. 1994. "Democratic Discourse and the Discussion of Literature." In *Integrated Language Arts: Controversy to Consensus*, ed. Lesley Mandel Morrow, Jeffrey K. Smith, and Louise Cherry Wilkinson. New York: Allyn and Bacon.

Soter, Anna O. 1999. *Young Adult Literature and the New Literary Theories*. New York: Teachers College Press.

Sperling, Melanie, and Sarah Freedman. 1987. "A Good Girl Writes Like a Good Girl: Written Response and Clues to the Teaching-Learning Process." *Written Communication* 4: 343–69.

Staley, Rosemary. 2001. *Teacher Professional Development: An Ethnographic Study of a Summer Institute of the South Coast Writing Project*. Ph.D. dissertation, University of California, Santa Barbara.

Stanford, Judith, ed. 1999. *Responding to Literature*. 3d ed. Mountain View, CA: Mayfield Publishing.

Sullivan, Patricia. 1994. "Writing in the Graduate Curriculum: Literary Criticism as Composition." In *Composition Theory for the Postmodern Classroom*, ed. Gary Olson and Sidney Dobrin. Albany: State University of New York Press.

Tierney, R. J., and P. D. Pearson. 1983. "Toward a Composing Model of Reading." *Language Arts* 60: 568–80.

Todorov, Tzvetan. 1978. *Genres in Discourse*. French ed. Cambridge: Cambridge University Press, 1990.

Touponce, William. 1991. "Literary Theory and the Notion of Difficulty." In *The Idea of Difficulty in Literature*, ed. Alan Purves, 51–71. Albany: State University of New York Press.

Traub, James. 2000. "What No School Can Do." *New York Times* (Sunday magazine supplement) 16 Jan.

Tuyay, Sabrina, Louise Jennings, and Carol Dixon. 1995. "Classroom Discourse and Opportunities to Learn: An Ethnographic Study of Knowledge Construction in a Bilingual Third Grade Classroom." *Discourse Processes* 19 (1): 75–110.

Vine, Harold, and Mark Faust. 1993. *Situating Readers: Students Making Meaning of Literature*. Urbana, IL: National Council of Teachers of English.

Vinz, Ruth. 2000. *Becoming (Other) Wise: Enhancing Critical Reading Perspectives*. Portland, ME: Calendar Islands Publishers.

Vygotsky, Lev. 1962. *Thought and Language*. Ed. and trans. Eugenia Hanfman and Gertrude Vakar. Cambridge, MA: MIT Press.

———. 1978. *Mind in Society: The Development of Higher Psychological Processes*. ed. M. Cole, J. Scribner, V. John-Steiner, and E. Soubermans. Cambridge, MA: Harvard University Press.

Wilhelm, Jeffrey. 1997. *"You Gotta Be the Book": Teaching Engaged and Reflective Reading with Adolescents*. New York: Teachers College Press.

———. 2001. *Improving Comprehension with Think Aloud Strategies: Modeling What Good Readers Do*. New York: Scholastic.

Wilhelm, Jeffrey, Tanya Baker, and Julie Dube. 2001. *Strategic Literacy: Guiding Students to Lifelong Literacy, 6–12*. Portsmouth, NH: Boynton/Cook.

Wilson, Nancy. 1989. "Learning from Confusion: Questions and Change in Reading Logs." *English Journal* (Nov.): 62–69.

Wimsatt, W. K., and Monroe Beardsley. 1954. *The Verbal Icon: Studies in the Meaning of Poetry*. Lexington, KY: University of Kentucky Press.

Woodward, Katherine, and Arthur Halbrook. 1999. "National Initiatives in English Language Arts." In *Alignment of National and State Standards: A Report by the GED Testing Service*, ed. Katherine Woodward, 39–64. Washington, D.C.: American Council on Education.

Yeager, Elizabeth, Anna Floriani, and Judith Green. 1998. "Learning to See Learning in the Classroom: Developing an Ethnographic Perspective." In *Students as Inquirers of Language and Culture in their Classrooms*, ed. David Bloome and Ann Egan-Robertson. Cresskill, NJ: Hampton Press.

Zancanella, Don. 1991. "Teachers Reading/Readers Teaching: Five Teachers' Personal Approaches to Literature and Their Teaching of Literature." *Research in the Teaching of English* 25: 5–33.

Zeiger, William. 1985. "The Exploratory Essay: Enfranchising the Spirit of Inquiry in College Composition." *College English* 47 (Sept.): 454–66.

Index